HOW ARE YOU GOING TO PAY FOR THAT?

HOW ARE YOU GOING TO PAY FOR THAT?

Smart Answers to the Dumbest Question in Politics

RYAN COOPER

ST. MARTIN'S
PRESS

NEW YORK

First published in the United States by St. Martin's Press, an imprint of
St. Martin's Publishing Group

HOW ARE YOU GOING TO PAY FOR THAT? Copyright © 2022 by Ryan Cooper.
All rights reserved. Printed in the United States of America.
For information, address St. Martin's Publishing Group, 120 Broadway,
New York, NY 10271.

www.stmartins.com

Designed by Steven Seighman

Library of Congress Cataloging-in-Publication Data

Names: Cooper, Ryan (Jounalist), author.
Title: How are you going to pay for that? : smart answers to the
    dumbest question in politics / by Ryan Cooper.
Description: First edition. | New York : St. Martin's Press, [2022] |
    Includes bibliographical references and index.
Identifiers: LCCN 2021016347 | ISBN 9781250272348 (hardcover) |
    ISBN 9781250272355 (ebook)
Subjects: LCSH: United States—Economic policy—2009- | United
    States—Economic conditions—2009- | United States—Social
    policy—1993- | United States—Social conditions—1980- | United
    States—Politics and government—1989-
Classification: LCC HC106.84 .C665 2021 | DDC 330.973—dc23
LC record available at https://lccn.loc.gov/2021016347

Our books may be purchased in bulk for promotional, educational,
or business use. Please contact your local bookseller or the Macmillan
Corporate and Premium Sales Department at 1-800-221-7945, extension
5442, or by email at MacmillanSpecialMarkets@macmillan.com.

First Edition: 2022

10 9 8 7 6 5 4 3 2 1

For Steve Randy Waldman, who carries the fire

CONTENTS

HOW ARE YOU GOING TO PAY FOR THAT?

INTRODUCTION

ADVERTISEMENTS OFTEN PROVIDE instructive lessons in economic conventional wisdom. Pay attention to ads on television, bus stop shelters, or YouTube and eventually you will see one for a "savings scold" business. These are the banks, financial services companies, and lifestyle coaches that make their living advertising strategies to save more money, often by hectoring people for not saving enough. They come in various flavors: Suze Orman, who caters to middle-aged women, promises that you can "be the master of your own financial destiny" with her financial advice products.[1] Dave Ramsey, whose branding is aimed more at conservative Christians, offers a "Financial Peace University" that you can sample with a fourteen-day free trial.[2] A man calling himself "Mr. Money Mustache," who skews more crunchy and environmentalist, promises early retirement through something called "badassity" (which in practical terms means saving about 50 percent of your income).

Savings scolds promise that people can improve their financial lot by being frugal and investing wisely. Theirs is an individualist creed that tends to implicitly blame people for financial misfortune. If you are poor or in debt—well, you should have made better decisions!

The coronavirus pandemic provided an interesting test case of what would happen if the whole population actually followed the savings scolds' advice all at once. In early March 2020, gripped by fear, the American populace abruptly stopped going to restaurants, movie theaters, gyms, and other public locations—which were closed by most state governments quickly afterward anyhow. Professional sports seasons were canceled. Airline travel plummeted by 96 percent.[3] The stock market fell sharply.

The federal government soon provided a huge economic rescue package to help people weather the crisis. As part of the CARES Act, it sent out $1,200 checks to most individuals, increased unemployment benefits, and provided hundreds of billions in grants to small businesses. That flood of money, plus the fact that most people weren't going out to spend money on their usual activities, meant the savings rate shot up to its highest rate ever recorded—from 7.6 percent in January 2020 to *33.7 percent* in April.[4]

What happened as a result? A nearly instant economic depression. New unemployment claims jumped from 256,000 to 6.1 million in three weeks, and the unemployment rate jumped from 3.5 percent to 14.8 percent.[5] The first quarter of 2020 saw gross domestic product (GDP, which is basically a summation of the whole of economic production) shrink by 1.7 percent in absolute terms, and GDP declined further in the second quarter, by a whopping 9.5 percent—probably the greatest single-quarter shrinkage in American history.[6]

Why did all this happen? Because income and savings do not exist in a vacuum—on the contrary, they depend on each other. When I spend money, I provide income for somebody else; conversely, my income must ultimately come from somebody else spending. If we all drastically cut back on our spending at the same time, then the economy just grinds to a halt.

It was an object lesson in both the impossibility of the broad population actually following the advice of the savings scolds and the fact of economic interdependence. *One* person might be able to accumulate a vast hoard of assets and retire at thirty by living a life of extreme frugality (if they are lucky and have a good-paying job), but because about two-thirds of the economy consists of consumer spending, the *people as a whole* cannot.[7] Indeed, despite the basic pitch of the scolds being about saving for retirement, none of the people mentioned above are actually retired themselves. Orman, 69, and Ramsey, 60, are running veritable advice empires, and while Mr. Mustache, 47, quit his job in software, according to a *New Yorker* profile, he makes $400,000 per year from affiliate links on his website.[8]

The pandemic, and the economic collapse it caused, briefly silenced one of the commonest questions in American politics: "How are you going to pay for that?" Though President Trump utterly bungled the executive branch's response to the virus (indeed, in the critical early stages his administration did largely nothing except downplay the pandemic and confiscate shipments of protective gear that were headed to hospitals and state governments), the CARES Act was passed without so much as a whisper of complaint about payment.[9] Large corporations first got $454 billion, to be doled out at essentially the sole discretion of treasury secretary Steven Mnuchin, and this was soon levered up into a $4.5 trillion loan program by the Federal Reserve. Small businesses got a loan program of $349 billion (later increased to $659 billion), in which the loans would be forgiven if the funds were spent on payroll or certain other expenses. As noted, unemployment insurance was dramatically (though temporarily) boosted by an additional $600 per week for most people who had been laid off. Hospitals got $50 billion to deal with pandemic expenses.[10]

Though the rickety American government struggled to implement the programs (particularly at the state level, where many unemployment programs have been deliberately designed to pay out as little as possible, meaning that many people who were eligible for benefits could not collect), all told it was a remarkably aggressive response to the financial aspects of the crisis—especially the unemployment portion, which made the program much more generous to lower-income citizens than similar programs in any European country.[11] Indeed, the extra $600 (so chosen because state unemployment systems were too janky and decrepit to give out 100 percent of someone's previous income, so Congress simply tacked on a flat amount) meant that many workers making less than the average wage were being paid more after being laid off.[12] For the lowest-income workers, it was *a lot* more.

In the initial panic—particularly when the stock market was collapsing—virtually no one raised concerns about where all of this money was coming from or how it would be paid back.

Questions like "How will you pay for that?" are rooted in a very old way of thinking that sees the economy as something outside human control. Instead of controlling economic production to achieve things we want—higher wages, for instance—we must bend ourselves to the inescapable economic winds. If someone wants better pay, they must educate themselves so they can get a better job. If jobs are being shipped overseas, that means American workers have simply become uncompetitive and must accept wage cuts. If we want a new social program, then every single dime must be accounted for through taxation beforehand, because the state can only be a burden on the economy. This is where savings scold thinking—the idea that economic outcomes are entirely the result of individual effort and decisions, and therefore people can *always* save as much money as they want, if they have sufficient willpower and smarts—comes from. This ideology is often called neoliberalism today, but it dates back all the way to the Industrial Revolution in the late eighteenth century. Because its central tenet is that property rights should be the inalterable foundation of politics, I will call it *propertarianism* (borrowed from the Ursula K. Le Guin book *The Dispossessed*).

Propertarianism has been crumbling since the 2008 financial crisis. It has been a long time since the early 1990s, when the Soviet Union collapsed and it seemed capitalism would rule forever. Political scientist Francis Fukuyama suggested in 1992 that capitalist liberal democracy would be the "final form of human government," leading to an effective "end of history."[13] Whoops!

The coronavirus pandemic shows one way in which the savings scolds are wrong. In times of crisis, the state must act swiftly to keep the entire economy from falling to pieces. But that is only part of the situation. It is not just the case that the state has to rescue people in times of emergency, or that we could fund social programs by cutting the military, though both of those are definitely true. The real deep-down truth is this: the *whole economy* is the result of human choices and actions, above all through the state. There is *no such thing* as an economic system that exists outside state support and control—especially in a huge, rich, and powerful country such as the United States, which controls most of the key levers of the global economy. The United States has an unparalleled ability to harness resources through its taxation power, its ability to print money, and its ability to control finance, trade, and economic production in general.

It is difficult for nations to become rich, but that task has already been accomplished in America. Our problem is that the economy has been rigged to serve primarily the needs of a tiny minority of ultra-rich people, instead of the whole population. The United States is in the bizarre position of having untold riches at its fingertips, yet a lousy standard of living for much of its population. We could make this country the world's most comfortable place to live—and not at the expense of poorer nations—if we only chose to make it so.

Following the initial burst of generosity from the CARES Act, fretting about spending quickly returned to the discussion of how to respond to the pandemic. Democrats repeatedly refused to leverage their control of the House of Representatives to include a rescue for state and local governments in the initial packages. Senate Majority Leader Mitch McConnell (R-Ky.) argued that state governments should not receive a rescue, saying instead they should declare bankruptcy.[14] It is unclear how that could even work, as states are not businesses that can be liquidated and sold off to their creditors, but almost certainly the objective was to get states to slash Medicaid, unemployment benefits, public employment, and public pensions (luckily, this did not work).

McConnell's attempt to prevent states from being rescued is a perfect example of what people really mean when they start whining about who is going to pay for things. Once Wall Street had its bailout package and Federal Reserve credit line,

McConnell and his ilk started leveraging the crisis to attack public benefits and employment. In his view, welfare programs and working for the government are prima facie illegitimate; the role of government should be to force people out into the labor market to work for private businesses making profits. He and other Republican senators were *disgusted* at the idea of paying people not to work. Lindsey Graham of South Carolina said that the $600 weekly unemployment boost would be extended "over our dead bodies."[15] It "makes it very difficult for many small businesses in Ohio and around the country to bring their employees back," said Rob Portman of Ohio.[16] "We should never pay people not to work," said John Cornyn of Texas.[17]

However, this reaction was not confined to the Republican Party. Democrats were patently reluctant to stand up to this argument, in part because of their long history of advocating the same objective. McConnell-style thinking can be seen in any of a dozen Democratic Party initiatives, from airline deregulation in the 1970s to welfare reform in 1996 to the Earned Income Tax Credit today. All were an attempt to achieve some social goal by bending society to serve the market economy, rather than the other way around.

This bipartisan type of thinking, and the oligarchy it underpins, are perhaps the biggest obstacles that stand in the way of making the United States a more equal and just society. In this book, I will outline where this ideology comes from, how it is not just wrong but has led to shattering social catastrophes, and what might replace it.

Future policymakers and ordinary Americans alike will have to shake off this notion that they are powerless in the face of global market trends. Indeed, we *must* do so if we are to confront the multiple enormous crises facing us: inequality, our malfunctioning and hideously inefficient healthcare system, climate change, viral pandemics, and more. Simply running on autopilot—that is, continuing with the status quo—will lead to certain disaster. But neither are any of these crises insurmountable. It will simply require political willpower: energetic social and labor movements, competent and loyal intellectuals who can translate their goals into policies, and visionary leadership with the fire and willpower to put those policies into law—all propelled by a confident belief that they are not head-in-the-clouds idealists but morally grounded pragmatists. My goal in this book is not just to educate progressives of all kinds on how neoliberalism colonized the minds of the American people but also to outline a replacement way of thinking that we can use to effect real change in this country.

PART I

HOW A WILDLY FALSE ECONOMIC IDEOLOGY CONQUERED AMERICAN POLITICS

A HISTORY OF A
SELF-IMMOLATING IDEA

LIKE MANY AMERICANS, my first serious economic decision happened when I decided where to go to college and what to study. When I was in high school in the first years of the 2000s and talking about the subject with my friends and family, one of the most important factors under consideration was the future earning prospects of prospective schools and majors. Harvard, Yale, Princeton, and Stanford were thought to be secure routes to success—so much so, in fact, that of those four I applied only to Stanford, thinking that was the only one where I had a prayer of being accepted. (I was rejected.) Meanwhile, business, computer science, engineering, and hard science were thought to be the most reliable career paths.

I ultimately chose chemistry as a major, and ended up going to Reed College, a liberal arts school that was more prestigious and more expensive than the University of Colorado at Boulder, which I had initially planned on attending. Reed gave me additional tuition aid when my parents and I begged for it, and it seemed like a decent risk. In the first of many lucky breaks, Reed ended up being dramatically cheaper than CU-Boulder because the Colorado state government repeatedly slashed its education subsidies as I progressed through school (which means I would have wound up paying more had I gone there), and because my need-based aid was bolstered when my sister entered school. In my final two years, I could pay my share for an entire year of school by working with my dad doing construction during the summer (the way almost anyone used to be able to do in the 1960s).

In my own mind, I chose chemistry because I liked my high school teacher in that subject, because I was reasonably good at it, and because it was a "salable trade," as my dad put it. That latter factor was continually emphasized throughout my college experience. I briefly considered switching my major to physics, as it was more fascinating to me (though I was much worse at it), but a friend talked me out of it by demonstrating the greater earning potential of a chemistry degree.

Though I was not great at planning my life—indeed, I ended up ditching chemistry immediately after graduating, and took up writing and journalism, which would turn out to be among the most doomed professions in America—I always took it for granted that one of the primary purposes of a college education is to learn something that can be used to earn a decent amount of money.

Since I graduated in 2008, that thinking has penetrated ever deeper into the university. Students today are racked with anxiety about the earning potential of their degrees—if only so they can pay off their student loans, which routinely mount into the six figures. Parents flip through college brochures assuring them that this school is guaranteed to land their child a good job. Colleges themselves now behave more like businesses, jacking up tuition to the highest level students can bear and stocking themselves with expensive amenities to attract new "customers."

Indeed, an ultra-expensive tuition is often considered a mark of quality—you get what you pay for, right? This bit of conventional wisdom, which might hold when you're buying a pair of boots, thus warps the question of how a young person should live the rest of their life. College is expensive, and people should strain every financial resource to get the "best" education they can, the thinking goes. I barely even considered the idea that I should be able to study more or less whatever I felt like, much less the idea that the economy and universities should be structured so that all students could pursue whatever academic subjects interested them.

This is just one aspect of a mind-set that saturates American culture. Of course eighteen-year-old college kids should pick a major with an eye toward the labor market returns over the next forty years. And if that doesn't work out, well, they'd better go back to school to learn something new. At a speech at the Brookings Institution in 2018, Joe Biden said this was even true of people with postgraduate degrees. "I just did Harvard's commencement and I pointed out if you graduated with a Ph.D. in astrophysics, if you don't go back for education you're obsolete in 10 years," he said. "You will be obsolete in 10 years. That's not hyperbole, that's a fact."[1] (So astrophysicists should go back for a *second* Ph.D.?) Or if there aren't any good jobs in your town, you'd better move to a more prosperous place. Poor white communities in Appalachia are that way because they "failed themselves," Kevin Williamson wrote in *National Review* in 2016.[2] "The truth about these dysfunctional, downscale communities is that they deserve to die. Economically, they are negative assets. Morally, they are indefensible," he argued. These people "need real opportunity, which means that they need real change, which means that they need U-Haul." Conversely, instead of businesses searching around for the best town in which to locate their headquarters, towns should entice businesses with tax breaks or other subsidies—or the government should create "opportunity zones" with special tax benefits.

In this and hundreds of other ways, the economy is viewed as something that operates basically on its own. The job of government is to nurture private business through private market institutions, and the job of the citizenry is to contort themselves to fit the market's ever-shifting whims.

Throughout this book, I will argue that this view is not only backward but impossible. The economy should serve the needs of the citizenry not only because it is morally right but also because all economies are necessarily the product of human decisions and actions. College students are obsessed with their future earnings prospects and people are forced to move across the country for work because of *policy decisions* made by the state. These decisions were harmful and unnecessary, and could easily be reversed or replaced.

It's a simple—even obvious—idea, but harder to fully internalize than it sounds, and it carries profoundly radical implications. To understand why, we must first begin with the origins of the idea of the economy as a self-regulating machine, how that idea came to dominate the United States, and how it has nearly destroyed this country on several occasions.

The field of what would become economics emerged as a distinct discipline in the late eighteenth century (at the time it was called "political economy"). The most important work in the early tradition was Adam Smith's *The Wealth of Nations*, published in 1776. This enormous, meandering, and brilliant work quickly became a classic. Smith argued—contrary to much conventional wisdom of the time—that countries become rich not through acquisition of gold, silver, or other natural resources but through labor, technology, and exchange. Dividing the production process into many separate labor actions allows each worker to be much more productive, while free trade allows different factories or countries to specialize and become more productive still.

Smith viewed trade as emerging from a "certain propensity in human nature . . . to truck, barter, and exchange one thing for another." A country becomes wealthy not through deliberate state action or planned cooperation but by allowing natural human instinct to work itself out. Ironically, the greed and self-interest of individual businesspeople provides for the greater good without any such intention on their part: "It is not from the benevolence of the butcher, the brewer, or the baker that we expect our dinner, but from their regard to their own interest. We address ourselves, not to their humanity, but to their self-love, and never talk to them of our own necessities, but of their advantages."[3]

His follower David Ricardo extended and systematized Smith's thinking with an elaborate mathematical apparatus, while his French contemporary Jean-Baptiste Say was more of a popularizer of Smith's ideas for a French audience (more on Say later).

I should note that Smith's modern reputation makes him out to be much more dogmatically pro-business than he really was. To today's ideologues at the Adam Smith Institute, he was like some forerunner of the Chamber of Commerce—a man who thought private entrepreneurs and businesses could basically do no wrong. And while Smith was generally in favor of commerce and suspicious of government regulations and taxation, he was also rather cynical about elites and business. Regarding feudal lords, he wrote:

> All for ourselves, and nothing for other people, seems, in every age of the world, to have been the vile maxim of the masters of mankind. . . . For a pair of diamond buckles, perhaps, or for something as frivolous and useless, they exchanged the maintenance, or, what is the same thing, the price of the maintenance of 1000 men for a year, and with it the whole weight and authority which it could give them.[4]

Regarding the state and property rights, he wrote, "Civil government, so far as it is instituted for the security of property, is, in reality, instituted for the defence of the rich against the poor, or of those who have some property against those who have none at all."[5] Karl Marx and Friedrich Engels said virtually the same thing in *The Communist Manifesto*: "The executive of the modern state is but a committee for managing the common affairs of the whole bourgeoisie"[6] ("bourgeoisie" meaning business owners).

Most important, Smith and his disciples made explicit room for public goods. Some "public institutions" and "public works . . . may be in the highest degree advantageous to a great society," Smith wrote, but they will clearly not be profitable to any individual or small group. That includes basic state machinery to administer the legal system and a military to defend the nation from attack; public infrastructure "for facilitating the commerce of the society," such as roads, bridges, and canals; and public education. He discusses in detail the best way of financing such programs—tolls in the case of bridges, but often general taxation in the case of schools.[7]

Nevertheless, most of these qualifications were set aside, and Smith became the patron saint of classical liberalism. This was the dominant political ideology of the nineteenth century, which advocated the rule of law, at least some civil liberties, and economic "liberty"—that is, low taxes, free trade, few regulations, no unions, and the gold standard. By this view, market institutions are supposed to be "self-regulating," as economic historian Karl Polanyi puts it in his book *The Great Transformation*.[8] Rather than the state controlling economic affairs with rules and regulations, things will work out for the best if private individuals and businesses are left to themselves. The market is all, and it should be trusted with all important decisions. So we return to modern college students' idea that they should study something that is reliably profitable, rather than what is most interesting to them.

Now, the idea of the economy as some all-knowing, omnipresent external force is always going to seem like common sense to many people—the vast majority of people in practice have almost no control over their economic destiny, just as medieval peasants had no control over the seasons or the weather. But the classical economists undoubtedly did lend credence to the idea of the self-regulating market. The bulk of Smith's ideas suggested that unregulated markets would work out most things by themselves, and that government "interference" would usually make things worse. Indeed, this notion is inherent to any conception of economics as a hard science, which is clearly what classical economists were aiming at. This idea also happens to be nonsense.

In physics, the objects of study always behave the same way under experiment—which means that if you launch a rock at precisely the same angle and velocity over and over (in a controlled environment), it will land in precisely the same place every time. This has allowed physicists to develop sophisticated theories of matter, energy, and motion that produced extraordinarily accurate predictions of physical phenomena (such as eclipses) and enabled the development of astounding new technologies. Isaac Newton started with a radical new theory of gravity, and eventually human beings flew a spaceship to the moon. Physicists, chemists, and biologists seem almost like wizards, using intellect and experimentation to pierce the veil of naive perception and uncover the deeper reality underneath.

Economists from Smith's day to now have obviously envied the prestige and authority of hard scientists and attempted to emulate their approach. Even John Maynard Keynes, who disagreed with the classical economists on most important points, called his 1936 magnum opus *The General Theory of Employment, Interest, and Money*—a very physics-style title. (Admittedly, calling it "The Contingent Theory" wouldn't have quite the same heft to it.)

The laws of physics that scientists attempt to describe with their theories are *immutable*—they can be overturned only if some previously unnoticed aspect of reality turns out not to fit with their existing theories. If there is some economic equation that describes human behavior in the same way that, say, Einstein's general relativity describes objects moving at very high speeds, then that means human beings are effectively imprisoned by the laws of economics. Nobody can cancel gravity through political mobilization.

There are no such economic laws, of course. There are guidelines, rules of thumb, and constraints, but no ironclad deterministic laws. In affairs of commerce there are always contingency, human agency, and planning. But as classical liberalism developed, elites in Britain—the first country to industrialize—made every effort to set up a "self-regulating" market system, which ironically meant a great deal of state planning.

Indeed, those efforts were already under way long before Smith published his book. As Eric Hobsbawm writes in his history of the period, *The Age of Revolution*, there were several key policy developments that enabled Britain to leap ahead economically. The British peasantry was largely evicted from common lands through a series of Enclosure Acts, the majority of which were passed between 1760 and 1830. The resulting mass of landless poor were forced into factory work through the Poor Laws, which viciously punished those without a job. Fresh supplies of raw materials and new markets for cotton textiles, the first industrial product, were obtained when the state conquered new colonies and opened up their markets. U.K. textile manufacturers obtained an effective monopoly on most of the international cotton trade, "aided by the aggressive support of the British Government," Hobsbawm writes.[9]

Internationally, the most important of these mechanisms was the gold standard, which embodied all the impossible intentions and paradoxes of classical liberalism. Under a gold standard (which took many different forms in practice), a nation backs its currency with gold—that is, it bases the amount of currency in circulation on the amount of gold it holds in its central bank, and promises to buy or sell gold at a fixed price in that currency.[10]

The basic idea was to make international trade function automatically. Businesspeople could conduct international commerce confident that all sales or purchases would be in hard currency (currency that could not lose its value). If a country ran a trade deficit—that is, importing more than it exported—then gold would drain out of the country, unemployment and interest rates would rise, and domestic prices would fall, with the result that imports would shrink, solving the imbalance. If a country ran a trade surplus, gold would flow into the country, creating a rise in spending, prices, and imports, and solving the imbalance in an opposite fashion.[11]

Classical liberals portrayed the gold standard as a natural and inevitable part of the economic system. In reality, it was a government program—as utopian an experiment in economic planning as anything ever tried by the Soviet Union. It took enormous state effort to make it work at all, and it backfired constantly. On one hand, there was an inherent bias in the way it treated countries with a trade deficit as compared with those in surplus. All deficits must have a corresponding surplus in some other country, because all trade happens on one planet. If trade should be balanced, then logically countries in surplus should be subject to as much pressure to cut their exports as those in deficit get to cut their imports.

In theory, the gold standard should work symmetrically, cutting imports in deficit countries and boosting them in surplus countries. In practice, the burden on deficit countries was much, much more painful. An inflationary boom, with rising incomes, employment, and spending, is generally a pleasant state of affairs. But a deflationary depression is not. Prices come down slowly, and in the meantime high unemployment ruins households and businesses by the thousands. Nations could and did end up with big chunks of their population needing state aid at a time when tax revenues had collapsed. Worse, as we will see, it is possible for surplus countries to cheat the gold system.

On the other hand, even wealthy countries often found the constraints of the gold standard extremely burdensome. As Polanyi argues, one of the drivers behind European colonization was the desire to set up bigger internal markets outside the gold system.[12] With people in Africa or Asia under the control of France or Britain and unable to resist whatever terms of trade the imperial power chose to impose, stable export markets and sources of raw materials could be established that were not subject to the ever-changing balance of trade between sovereign powers.

As a side note, another driver of colonization was inequality. As journalist Matthew Klein and economist Michael Pettis write in their book, *Trade Wars Are Class Wars*, there is a declining marginal propensity to consume—meaning that the richer people are, the more of their income they tend to save (at least in a capitalist country; see below for a discussion of pre-capitalist societies).[13] By itself, a very unequal country will tend to fall into an indefinite quasi-depression, because its working classes do not have enough income to buy what they produce. And indeed, as the countries of Western Europe developed over the nineteenth century, they became hugely unequal. This problem was "solved" by imperialism and colonization—violently roping other countries into trade systems such that they have no choice but to buy the surplus production. That way, the economy at the imperial center can keep growing without having to transfer income from the rich to the poor. India, for instance, accounted for about half of the GDP of the British Empire in 1870—but most of that economic activity was geared to support British manufacturers.[14] We will explore inequality, which has become a central fact of the modern economy, in more depth later.

The whole apparatus of classical liberalism was plainly biased toward the richest countries, which were generally huge exporters, and further biased toward the rich in those countries. It is not a coincidence that the first advocates of free trade emerged from the United Kingdom, because that country industrialized first and hence had a big head start in industrial productivity. Free trade is beneficial to such a country because its domestic industry can outcompete any other.

But it can be incredibly destructive to poorer countries whose domestic production cannot compete. Indeed, before the Industrial Revolution, India and China were the major world producers of textiles—typically high-cost, high-quality goods produced on hand looms. Not only did Britain outcompete Indian production with its textile factories, but it forced India into the British marketplace as a colonial overlord. It did the same thing to China during the Opium Wars. Cheap British imports flooded in and destroyed the domestic manufacturing base in both countries (often called deindustrialization). India, especially, became a relatively much poorer country (one study estimates that India's output per person declined from over 60 percent of the equivalent British figure in 1600 to less than 15 percent by 1871) dedicated mainly to producing raw materials for British industry, and consuming the resulting imports.[15] Tens of millions of Indians lost a major source of income, which badly exacerbated numerous famines when the price of food rose beyond what the poor could afford. As a result, tens of millions of people died of hunger over the whole history of British India.[16]

Early policymakers in the United States recognized the danger of deindustrialization immediately, and slapped tariffs on imports to protect their infant industries. For well over a century, the tariff was an article of faith among Whig and Republican politicians representing industrialized sectors of the country, as they recognized that unrestricted free trade would strangle American industry.[17] (On the other hand, Democrats representing cotton plantations in the South, which relied on slave labor, favored free trade so they could supply British factories—a tension that was eventually resolved by the American Civil War.) East Asian countries that became wealthy after World War II, including Japan, Taiwan, and South Korea (and later China), followed the same path of early domestic protectionism and controls.[18]

The larger point is that classical economics and classical liberalism as they functioned in the nineteenth century were not some scientifically accurate—or even politically neutral—description of how societies function. They were heavily slanted in favor of wealthy countries, and especially the large business owners in those countries. Classical liberalism was part of how the British elite exercised what political theorist Antonio Gramsci calls "hegemony" over the rest of the country.[19] It was a way of thinking (or ideology) that explained and justified the prevailing political order, and came to be taken for granted by a critical mass of the population. Nineteenth-century Britain, with its enormous share of world trade and its colonies that eventually covered a quarter of the earth's landmass, arguably dominated the globe to a greater degree than any other country before or since. Classical liberalism provided an excuse for the capitalist domination of colonies abroad and the poor living standards of the working class at home.

All political orders need some kind of dominant ideology, or mental glue, to hold them together and obtain buy-in, or at least grudging tolerance, from the bulk of the population. Feudal countries had the idea that society was naturally divided into three parts: peasants, who worked the land; nobles, who protected the community; and priests, who provided moral and religious instruction. The Soviet Union had Marxism-Leninism—a sort of secular state religion developed by Stalin that purported to explain all history and politics for all time, and portrayed the USSR as the leading edge of a future utopia. Most dictatorships have a cult of personality around the leader. Nineteenth-century Britain, and modern propertarian nations today, have the idea that the self-regulating market is the purest expression of liberty.

A hegemonic ideology gains strength when it provides obvious success. During the nineteenth century, British liberals saw their country become the strongest great power by far, piling up unprecedented riches. Under these circumstances, disputes with trade unions and the horrible poverty in great swaths of society were easily swept under the rug.

However, a hegemonic ideology can crack during a crisis—if reality diverges too far from the ideology's tenets and predictions, particularly as the result of a social calamity, the ideology can lose its broad credibility or even be abandoned by its own proponents. That is precisely what killed off classical liberalism and the self-regulating market between 1914 and 1929—though only temporarily.

In 1910, the British journalist Norman Angell wrote a book called *The Great Illusion* (expanding on a pamphlet he had written the previous year).[20] He made the quintessentially liberal case that wars between great powers were irrational, because the economic affairs of nations had become so complex and deeply intertwined, and because wars had become so expensive. Unlike in Roman times, it was impossible to loot conquered nations, because their wealth consisted not in hoards of gold or grain but in factories and trade relations that a war would inevitably disrupt. Moreover, it was no longer possible for a country to cover the cost of a war, much less profit from it, by forcing the loser to pay, as a modern full-scale military, with its hundreds of thousands of troops, all their associated arms and equipment, and expensive ships and artillery pieces, would cost far more than any aggressor power could possibly extract.

Therefore the "elaborate interdependence" of national economies would serve as the "real guarantee of the good behavior of one State to another," Angell wrote.[21] Any war that did break out surely would not last long, as states would be slammed by the consequences. The book was a massive hit, and Angell became something of a celebrity. Unfortunately, just four years later a prolonged general war did indeed break out—and it would prove to be the bloodiest war in European history up to that point.

Now, as noted earlier, European colonial aggression actually was quite profitable. Political conquest was indeed economically "rational" in that circumstance. But Angell turned out to be completely correct about the consequences of a general war between major powers. The economy of Europe was shattered by World War I, and all of the combatant powers quickly piled up virtually unpayable debts, mostly to the United States. Yet states kept on fighting even at grotesque cost in lives and treasure. Once the European powers had locked themselves into two great blocs, and once the war had started, national pride, fear of defeat and humiliation, and sheer bloody-minded stupidity kept the carnage going until entire societies fell to pieces.

In a single battle at the river Somme in 1916, the two sides suffered more than half a million casualties each.[22] That, and the strain from several other battles, nearly broke the French military, which witnessed mass mutinies and desertions in 1917. Gargantuan Russian losses and economic disaster dissolved the legitimacy of the Russian monarchy, which fell to a liberal revolution in 1917, and then to a communist one later that same year. Lenin withdrew Russia from the conflict, leaving Germany able to muster its full resources on the Western Front. Germany nearly overran the Allies in 1918, but they turned back the German forces with American support. The exhausted German state fell apart, and a revolutionary democratic government took power. And while the Ottoman Empire proved far more formidable than the Allies had presumed, it too was eventually defeated and dismantled.[23]

Angell was right about the economics, but utterly wrong about the politics. It turned out that economic development had banished none of the demons of international politics—in fact, liberal capitalist development had made war more destructive than ever. But when the dust settled, liberals attempted to resurrect the prewar system. There was no immediate restructuring of the enormous wartime debts—on the contrary, Germany was saddled with huge reparation payments, for supposedly starting a war that had in fact been caused by colonial competition, economic inequality, the European alliance structure, and diplomatic bungling.

Throughout the 1920s, wealthy nations kept trying to resurrect the self-regulating market. They clung to the gold standard, low tariffs, and low taxation. This worked tolerably well for some countries, including the United States, which had suffered no physical devastation and comparatively few casualties and which was the major creditor for all the combatant powers. It was horrible for the United Kingdom and Germany. In 1925, the former legally fixed the value of the pound (or, pegged it) to its prewar level of 4.86 American dollars. This was far above the prevailing prices for goods and services (or, price level) in Britain, which required grinding deflation—that is, keeping unemployment high and spending low, so prices would gradually fall. (Lower prices, of course, mean money is worth more.) This decision had the further toxic effect of making foreign imports into Britain cheap, but British exports expensive, which harmed its domestic industries.[24] All throughout the 1920s Britain was in a moderate depression, with millions of unemployed and serious labor unrest. The German economy flailed under the burden of reparation payments, poor terms of trade, and political instability, falling into hyperinflation in 1921–23. Things stabilized afterward, but only because of a flow of loans from the United States.

Worse, both France and the United States cheated on the gold standard.[25] France had done the opposite of what Britain chose to do, undervaluing its currency and gaining a big export advantage. America had a similar surplus thanks mainly to not being devastated in the war, and so gold flowed into both countries. But instead of allowing the inflationary boom that would have been required under gold standard rules, their central banks "sterilized" the gold—basically taking possession of it without increasing the money supply, which meant it largely vanished from the international market. They effectively prioritized keeping down domestic inflation and maintaining trade competitiveness at the cost of breaking the world trade system and stoking international tensions (a kind of beggar-thy-neighbor stance we'll see again).

The international economy limped along until 1929, when calamity struck. The gigantic bubble in the American stock market collapsed starting in September of that year, which landed a devastating blow on an economy that was already starting to falter, and sparked the worst economic crisis in world history. The broader causes of the Great Depression will be discussed in later chapters, but for our purposes what matters is that economies around the world were crushed, and orthodox liberal policy only made things worse.

Financial panic spread around the world, as many foreigners had been invested in the New York boom. Uncontrolled bank runs took hold in hundreds of cities, and multiple countries suspended payments of their sovereign debt. Banks failed and businesses and individuals lost their savings, dragging more businesses under as sales and profits dried up, which threw yet more people out of work, and so on. In the United States, industrial production fell by 46 percent, and unemployment soared to 25 percent—one out of every four workers was out of a job.[26] In the United Kingdom, unemployment hit 23 percent; in Germany, 30 percent.[27] Overall, global industrial production fell by almost 40 percent, and world trade fell by 30 percent.[28]

As economist John Kenneth Galbraith writes in his book *The Great Crash*, initially President Hoover responded by cutting federal taxes. That was at least a small step in the right direction, as it put more money in some people's pockets. But the effect was negligible, since barely anyone paid any taxes at the time. "Thereafter policy was almost entirely on the side of making things worse," Galbraith writes.[29] This was true in all the rich countries at first. Orthodox liberalism recommended "sound currency" (that is, the gold standard) and a balanced budget, which ruled out any scheme to increase employment and production by devaluing the currency or borrowing to spend on public works; indeed, it meant tax hikes and cuts to government spending to balance the budget in response to collapsing tax revenue, which only threw more people out of work and made the problem worse. Say's law of classical economics (named after the aforementioned Jean-Baptiste Say) held that all production would create its own demand, implying that the kind of self-perpetuating collapse in spending and employment happening around the world could not happen. "The economic advisers of the day had both the unanimity and the authority to disavow all the available steps to check deflation and depression," writes Galbraith.[30]

Other countries followed the same path to hell. In 1931, the British Labour government implemented sweeping benefit cuts, wage cuts for public employees, and tax hikes.[31] (To be fair, the United Kingdom did later break with orthodoxy, but only under intolerable pressure. Hemorrhaging its gold reserves, it left the gold standard in 1931. Most of its close trading partners followed suit.) German chancellor Heinrich Brüning implemented similar measures between 1930 and 1932, attempting to deflate the German economy back to competitiveness and trying to demonstrate that its reparation payments were unsustainable.[32]

The United States clung to gold and austerity for as long as Hoover remained president. He did try a variety of penny-ante schemes to reverse the damage, such as modest spending programs and attempts to induce private philanthropic efforts, but these were swamped by the scale of the crisis. Even when Franklin Roosevelt, promising a program of public works and sweeping state action to attack the Depression, obliterated Hoover in the 1932 election—the presidential vote saw a partisan swing of 35 percentage points compared with the 1928 election—Hoover clung ever tighter to orthodoxy in the months between the election and when the new administration was inaugurated.

Hoover had ferociously attacked FDR's New Deal during the 1932 campaign. In one speech, he said it would "break down our form of government. It would crack the timbers of our Constitution . . . Free speech does not live many hours after free industry and free commerce die." In another speech, he said that "so-called new deals would destroy the very foundations of the American system of life." Roosevelt's tariff policy meant "grass will grow in the streets of a hundred cities, a thousand towns; the weeds will overrun the fields of millions of farms." During the transition period between administrations that winter (which lasted from November to March in those days), he repeatedly attempted to bait Roosevelt into abandoning his entire program, asking him to participate in various conferences and committees that would tie his hands policy-wise. As Hoover admitted in a letter to his friend Senator David Reed (R-Penn.), the effect would be to make FDR endorse "the whole major program of the Republican administration" and abandon "90 percent of the so-called new deal." Just days after Roosevelt was nearly killed by an assassin in February 1933, Hoover sent him a nine-page letter demanding once again that the New Deal be abandoned.[33]

Roosevelt, of course, would have none of this, and indeed put through the New Deal immediately upon taking office. As we'll see in chapter 2, contrary to Hoover's apocalyptic predictions, the New Deal worked pretty great. Grass did not, in fact, grow in the streets of a hundred cities. On the contrary, American roads and bridges were dramatically improved by gargantuan public works programs. Growth and employment exploded during FDR's first term, and while economic woes did return in 1937, it was because Roosevelt attempted to balance the budget Hoover-style before full employment was reached. The titanic borrowing and spending to mobilize for World War II finally licked the Depression for good.[34]

But rather than admitting his error, Hoover doubled down on his hatred of Roosevelt and his economic policy. He spent the rest of his career ensconced in conservative think tanks, writing books and pamphlets attacking FDR and the New Deal and arguing that the 1920s free-market system was not to blame for the Depression. He died in 1964 before finishing a big history of the Roosevelt administration, *Freedom Betrayed*. This was actually published in 2012, and turned out to be a nearly thousand-page unhinged assault on Roosevelt and everything he did, from the New Deal to winning World War II (Hoover argued the United States should not have supported Stalin against Hitler).[35]

This was odd behavior for a politician. Even when economic crisis was threatening the integrity of the United States, and even when his predictions were disproven, Hoover stayed the course. Clearly, he had a commitment to the notion of a self-regulating market that transcended evidence and his own political interest.

Once again, we see political ideology at work. In the most brilliant essay about the politics of depression ever written, "Political Aspects of Full Employment," the Polish economist Michał Kalecki explains this tendency.[36] Hoover was not the only one holding on to orthodoxy—before 1933 big business in the United Kingdom, France, and Germany also opposed programs to ease the Depression, even though the crisis was badly harming them, and even though spending on public works or other stimulus measures would increase their profits.

The reason is that government spending programs reduce

the power and status of business owners. "Obstinate ignorance is usually a manifestation of underlying political motives," Kalecki notes. Without state action, the economy's health "depends to a great extent on the so-called state of confidence. If this deteriorates, private investment declines, which results in a fall of output and employment."

> This gives the capitalists a powerful indirect control over government policy: everything which may shake the state of confidence must be carefully avoided because it would cause an economic crisis. But once the government learns the trick of increasing employment by its own purchases, this powerful controlling device loses its effectiveness. Hence budget deficits necessary to carry out government intervention must be regarded as perilous. The social function of the doctrine of "sound finance" is to make the level of employment dependent on the state of confidence.

Second, direct government subsidies of individuals undermine the capitalist labor system, which is geared around forcing people to work for whatever business owners are offering. Here "a moral principle of the highest importance is at stake. The fundamentals of capitalist ethics require that 'you shall earn your bread in sweat'—unless you happen to have private means," Kalecki observes. As noted previously, the British state expended great effort to create a pool of cheap factory labor in the early Industrial Revolution. And the belief that Kalecki describes is alive and well today; many modern American politicians still view the primary job of state policy as whipping people into the labor market. Notably, it was the major objective of welfare reform in 1996, which abolished a New Deal poor relief program for mothers so that they could earn "a paycheck, not a welfare check," as President Clinton said when announcing the program.[37]

Third, full employment threatens the authority of business by empowering workers. When jobs are plentiful, workers can quit over low pay or oppressive conditions, or organize into labor unions to force their employers to improve pay and conditions, without fear of destitution from job loss. "The social position of the boss would be undermined, and the self-assurance and class-consciousness of the working class would grow. Strikes for wage increases and improvements in conditions of work would create political tension," Kalecki writes. Capitalists might have to offer higher wages, grant union recognition, or, worst of all, allow labor to have some influence over how the business is operated.

In short, the quiet political philosophy behind classical liberalism holds that capitalist business owners should rule. The self-regulating market is a facade covering political domination by business owners. Thus the name "propertarianism," because its main practical tenet is that the owners of property should exercise political command over society. New Deal–style policy was a threat to these values not only because it dethroned capitalists from their accustomed place at the top of the social pyramid but also—indeed, especially—because it proved they did not deserve that place. That is why furious American plutocrats refused to speak Roosevelt's name, calling him "that man in the White House."[38] Retired Marine Corps general Smedley Butler testified before Congress that in 1933, several conservative business owners had recruited him to lead a fascist militia that would overthrow FDR in a coup.[39]

Despite all that resistance, the program of classical liberalism and the self-regulating market was obviously unworkable. Economic catastrophe shattered its legitimacy, and it was indeed overthrown across the world. In some countries, including the United States, Canada, and the United Kingdom, democratic governments saved themselves by ditching orthodoxy and inaugurating a broadly left-wing policy of intervention and experimentation that reversed enough of the damage to preserve the state—even though in the latter two countries conservative parties led government for much of the period. By contrast, failure to solve the crisis in Germany inflamed extremism on the far left and especially the far right, which eventually destroyed the Weimar Republic. In elections in July 1932, parties formally committed to abolishing democracy, the Nazi Party and the German Communist Party, won a majority in the Reichstag, making normal parliamentary government impossible. Eventually President Paul von Hindenburg appointed Adolf Hitler chancellor; he quickly abolished the republic, made himself dictator, and threw orthodoxy out the window. He then solved the Depression quickly and easily, through ditching the gold standard and vast spending on public works, especially rearmament.[40]

Conceiving of the economy as a self-regulating system that is external to politics may seem rather dull, and to be fair, the ideology is not as strong today as it was in the late 1920s—as shown by the enormous spending packages across the world to fight the coronavirus pandemic. But it is still a dangerously attractive doctrine. Balanced-budget fixations quickly returned after the panic of 2008, and they might again long before any post-pandemic recovery has been achieved. During the Depression, wise leaders such as Franklin Roosevelt realized that democracy cannot survive when the economy will not function and great swaths of the population are going hungry. Failure to provide for the needs of the citizenry erodes the legitimacy of the state and inflames extremist politics.

To counter that, one needs to arm oneself with a different way of thinking about the economy—viewing it correctly as a product of human agency and choices. The economy is a political creation, and it can be changed through politics. That will be the subject of chapter 2.

2

COLLECTIVE ECONOMICS

IN ONE OF THE BITS IN HIS 1999 comedy special *Bigger and Blacker*, Chris Rock complained about President Clinton's modest tax increases. "The one thing Clinton did I didn't like: raise taxes. Taxes all high and shit. You know what's fucked up about taxes? You don't even pay taxes. They take tax. You get the check, money gone. That ain't a payment, that's a jack." The audience roared.

This is a perfect example of propertarian ideology. By Rock's view, *all* the labor income produced by his work, including tax payments of all kinds, rightfully belongs to him, and when his employer directs part of his paycheck to the government, that's a taking of his property.

Now, most people would surely agree that tax payments aren't *really* like a robbery, and most will admit (however grudgingly) that taxes are generally worth paying so that the government can fund Medicare, the military, and so forth. No doubt that includes Rock himself, who after all was just making a joke. But the joke depends on a shared understanding that even if taxes fall short of theft, they are still somehow a taking from a paycheck that would have been larger if it weren't for the grabby hands of the state. From this naturally follows a whole set of propertarian beliefs: that people are in-dividually responsible for what they earn, that government regulations are an imposition on a pre-political economy that will in all likelihood get in its way, and therefore where possi-ble government should let businesses and individuals do what they want "free" of state control.

But Rock is wrong. In this chapter I'll outline what I'll call "collective economics," which emerges from consideration of the inescapable fact that the whole American economic machine is a huge collective enterprise wholly dependent on government laws, regulation, and spending, as well as the daily activities of the whole American people and their prior economic history. Without the government, or without the broader population of people building, selling, working, and spending every day, there would be no money, no paychecks, and no economy.

To begin, Rock's joke turns on property rights, which are enforced in various ways by federal, state, and local govern-ments. Again, most understand that one role of the police and courts is to protect people from theft or trespass. But few take this to its clear logical conclusion—that having access to the state's violent authority is *what it means* to own something. People tend to think of property as a relationship between a person and an object: this is *my* house, *my* car, and so on. But property really is a relationship between people. Prop-erty is a legal construct whereby if someone takes or accesses something without the legal owner's permission, the owner can call the cops or sue to force that person to stop. You own something if the state says you do.

So now we're in a position to understand the problem with Rock's bit. The reason his taxes are not a "jack" is that the money *does not belong to him.* Those taxes are legally owned by their recipients—retired people on a Social Security pension, people on Medicare or Medicaid, all the various government bureaucracies, and so on. To attempt to keep that tax money through some kind of trick would be actual theft—namely, the crime of tax evasion. Indeed, it would be literally impossible to create a tax-free society. Even the most bare-bones state imaginable would require at least some tax revenue to run a system of police and courts. (Alternatively, if the police and courts were funded with printed money, the state would need to tax to forestall inflation, as we'll discuss later.)

But leaving aside the state, there are further aspects of economics that are inescapably collective—even within the purest market institutions—in a way that goes beyond moderate liberals' recognition of economic interdependence. For instance, during the 2012 presidential campaign, Barack Obama referenced the fact that private businesses depend on public infrastructure such as roads and bridges:

> If you were successful, somebody along the line gave you some help. There was a great teacher somewhere in your life. Somebody helped to create this unbelievable American system that we have that allowed you to thrive. Somebody invested in roads and bridges.
>
> If you've got a business—you didn't build that. Somebody else made that happen.[1]

Republicans pulled the "you didn't build that" line out of context to make it seem as though Obama meant that entrepreneurs had literally nothing to do with the businesses they start. They even made this ridiculous, false interpretation a central element of the 2012 Republican National Convention. But while Obama didn't mean what some Republicans claimed he meant, it is actually true that even the market activities of private businesses are inherently dependent on the rest of society. Even if we set aside the whole state firmament of laws, regulations, and so forth, entrepreneurs do not build most of what makes their businesses succeed.

First, every private business must have a population of potential customers with money in their pockets—and for a modern business of any size, that population must be large. A mass consumer base providing a market for mass-produced goods is what makes any developed economy function. Without a class of people with hundreds of dollars to spend on gadgets, there would be no Apple or Microsoft. (As we'll see, governments have historically done a great deal to create and maintain middle classes, but we're just considering the market function of people's spending here.)

Second, the overall productivity of the economy, and hence the income of the public and entrepreneurs, is largely due to the historical legacy of past growth. Each generation has seen substantial progress, but the process of a nation becoming wealthy gets easier the longer it goes on, due to the dynamics of compound growth—it took the United States about 135 years to progress from $2,500 of GDP per person in 1800 (in 2011 prices) to $10,000, but just another 75 years to reach $55,000.[2]

Beyond that, production, as well as the ongoing innovations in private firms, depends upon a vast collection of knowledge—fundamental science and mathematics, manufacturing, management, advertising techniques, and so on—that was discovered at tremendous effort by people in the past, almost all of them now dead. This is sometimes difficult to picture when discussing private businesses, but consider physics: without the brilliant work of people such as Michael Faraday and James Clerk Maxwell there would be no electricity and no computer technology. Without people such as Marie Curie and Niels Bohr there would be no nuclear energy. Without Albert Einstein's work there would be no GPS and no lasers.

Indeed, even by pointing out these famous geniuses I am presenting a somewhat skewed view of how scientific discovery happens. Science is also very much a collective enterprise, where students get their start by studying the theories and discoveries of people in the past (or "standing on the shoulders of giants," as the saying goes), and practicing researchers almost always work together in groups, some of them very large. Anyone who has ever tried to solve a tricky problem knows how helpful an informed collaborator can be—providing critiques of one's ideas, or suggestions for improvements, or different ideas altogether, which one might then critique in turn.

The collective nature of science can be seen even with people who are working completely apart from one another. Historians of science have demonstrated that many pioneering scientific breakthroughs are "co-discovered" by different people or groups working independently.[3] Charles Darwin and Alfred Russel Wallace developed the concept of evolution at about the same time. Dmitri Ivanovich Mendeleyev and Lothar Meyer developed the periodic table of elements within a year of each other, working apart. The law of conservation of energy was discovered by no fewer than four people at once.[4] It appears achievement sort of pulses through the whole scientific community, and Nobel Prize–winning work is more often the vector by which collective discoveries break out than the product of heroic geniuses working on their own.

Now, individual effort, talent, and initiative are of course very important in science, and pioneering discoveries are certainly worthy of the highest praise. But every sensible scientist knows that they are only a small part of a vast collaborative machine stretching back hundreds of years.

What is true of pure science is even truer of entrepreneurship. Competition is the engine that makes the whole capitalist system go—business owners are constantly watching their competitors and attempting to borrow, copy, or improve their products. The American steel industry, for instance, was kicked off by a man who licensed technology from British inventor Samuel Bessemer.[5] But if licensing ideas or patents is unfeasible or too expensive, entrepreneurs will often just take ideas outright. In the early eighteenth century, a British entrepreneur named John Lombe learned how to build a silk spinner by getting a job in an Italian silk factory under a false pretext—thus stealing some of the technical know-how that seeded British textile mass production in the Industrial Revolution.[6] (German and American companies later stole the same information from the British.) Steve Jobs stole the idea of the graphical user interface (the method by which practically every computer today is operated) from a technical demonstration at Xerox. "I thought it was the best thing I had ever seen in my life," he later said in an interview. "The germ of the idea was there and they had done it very well."[7]

Finally, workplaces themselves have an inherently collective nature. All depend on shared knowledge and relationships to work—anyone who has worked at a new job knows that it takes some time to understand the peculiarities of each business's systems and procedures, whom to ask for help when things aren't working, and so on. Some of these procedures are designed by entrepreneurs, but just as often they are informally set up between workers on the ground.

Let's return to the state, which carries out dozens of important functions in addition to the bedrock of the legal system. Money itself is quite literally created by the U.S. government, and its value is managed by a government agency—the Federal Reserve (or Fed, for short). Corporations are also a state creation: they are chartered by state governments, and get special protections from legal liability. Stock and commodity markets are elaborately regulated by the government to prevent fraud and preserve the integrity of the market. Labor contracts are similarly enforced by government courts. The state educates future workers—in the United States, some 90 percent of children go to public primary and secondary school (and in other countries that percentage is even higher).[8] About three-quarters of American students who pursue education after high school go to public colleges or universities.[9]

All modern states dedicate substantial resources to protecting the quality and purity of food and medicine, ensuring the safety of transportation, delivering mail and packages, and building basic infrastructure such as roads, bridges, trains, airports, and public transit systems, along with dozens of other functions vital to the daily business of commerce.

In short, the whole economic edifice of business, profits, workers, and so on rests on the state's structural foundation. This means that the common neoliberal objective of "deregulation" is all but impossible. All such policies amount to *redefining* the state's role in the economy, not reducing it—indeed, the side effects of such policies often cause problems that require much more blatant and coercive state action. Financial deregulation in the late 1990s and early 2000s, for instance, helped cause the 2008 banking crisis, which forced the state to take emergency measures to keep the banking system from collapsing—

including straight-up nationalizing the world's largest insurance company, AIG.[10]

All this is a reflection of basic human nature. Evolutionary psychologists often advocate a lot of hokum, but one idea of theirs that is definitely correct is that humans are, like most primates, deeply social creatures. Humans have always lived in large groups with an elaborate social structure, in part because human children are extraordinarily helpless when they are born. Our brains are very large relative to our body size, but the fact that babies are delivered through the mother's pelvic girdle means much of that brain growth takes place after birth. An infant's brain grows in size by 64 percent during just its first ninety days of life—yet a baby still takes around a year to even learn to walk, while a baby horse or giraffe can stand within minutes of being born.[11]

Any human community therefore requires some division of labor to allow for such an extended period of child-rearing. In hunter-gatherer communities, adults gather food for mothers with infants, and older relatives often care for toddlers later so that parents can join in on hunting or gathering expeditions. The older hunters and foragers teach the younger ones the extraordinarily difficult business of stalking prey or distinguishing between thousands of different plant species.[12]

All human beings who have ever lived were born into an inescapable network of interdependency. We live because our mothers construct our infant bodies inside themselves and give birth to us, at considerable personal risk, and then our parents nurture us for years afterward. We learn to speak languages that evolved over centuries. We are educated by other members of the community, who almost never have been solely responsible for developing the concepts they inculcate. Today, virtually all of us go to work at companies we did not create, whose success is very largely due to background conditions nobody involved with the firm had anything to do with. Collective economics is simply a fact of human existence, and always has been.

The picture I'm painting here of how the economy works clashes with the vision of both Marxists and neoliberals. In his magnum opus *Capital*, Karl Marx espoused a "labor theory of value," which holds that all increases in economic production are at bottom the product of worker effort. The argument is extremely complicated, but one can intuitively see the appeal of it—no production can happen without workers, and workers also must build the machines and factories that are used for production. It is surely at least partly right.

By contrast, as we saw in chapter 1, propertarians hold that growth comes from three things: capital, labor, and technology.[13] The math is complicated, but the basic picture is simple to understand—take work, add factories and machines, and then add another term to account for technology. That too is at least partly right. But more insidiously, propertarians also have a "marginal productivity" theory of distribution. This was developed by economist John Bates Clark (who has an important economics prize named after him). In an essay, he argued that "the distribution of the income of society is controlled by a natural law, and that this law, if it worked without friction, would give to every agent of production the amount of wealth which that agent creates."[14] The idea of marginalism is that economic agents make their decisions on the margin—for workers, whether to work one additional hour at the prevailing pay rate; for firms, whether to produce one additional unit of output; and so on. In an imagined perfectly free market, the marginal productivity of labor should exactly equal the actual wages paid out—that is, employers would pay workers precisely as much as they have personally contributed to the firm's production.

Neither of these models is satisfactory. On the Marxist side, a strict version of the labor theory of value is clearly false. However one defines value, certainly some of it comes from nature. The same seeds planted and cultivated in the same way can deliver enormously different crop yields depending on the fertility of the soil. The American Midwest is an agricultural powerhouse in part because of huge deposits of loess piled up by moving glaciers thousands of years ago.[15] Tools can also increase a worker's productivity not only by allowing her to leverage her own strength or the past effort of the workers who built the tool but also by harnessing energy from nature via machinery that requires natural resources to create. A heavy steel power hammer used in an industrial forge can exert hundreds or thousands of times as much force as a blacksmith using her arm because it uses electricity to drive a hammer too heavy for a single person to even lift.

(Also, while Marx took the concept of the labor theory of value from the classical economist David Ricardo, it's not hard to see the obvious political subtext of the idea that workers are responsible for all economic value, while capitalist owners merely skim off profits from workers' labor.)

The neoliberal production model is probably more accurate in that it includes technology, and while it can be useful in some technical contexts, it is comically simplistic. Growth is portrayed as simply trundling along on its own, driven at bottom by technological advances about which the model has nothing to say. Indeed, the technology factor (known in this theory as the "Solow residual") is simply a fudge factor—what is left over after accounting for labor and capital.[16]

The marginal productivity distribution model is also technically useful but politically toxic. It holds that everyone gets the income that they create personally. The attraction for the rich is obvious: their income is held to be what they earned through hard work, while the poor can be blamed for not being productive. Conservative and libertarian economists have used this idea to defend the moral worthiness of market income distribution, to assert the rights of the top 1 percent, and even to argue that CEOs are perhaps underpaid.[17]

These political conclusions from marginal productivity theory are absurd—far more so than the labor theory of value. As a description of how an economy functions, the theory is false. As economist Amartya Sen argued in a famous essay, it cannot even be used to suss out which portion of total output has been produced by each of the components, which virtually always involve more than one person:

> Production is based on the joint use of different resources, possibly provided by different people, and it is not in general possible to separate out who—or even which resource—produced how much of the total output. There is no obvious way of deciding that "this much" of the output is owing to labor, "that much" to raw materials, "that much" to machinery, and so on. In economic theory, a common method of attribution is according to "marginal product," i.e., the extra output that one incremental unit of one resource will produce given the amounts of other resources. This method of accounting is internally consistent only under some special assumptions, and the actual earning rates of re-

source owners will equal the corresponding marginal products only under some further special assumptions.

But even when all these assumptions have been made—quite a tall order—it is still arbitrary to assert that each resource's earnings reflect the overall contribution made by that resource to the total output. There is nothing in the marginalist logic that establishes such an identification.[18]

The problems get even worse when one considers businesses in separate markets, because their incomes can gyrate wildly due to external factors without any change in the process of production. Two companies might see a giant divergence in their income thanks to random circumstances—for instance, face mask manufacturers saw a huge spike in demand thanks to the coronavirus pandemic, while airplane manufacturers saw a huge collapse.

Finally, there is the need to distinguish between what a person produces and what is produced by resources that he happens to own. The moral appeal of giving more to "those who are more productive and contribute more to output" does not readily translate into giving more to "those who own more productive resources that contribute more to output."

All this leads to a general conclusion: Economic production is an *inescapably* collective activity. As done in the United States today, it requires workers, businesses, the government, inventors and scientists, and especially a past history of economic growth and technological achievement. It is not possible to break down which share of output is created by each part of the system, because without any one of them there would be no production. Without natural resources there could be no factories or businesses, but without workers the factories and services would not function. Without the state the whole thing could not even get off the ground in the first place. (However, there is one type of person that really can be extraneous—the capitalist business owner. Firms can and do operate perfectly well owned by their employees, or by the state.)

Now that we have a firm grasp of the most important fact about economics, that of interdependence, we are in a position to develop a rough sketch of how economic policy works. The point here is not to try to advance a new technical model to displace existing ones (I am neither interested in doing that nor qualified to do it) but to set forth a pragmatic picture that cuts away the ideological dross and allows us to focus on the important moral and political questions.

The best place to start, in my view, is with production. *Why* nations have become rich has long been the subject of intense debate, but the basic mechanics of the process are not too complicated. There are two sides to the story. One is the buildup of productive capacity in the form of entities that produce goods and services; these entities become ever more productive through the application of new technological improvements. On the other, there is the buildup of a consumption market for the products these entities produce.

That sounds simple, but there are a lot of potential pitfalls. Successfully balancing these two sides requires a complex dance involving saving (that is, the difference between income and spending), investment, and consumption to keep growth chugging along. By itself, a nation needs both continual progress in its productive capacity and continual increase in the incomes of the mass population to buy the resulting products (or a continual increase in new export markets for the same purpose). That raises several potential roadblocks to growth. First, it is patently quite difficult for a poor nation to start moving up the development ladder, as shown by how long it took Britain to touch off the Industrial Revolution and by how many nations remain poor today. Poor countries have little domestic capital to tap for investment, and they have few prospects for domestic markets in any case precisely because they are poor. Foreign investors may be crooked or looking to brutally exploit cheap labor. Most development success stories, from Britain to China, have relied on a competent state that can tailor its policies to the conditions prevailing at the time.[19] In general, a state is always the necessary backbone for any development strategy—there is always new public investment needed, new problems to solve, new parasitic criminals to root out, basic administrative tasks to carry out, and so on. Without an honest bureaucracy, the most profitable business activity will quickly become riddled with fraud and extortion.

Investment is a particularly tricky question. In many economic theories and in the national accounts data used by governments, investment is set as equal to savings by definition. Propertarian economists from the classical period to today typically portray this relationship as causal—holding that investment is caused by people saving money.[20] This has the handy political benefit of crediting rich people for funding ongoing investment and touching off sustained economic growth in the first place. And to be fair, it is surely at least possible for individual investments to happen in this fashion. (I did this myself in 2020 by saving up a lot of money during quarantine, then spending it on solar panels for my home's roof.)

But the relationship does not hold in general. As economist Joan Robinson argues in her book *Introduction to the Theory of Employment*, the arrow of causality typically goes the other way: investment causes saving. When an entrepreneur or the state chooses to invest, that raises the income of the people who are hired to build the investment, which increases their rate of saving (because, as noted earlier, people tend to save more as their income increases), and it all balances out in the end. She writes: "Saving is equal to investment, because investment leads to a state of affairs in which people want to save. Investment causes incomes to be whatever is required to induce people to save at a rate equal to the rate of investment."[21] Conversely, as we saw in the introduction, the sudden huge increase in the rate of saving across the population in early 2020 caused mass unemployment instead of mass investment. We can increase savings by increasing investment, but not the other way around. As Robinson argues, it is a common occurrence in capitalist countries for private entrepreneurs to fail to provide enough investment to achieve full employment. In that case, it falls to the state to make up the difference—otherwise production and growth will stall.

Finally (and relatedly), without tight regulations and heavy taxation on the rich, income inequality tends to grow, and this is a drag on growth. As noted previously, if too much of the national income flows to the rich, who disproportionately save it instead of spending it, the working classes will not have enough income to consume what they produce. That in turn tends to drag down private investment, because investments are only as profitable as their prospective mass market—there is no point in building a shoe factory if the population of potential customers does not have money to spare to buy shoes.

Currently, the United States has about the most productive large economy in the world, roughly tied with France's and Germany's.[22] It is extremely unequal, and has suffered as a result, but as a practical matter it has tremendous economic strength. Across the country, there are millions of businesses that produce goods and services—cars, electronics, medical treatments, haircuts, and so on. These are mostly sold through some kind of market and bought by the consuming population, most of whom get their income by working at those very businesses.

Not all income goes to labor, of course. Businesses make profits when their income exceeds what they spend on overhead, and those profits are collected by the owners of the firm (this has consistently been about 30 percent of national income in the United States).[23] Those firm owners might keep the profits, or spend them on investment in new buildings, machinery, tools, and so on, providing income to construction or supplier firms, who in turn provide income to their own workers. This *circulation of spending* is what makes any advanced economy function—a nation is prosperous when its money is going around and around, all workers are employed, and all businesses are operating at top speed.

That state of affairs has been comparatively rare in modern times. In the financial crisis of 2008, for instance, the process of circulation was strangled by a panic in the banking sector that quickly spread to all parts of the economy. Many businesses went bankrupt, throwing all their workers out of a job and removing whatever spending they had previously dedicated to investment and supplies. Other businesses who had relied on those sales were in turn driven under or forced to cut their shifts, which cut overall spending more, and so on.

That is an *economic depression*. A modern economy is vulnerable to self-perpetuating collapses in spending that lead to mass unemployment and idle productive capacity—the bizarre situation in which people go hungry and shoeless while crops rot in the fields and factories sit silent for lack of customers.

Things haven't always been this way. In premodern societies through most of the nineteenth century, even in rich countries, the majority of people worked in agriculture, and in times of economic crisis most people could resort to subsistence farming to preserve a basic standard of living. But as economies became more and more productive, a greater and greater fraction of people have moved into wage labor. Today in the United States, just 1.3 percent of workers are on farms (which are heavily subsidized to boot), and most people require paychecks for their daily sustenance.[24] Indeed, even most farmers today require sales and wages to live—an industrial dairy farmer cannot live on milk alone.

Neoliberals, like their classical liberal forebears, often argue that depressions are simply a fact of nature, or some kind of just punishment for past excess. Herbert Hoover's secretary of the treasury, Andrew Mellon, famously said this about the Great Depression: "Liquidate labor, liquidate stocks, liquidate the farmers, liquidate real estate. It will purge the rottenness out of the system."[25]

But this idea is false. A depression causes pointless waste and misery, and the state can solve the problem quickly and easily by stepping in to restore the missing spending—that is, *stimulating* the economy. It can increase the money in the citizenry's pockets by lowering taxes or increasing spending (on public works, for example, or through simple cash handouts). Or it can increase the supply of credit through the central bank, which has various ways to induce more lending.

On the other hand, if an economy faces the contrary problem of spending running well ahead of increases in economic production, resulting in economy-wide price increases as people bid against each other for labor, goods, and services—that is, high inflation—then the government can *slow* the economy by hiking taxes, cutting spending, or restricting the supply of credit (often called austerity).

These two situations illustrate an important side fact: we know an economy has reached full employment and production when we start seeing sustained upward pressure on prices. This has not happened in any major economy since the 2008 financial crisis. Just witness the measured inflation rate in the United States, which has been bumping along well below the Fed's 2 percent target for almost that entire period (implying there could be more jobs and production without any pressure on prices).[26] For the foreseeable future, restoring full employment would be priority one for any sensible government.

People often get confused about where the money for economic stimulus can come from. It seems as though it can't just come from nowhere, right? And if the government borrows tons of money, then surely it will have to pay it back. Mainstream media coverage fuels this perception by ceaseless scaremongering about the national debt. If individuals have to "tighten their belts" during hard times, then surely the government should do the same.

In fact, a major state has unique powers that allow it to stimulate without limit so long as the economy remains depressed. In times of crisis, there is enormous demand for safe assets—and there is none safer than U.S. debt, because if the American government collapses, the whole world economy would go up in smoke. Furthermore, if a country borrows in a currency it controls, as the United States does, the central bank can simply buy up the debt itself, effectively financing the borrowing with printed money. (Indeed, there is no reason why the central bank couldn't just hand out printed money directly to citizens as a stimulus policy.) Again, there can be no economy-wide, sustained inflation so long as there is ample idle capacity in the economy.

So the *money* for stimulus comes from nowhere, because it can be created infinitely at zero cost, but the *real resources* that matter—the workers, raw materials, goods and services, and so on—come from the whole society. Depressions are easy to resolve because the entire problem is that gobs of useful stuff are literally lying around idle. All the government has to do is force enough spending into the system to get the process of circulation started again.

But fighting depressions is just the start of choices that states can make to shape their economies. The important thing to realize for our purposes is that the economic machine depends at every point on state rules and policies, and those can be radically altered without impeding economic production whatsoever—on the contrary, they can improve it, as we will see in chapter 3. How much workers collect in income for how many hours of labor, the rate of corporate profit, who owns the businesses, the characteristics of the markets they operate in—states have enormous latitude to change all these outcomes and more.

Sensible economic policy therefore should start with a moral ideology—a vision of a just society—and then arrange economic institutions that can achieve it. I am partial to the arguments of Amartya Sen and Martha Nussbaum, who have constructed an elaborate "capability approach" that values every person's well-being as defined by their capability to achieve what they have reason to value.[27] By this view, economic and social institutions should be constructed such that all people have the resources and education to live a full, satisfying life.

Philosopher John Rawls has a similar system, imagining a social contract set up behind a "veil of ignorance."[28] Roughly speaking, the idea is that if one had no idea where one would land in an income distribution, one would logically construct a society that was as equal as possible, so long as that equality didn't interfere too much with the overall wealth of society.

However, one could equally well substitute the teachings of Jesus Christ, who said that those who care for the worst-off people in society (prisoners, the hungry, the poor, or immigrants) not only will be sent to heaven but, in caring for those groups, are caring for Christ himself: "Inasmuch as ye have done it unto one of the least of these my brethren, ye have done it unto me." Or one could follow the words Thomas Jefferson put into the good old Declaration of Independence: "We hold these truths to be self-evident, that all men are created equal, that they are endowed by their Creator with certain unalienable Rights, that among these are Life, Liberty and the pursuit of Happiness."

Not all share such views, of course. The other basic tendency in political-moral reasoning is hierarchy—the idea that people should be ruled by an elite and that subordinate classes must be kept in their place, by force if necessary. As Corey Robin writes in his book *The Reactionary Mind*, this kind of instinct is at the heart of conservative politics. When downtrodden groups—like Black Americans in the 1960s during the civil rights movement—try to liberate themselves, there is very often a backlash from groups with higher status demanding they be put back in their "place." The great bulk of political history since the French Revolution has centered around the contest between subordinate groups trying to break free of domination and the beneficiaries of status quo privilege trying to stop them.

Expressed this way, conservatism sounds unpleasant, but I reckon just about everyone has a little conservative in them. It can be felt in the surge of anger you feel when someone has broken into your car, or the nostalgic disappointment you feel when you find that a favorite childhood tree has been cut down. Packaged properly, a conservative message can plainly appeal to a large mass audience, as evidenced by the success of the Republican Party and the British Tories over the last seventy years. But it also explains part of the appeal of neo-liberalism. As we've seen, neoliberalism enshrined the political domination of property owners, and was often sold with thinly disguised racist backlash rhetoric. In 1996, the cover of the then-neoliberal magazine *The New Republic* featured a cover story demanding the passage of the welfare reform bill—and the illustration accompanying the story showed a single Black mother smoking a cigarette.[29]

The ostensible technical reason for the welfare reform bill was to get poor single mothers to work, but the real political fuel for it was a visceral desire to punish and discipline the poorest people in the country, who were disproportionately nonwhite. Similarly, when the propertarian Liberal Republicans ran a candidate for president in 1872, they ran on a platform of free-market capitalism and taking away the civil rights of freed slaves. Propertarian "self-regulating" market institutions tend to produce economic calamity, which makes them unpopular, but if they can be hooked into conservative moral politics, they can help politicians win elections over and over.

In any case, once one has a moral objective defined, then one can choose economic policies appropriate for that goal.

(I will take for granted that the reader shares my egalitarian Christ/Jefferson/Sen opinions; if not, you can consult some Oswald Spengler.) As a simple, basic objective, we should try to wrench inequality down as far as possible, so long as it does not disrupt the system of production too much.

But you don't have to be a political philosopher or a theologian to work out a basic moral framework. Ultimately a rough-and-ready egalitarianism is sufficient for almost all political purposes. A brief glance at American politics and institutions proves beyond any question that the current system is grossly unfair and dysfunctional. The current American elite do not deserve in any way to rule the people, and there is every reason to overhaul our society to make it drastically more equal.

So what does that mean in concrete terms? In the rough sketch given here, I have left out the welfare state, but that is a foundational part of the economies of all advanced countries, even the United States. Across all of the states that belong to the Organisation for Economic Co-operation and Development (OECD), states spend an average of about a fifth of their production on social support programs.[30] The main point of these policies is to spread out the distribution of income, because classic capitalist institutions distribute income only to workers and owners of property, regardless of their needs— leaving out people who have no wealth and can't work, and often bankrupting the sick. So on the one hand, that means setting up an income stream for all people who cannot or should not work—children, students, retired and disabled folks, the unemployed, and so on. On the other hand, policies such as a child allowance, maternity grant, or paid family leave provide extra income to account for expenses related to rearing a family, something that tends to occur early in the life cycle, when people are generally at their lowest earning potential. Other programs, such as universal healthcare (covered in chapter 7), give people not just the ability to go to the doctor when needed but also the security to know that they will not be bankrupted by an expensive illness.

In addition to providing income security for all people whether they work or not, a complete welfare state that applies to all categories of nonworkers radically changes the nature of the labor system. Under classical capitalism, people are forced to go seek work out of fear of destitution, and many cannot get a job even when they try. Stories abound about Americans working grueling hours just to pay the bills, or being driven into poverty for lack of work, and no doubt many readers have experienced that pressure themselves. But with a full welfare state—including an unlimited basic unemployment allowance, as exists in Finland—nobody has to work to survive.[31] Instead, if businesses and government need work to be done, they have to *coax* people into it with decent hours, pay, and benefits. And this can work just fine—indeed, in Finland the fraction of prime working-age people (aged twenty-five to fifty-four) who are either employed or looking for a job is more than 5 percentage points higher than the comparable figure in the United States as of 2019.[32]

The labor system can be made even more just with unions, as we'll discuss in more detail in chapter 11. Workers are said to participate in a "labor market," but work is not really a commodity, because it cannot be preserved and held back for a better price. In any particular hour, either you work and collect wages, or you do not and that hour is lost forever. That may be a harmful loss of income, even if cushioned by the welfare state, if one has mortgage payments, childcare bills, or other expenses, as most people do. On the other hand, an employer can often find someone to take your place if you refuse the offered wage, or can wait you out until you crack.

In other words, there is a gigantic power imbalance in any labor "market" in favor of employers. That is why for thousands of years workers have attempted to band together in organizations to increase their collective leverage. A firm might be able to cast aside one disgruntled worker, but not all of them simultaneously if they are organized. A union can thus force the company to sign a contract guaranteeing relatively equal wages for all employees, protections from unjust termination or workplace abuse, and benefits such as paid vacation days.

Unions are nearly dead in the American private sector, but they have been effectively institutionalized in many European states. In Austria as of 2016, 98 percent of workers were covered by a union contract, while the figures in Belgium and Iceland were 96 and 92 percent, respectively.[33] This can be achieved in a number of ways—with the "Ghent system" (which originated in Belgium but is the norm in Nordic countries today), for instance, unions are made responsible for unemployment insurance, and most all workers join up so that they don't miss out on that benefit.[34] Or with "sectoral bargaining" in Austria, union leaders and management negotiate a contract for a whole economic sector, and then the state extends the resulting contract over the entire workforce.[35]

As a result, the distribution of wages in these countries is dramatically compressed. In Nordic countries, the top tenth of wage earners make between 2.3 and 2.5 times as much as the bottom tenth of wage earners, while in the United States they make over five times as much.[36] Incidentally, if unions are strong enough, then a minimum wage policy becomes unnecessary, because wage contracts keep all workers well above the poverty line. Indeed, in Finland a conservative business lobby recently proposed a minimum wage partly on the explicit grounds that it would weaken the collective bargaining system.[37]

Then there is ownership. In the United States, wealth ownership is grotesquely unequal—the top 10 percent of households own nearly 75 percent of the national wealth, and the top 1 percent own nearly 40 percent.[38] The bottom half of American society owns virtually nothing. But it doesn't have to be this way. In European countries, wealth concentration is markedly lower, particularly in Norway, where the state owns fully 75 percent of the national wealth, excluding owner-occupied housing—including the country's largest oil company, largest telecommunications company, and largest bank.[39] It's as if the U.S. government owned ExxonMobil, AT&T, and JPMorgan Chase. There is no reason for a tiny minority to exercise dictatorial control over national businesses—indeed, even in the United States many corporate enterprises function perfectly well when they are owned by their workers (such as the King Arthur Baking Company or New Belgium Brewing) or owned by the state. The American government owns the United States Postal Service and the Tennessee Valley Authority, which are functional and successful enterprises despite decades of propertarian attacks (though Donald Trump did terrible damage to the USPS in 2020, seemingly as part of an attempt to prevent Democrats from voting by mail; at time of writing plans were afoot to repair it).

Finally, there is the structure of markets. Many leftist writers view markets with suspicion, because they are the means by which so much current injustice is perpetrated. And indeed, as we'll see in chapter 7, a market is wholly inappropriate for structuring a service such as healthcare, because many injuries or illnesses are far more expensive to treat than even an upper-middle-class person can afford to pay out of pocket, and rationing by price means that those who cannot afford treatment would die. (The Byzantine labyrinth of Obamacare regulations shows just how much government regulation is necessary to create even a poor simulacrum of a health insurance market.)

However, the structure of a market is just as important as whether a market exists. Who sets the rules of the marketplace, the number of firms offering their goods for sale, and the background level of income inequality have enormous influence on how a market functions. If a single company controls the entire supply of some good (that is, if there is a monopoly), then it has free rein to soak the customer. Or if a company controls the market itself, it can use its leverage to squeeze both suppliers and consumers. John D. Rockefeller did exactly this with railroads to roll up his oil empire during the Gilded Age.

Amazon and Walmart, for instance, are notorious for forcing price discounts onto companies that sell items in their stores, so that they can gobble up more market share. Competing on quality becomes very difficult in such a situation, and those stores tend to become flooded with cheap junk. And with Amazon unwilling to spend the money necessary to truly police its gigantic marketplace, counterfeiting and fraud have become major problems on the platform.[40] Greed and power can easily overwhelm any other factor in a marketplace and cause it to behave in bizarre and toxic ways.

It follows that for even the simplest market to function as advertised, we require an elaborate structure of state policy. Indeed, as we'll see in chapter 3, even capitalists have often been forced to create rules and standards in markets they control to tamp down on cheating and fraud.

On the other hand, if there are a reasonable number of competitors in a market, and companies can set their own prices, and the population of customers has a relatively equal amount of income, and the goods in question are not subject to some emergency-induced shortage (in which case rationing should be used to ensure everyone can get what they need at a fair price), then a market is a perfectly functional way to distribute things.

At any rate, fully recognizing the fact of economic interdependence appears to be a difficult thing for politicians. Even Franklin Roosevelt, whose entire 1932 campaign was themed around the idea, failed to fully internalize it. In his address to the Democratic National Convention in July of that year, he endorsed a collective view of economic policy:

> Our Republican leaders tell us economic laws—sacred, inviolable, unchangeable—cause panics which no one could prevent. But while they prate of economic laws, men and women are starving. We must lay hold of the fact that economic laws are not made by nature. They are made by human beings.

But Roosevelt remained leery of budget deficits, and tried to pay for as much of his New Deal programs as possible with increased taxes, mainly on the rich—which limited their stimulative effect. Then in 1937 he attempted to balance the budget long before full employment had been reached, which tipped the economy back into recession and caused his party to lose many congressional seats in the 1938 midterms. More than seventy years later, Barack Obama's premature focus on budget deficits weakened his administration's response to the 2008 financial crisis, leading to a sweeping defeat for the Democrats in the 2010 midterms that cost them control of multiple state legislatures and the House of Representatives. Time and time again, we have seen that submitting to propertarian orthodoxy spells disaster for any incumbent party.

In the following chapters, I will explore various aspects of collective economics, and detail how the United States can become a far better place to live by fully embracing this idea—not quitting halfway as Roosevelt did. But first, let's consider how the tentative collective system of the New Deal was destroyed.

HOW NEO-PROPERTARIANISM CONQUERED THE WORLD

THE GREAT DEPRESSION DESTROYED classical liberalism. As we saw in chapter 1, it was already dying thanks to World War I and the difficulties of the 1920s, but the 1930s finished it off. After World War II ended, it was plainly obvious that the malfunctioning international economy had been a major factor in bringing Hitler to power, and the resulting war was the bloodiest in history. Something had to be done to keep that from happening again.

This led to a radical change of political thinking at all levels of society. Elites in almost every country abandoned propertarianism and the self-regulating market, while the broad population came to expect government action to deal with economic problems. Above all, there was a firm consensus that mass unemployment and depression must be avoided at any cost. Interfering with property rights or exchange rates, jacking up taxes, canceling debts, or just about anything else was now worth considering—whatever the side effects, they could not possibly be worse than Hitler.

That urgency fueled the creation of numerous economic institutions and mechanisms to control the world economy. These structures and thinking reflected a new hegemonic ideology dubbed "Keynesianism," after John Maynard Keynes, though it bore little resemblance to what the man himself advocated. American economists led by Paul Samuelson produced a school of "New Keynesianism" that was essentially old classical economics with some additions bolted on to deal with recessions and government spending. Keynesianism came to mean little aside from the idea that the government could fight recessions by spending money—a gross oversimplification. Keynes's disciple Joan Robinson, who had helped write his *General Theory*, called this "bastard Keynesianism."[1]

Still, the system basically worked. For about three decades there was full employment, fast growth, and relative political peace across the rich world—quite a feat, considering that we had just emerged from two of the most destructive and costly wars in human history, one right after the other.

In the previous chapters, I've argued that the economy, far from being a naturally occurring phenomenon that should be left to its own devices, is an inherently collective system that must be treated as such, both to maximize national and international prosperity and to improve the quality of life of as many people as possible. Making that the foundation of world policy led to the greatest economic boom in history. And yet by the 1990s propertarianism and the self-regulating market once again ruled the world, eventually driving the economy and global politics into the exact same ditch of economic crisis and political extremism it had crashed into in the 1930s.

How could this have happened? Well, the world economy ran into a fresh set of troubles in the 1970s, and a new class of propertarians was ready to pounce on the opportunity and mount an incredibly successful assault on the Keynesian consensus—one that we must study if we want to have any hope of regaining control of our future.

The story of our backslide into neoliberalism begins in 1944, during the Bretton Woods conference at the height of World War II. Diplomats and economists from the Allied countries (including Keynes) gathered at a resort in New Hampshire to iron out an agreement on how to run international trade. The basic plan was to construct a managed trade system that would forestall the problems of the 1920s and 1930s, when the gold standard, competitive devaluation, and general chaos had unleashed hell.

Keynes had a brilliant idea for an "International Clearing Union" that would manage trade through a new currency, the "bancor," to be used only for settling international trade accounts. The objective was to encourage *balanced* trade, so unlike the gold standard, there would be strict mechanisms pushing against both surplus and deficit. The system would be open to every country in the world. Each would pay a membership fee in proportion to its total trade, which would be used for settling international accounts. Countries with a trade surplus would get a bancor credit to their account, while those in deficit would have a deduction. Exchange rates were to be fixed, but still adjustable in case of problems. Get too far into deficit, and you would be required to devalue your currency to cut imports—but get too far into surplus, and you would be required to increase your currency's value to cut exports. There would be a further progressive tax on bancor accounts to discourage trade imbalances. And there would be no possibility of cheating.

Since all trade would be eventually settled in bancor, all

trade deficits and surpluses would eventually cancel each other out—preventing the kind of galloping collapse in international payments that was seen in the 1930s. As Keynes wrote, the basic "principle is the necessary equality of credits and debits, of assets and liabilities. If no credits can be removed outside the clearing system but only transferred within it, the Union itself can never be in difficulties."[2]

Alas, power politics ruled out Keynes's idea. The United States was emerging from the war as by far the most powerful country on earth. Europe, China, and Japan were physically devastated and had lost tens of millions of people—the Soviet Union alone, which had done the great majority of the fighting against the Nazis, had suffered perhaps 27 million deaths.[3] By comparison, the United States lost only about 400,000 people, and its territory was virtually untouched by conflict.[4] By 1945, it accounted for something like a third of the whole world economy.[5]

Therefore Keynes's idea was shelved, and the resulting Bretton Woods system was a much more haphazard affair, geared around American needs and power at the moment. All participating countries—the United States, Japan, Europe outside the Soviet bloc, and Australia (the Soviets attended the conference but refused to join)—would theoretically tie their currency to gold, but in practice tie it to the dollar. They would be required to keep their exchange rates within a 1 percent boundary. All the pains of adjustment were to fall on countries with a trade deficit—the United States was at the time the largest exporter in the world—though the International Monetary Fund was set up to extend loans to countries with balance-of-payments difficulties (for instance, if a country was struggling to obtain gold or dollars to finance a trade deficit).

Probably more important, the wartime controls on finance were largely kept in place. After the international financial contagion of 1929–33, policymakers looked at the international movement of capital with considerable skepticism. Trading commodities was fine so long as you kept the trade balanced, but flows of money—particularly "hot" money in the form of short-term investments or speculative gambles—were rightly viewed as highly dangerous. Strict capital controls were kept in place in most countries, allowing for little but long-term investment. This was more a result of inertia than deliberate planning, but it was an extraordinary success—banking panics virtually ceased in the Bretton Woods participants, only to return in force when the system collapsed and domestic controls were rolled back.

Elsewhere, American selfishness was at least somewhat farsighted. U.S. negotiators realized that now that the war was over, a great chunk of their pristine industrial capacity would go to waste unless foreign countries had enough income to buy American products. Thus in 1948 U.S. policymakers proposed a big reconstruction grant—not a loan, remarkably—for war-ravaged countries: the Marshall Plan, named after Secretary of State George Marshall. The conditions were relatively modest, requiring mainly a reduction in trade barriers and some adoption of American business practices. The main point was to kick-start the European economy to stave off depression, encourage Europeans to buy American exports, and build up Europeans' own internal production and export capacity from there.[6]

The impending Cold War, which was already taking shape, played a major part in this design. A wealthy and prosperous capitalist bloc was considered vital for containing the spread of communism. That was particularly important for

West Germany, which otherwise might have been broken into more pieces. Germany had been the economic engine of Western Europe for decades, and it was thought better to keep it strong to provide a bulwark against communism, rather than break it up to forestall the risk of another Hitler. Poorer countries, unfortunately, were largely left out. Indeed, even in Europe richer nations got more money than poorer ones, since it was thought they were key to recovery. (To be fair, there was a much darker side to this story: In the name of anticommunism the United States would assist in or carry out mind-boggling atrocities across the developing world, up to and including outright genocide in Indonesia. There, in response to an abortive coup attempt that was falsely blamed on the Indonesian Communist Party, right-wing forces carried out a mass butchery of communists and suspected leftists between 1965 and 1966, with the support of the United States, that left perhaps a million dead.[7])

Despite these flaws, the combination of the Marshall Plan and Bretton Woods was one of the most striking examples of international generosity and effective statesmanship in history. Under the American umbrella, Western Europe and Japan did indeed rapidly recover and rise to an American standard of living. The German-French border region, which had seen wars occur with clockwork-like regularity for hundreds of years, became a quiet, peaceful place. Indeed, most European countries harnessed their new wealth far better than America itself, building out comfortable welfare states while the United States built only a few modest additions to the New Deal.

The three decades after World War II were probably the best historical period ever for the working classes of wealthy Western countries, all things considered. Wages were growing, housing, medical care, and education were affordable, and jobs were plentiful. Of course, many people were partly or entirely excluded from the social bargain—African Americans in the United States, immigrants in European countries, and so on. Poorer countries did less well, although some, such as South Korea and Taiwan, did manage to start climbing up the development ladder.

But the economies of social democracies in Europe and the New Deal in America ran aground in the 1970s. One problem was inflation in the United States, where the government started up Medicare and Medicaid and fought the Vietnam War without increasing taxes enough to compensate. That stoked the economy, which was already hot thanks to a massive expansion of the workforce (discussed shortly), and led to steady price increases and a stronger dollar, pushing the United States toward a trade deficit. The United States was the central pillar of the whole Bretton Woods system, and that system was not designed to accommodate an inflationary America. Yet President Nixon manipulated the Federal Reserve away from slowing price increases, for fear that a recession would cause him to lose the 1972 election.[8]

Equally important were the increasingly successful efforts of financiers to squirm out of the Bretton Woods financial controls. One of the most important of these was Regulation Q in the United States, which capped the amount of interest banks could pay on deposits. In the mid-1950s, when British interest rates were higher than those allowed by this rule, U.K. banks hit upon the idea of borrowing U.S. dollar bank deposits and using them to back higher-interest loans in pounds—thus making a quick profit on the difference between the pound interest rate and the dollar one.[9] This arbitrage was simple and hugely profitable, and soon many other banks, including American ones, were involved in similar trades.

That was the origin of the "Eurodollar" market, meaning finance conducted in dollars outside the United States. This exploded in size over the 1960s, growing from $5 billion in 1963 to $37 billion in 1969.[10] Both European and American regulators, already heavily under the influence of bankers by this point, decided this market was not their jurisdiction— effectively creating a new financial and monetary system completely outside any state regulation. Skyrocketing hot money flows further strained the exchange rate system, both through market effects and through speculative attacks on currency values.

It's worth going through an exchange rate attack as a potential example of pure financial predation. In a fixed exchange rate system, a country's central bank needs a store of reserves to defend the value of its currency in the market— under Bretton Woods, those reserves could be either in gold or in dollars. Speculators accumulate big piles of currency, then sell them to the central bank, depleting its reserves. Simultaneously they bet against the target country's stock market, or take out loans in the target currency and then exchange that money for a different currency, or both. If the attack succeeds (and they often have), countries are forced to devalue sharply, causing a stock market crash and sometimes a recession. But the speculator makes a quick profit from the stock bet or from repaying the loan in a much less valuable currency. Sometimes exchange rate speculators justify their acts with the argument that they are preventing imbalances from building up and creating worse damage later down the road (as George Soros did when he attacked the British pound in 1992).[11] This may be somewhat true on occasion, but the argument is extremely self-serving at best, and most such attacks clearly lack even this excuse.

After Bretton Woods collapsed, such things happened much more frequently. The 1997 financial crisis in Southeast Asia, for example, was touched off by a speculative attack on Thailand's baht (which the Thai government had pegged to the dollar), which caused knock-on disasters that eventually engulfed countries from Russia to Brazil.[12] The resulting economic carnage—Indonesia's GDP fell by almost 60 percent in two years, and did not recover for a decade—cannot possibly be justified by any kind of reference to "imbalances."[13] Toppling Thailand off its dollar peg was purest bloodsucking parasitism. That kind of behavior is extremely common in finance, and it is often tremendously disruptive to the lives of ordinary people. Businesses go bankrupt and regular folks lose their jobs or savings, just so that rich bankers can make a quick buck. Bigger states can halt this sort of thing with legal coercion, but by the 1970s, thanks to the influence of financiers and propertarian ideology, they no longer wished to try.

At any rate, years of inflation and speculation strained the Bretton Woods system and put pressure on the dollar gold peg of $35 per ounce. Gold flowed out of U.S. reserves, as it was more valuable on the open market. French president Charles de Gaulle famously exchanged his dollar reserves for American gold in protest at United States economic dominance.[14] After trying various measures to prop it up, the United States went off the gold standard in 1971, allowing the value of its currency to float against all others, and that was that. As economic historian Adam Tooze writes, "Fiscal deficits and trade imbalances destabilized the Bretton Woods system. But if its foreign exchange controls

had not been constantly under assault from private speculation, the system might have survived."[15]

Things only got worse as the 1970s progressed, with both
inflation and unemployment dogging the economy. Domestically, a new school of self-described "neoliberals," which had
been organizing since the 1950s, seized the opportunity to
mount an all-out assault on the Keynesian consensus. The
high inflation of the 1970s was combined with high unemployment (a combination deemed "stagflation"), which was
supposed to be impossible according to the popular understanding of Keynesianism. Again, this was not Keynes's idea;
it came from Paul Samuelson, who produced a "Phillips
curve" (based on the work of another economist, William
Phillips) showing a smooth trade-off between inflation and
unemployment—with high unemployment one would have
low inflation, and conversely high inflation during low unemployment, regardless of circumstance. The presence of high
unemployment and high inflation simultaneously was seen as
a blow to the prestige of Keynesian economics.

Advocates of the status quo were on the back foot. They
struggled to unite on a consensus explanation of what was
happening, and what should be done as a response. The
neoliberals pounced, blaming stagflation on the Keynesian
attempt to steer the economy, and proclaimed the entire ideology discredited. They advocated an updated form of the
old classical liberalism in response.

Milton Friedman was an important thought leader among
American neoliberals, who were centered around the economics department at the University of Chicago—a group

that would come to be known as the "Chicago School"—and he advanced an argument based on "rational expectations." The idea is that everyone behaves like an economic agent who has perfect information—that is, all people act like self-interested businesspeople who can predict the consequences of their future actions in profit terms with complete accuracy. By this view, inflation was happening because expectations of increasing prices had become baked in. Because people had supposedly anticipated the government's attempts to stoke the economy with stimulus, it did not work. The result was increasing prices while unemployment remained high.

Chicago's Robert Lucas developed this thinking into a general attack on the whole Keynesian approach. His critique held that policies based on models using historical data—that is, Keynesian models—might not be any good, because people holding rational expectations would change their behavior in response to new policies. Instead, economic models should be based on rational "microfoundations" (that is, the idea that all people are independent, self-interested profit-maximizers), which were assumed, without any kind of systematic test, to produce more accurate models than the Keynesian variety.[16]

The heavy political slant here is obvious: all policy that regulates markets should be treated with severe skepticism. Thomas Sargent and Neil Wallace, two other neoliberal economists, even summed it up as the "policy ineffectiveness proposition."[17] Policy in this case of course does not refer to property laws, or the corporate legal structures that allow markets to exist in the first place; neoliberals welcome those (or pretend they do not exist). Rather, the target was the policies and programs that comprised the welfare state, as well as regulations to protect the environment and the working class. Of course, neoliberals admitted certain hypothetical circumstances in which regulation would be appropriate, but they placed the burden of proof upon those proposing such regulation. Anything that might "interfere" with the self-regulating market was bad until proven otherwise. (Legal scholar Cass Sunstein would explicitly enact this double standard as President Obama's regulatory czar, forcing agencies to jump through a slew of flaming hoops before promulgating any new regulation, which disastrously slowed the administration's response to the financial crisis and climate change.[18])

Under this view, markets were once again an inescapable, pre-political institution, and all policies must by definition take this into account. At bottom, these neoliberals simply assumed government should generally not try to improve the lot of the working class or the poor too much (the benefits for capitalists of property rights went mysteriously unexamined), because it would probably make things worse. Property was once more sacrosanct.

The most extreme use of rational expectations was the Real Business Cycle (RBC) school of thought, which argued that depressions caused by demand shocks (that is, the kind of self-perpetuating collapse in spending seen in the Great Depression) *cannot* happen—instead, recessions and unemployment are always the result of rational, efficient adjustments to developments on the supply side of the economy.[19] You can probably guess the policy conclusion: government should not try to fix recessions with monetary or fiscal stimulus.

Of course, the neoliberals were talking nonsense. It is flatly ridiculous to think RBC models explained all recessions, or even that many of them. If there had been a supply shock in

1929, for instance, then prices should have risen in response. Instead, they fell for the next four years straight. And only someone who has internalized the idea that markets are free-standing, pre-political institutions could believe that Robert Lucas's critique is a super-insightful observation. He did have a point that government policymakers must take the citizen-ry's reaction to their decisions into account, and it is probably fair to say that by the 1960s many of the bastard Keynesian economists had gotten overconfident about their ability to steer the economy. But the broader political goal that Lucas and the Chicago School were trying to establish—essentially that the government shouldn't build a welfare state, increase taxes, regulate the banks, or try to boost employment, be-cause people will adjust their behaviors in unpredictable ways to new rules—is absurd. If that is a decisive blow against wel-fare and regulation, then it is a decisive blow against all eco-nomic systems of any kind.

Of *course* people's behavior is influenced by economic rules. But that is true of all social systems, economic or otherwise, because people's behaviors are extraordinarily malleable. One natural experiment involving baboons is instructive. A study in 2004 examined how a troop of baboons dominated by large and aggressive males changed after all those domi-nant males caught tuberculosis and died.[20] With only smaller, gentler males remaining, the culture of that troop underwent a dramatic shift, moving from a social structure character-ized by endemic bullying and fighting to one with much more peaceful grooming. Conflict was still there, of course, but it tended to be resolved with peaceful methods, and the fighting that did happen was more between equally matched baboons, instead of a big one picking on a small one. Remarkably, the culture of that troop persisted even after all those original males had died off and were replaced by others coming in from outside. The new males were acculturated to the group norms, and learned to behave less aggressively.

Obviously, humans are not baboons. But it seems highly plausible that this is basically similar to why different human societies can have drastically different behavioral norms— consider premodern tribes who worshiped their ancestors and shared food in common, medieval peasants who accepted the divine right of kings and performed free labor for feudal lords, and people today who believe in democracy and corporate employment contracts. Human societies have much more complexity and choice than baboon societies, but the point is that behavioral norms are to a great degree the product of culture and learning, not the other way around.

Karl Polanyi studied premodern societies, and discovered in about five minutes that there is no evidence of an inbuilt propensity for "rational expectations." These societies were not remotely governed by individual self-interest, and trade for personal profit was a small part of such societies, if it existed at all. Instead, people's behavior was largely determined by status and tradition.

Hunter-gatherer societies, for instance, virtually always shared all the results of hunting and foraging collectively— even with hunters who failed to bring anything home. The potential problem of shirking was avoided by status within the tribe being based on one's level of selflessness. As a result, "the premium set on generosity is so great when measured in terms of social prestige as to make any other behavior than that of utter self-forgetfulness simply not pay. Personal character has little to do with the matter."[21] Conversely, behaving like a business owner—that is, a selfish chiseler—was a route to social ostracism and even exile.

From a biological standpoint, this sort of behavior makes a great deal of sense. Human beings are weak and rather defenseless on an individual level; our status as world super-predator depends on large-scale cooperation, memory, and intelligent strategy. Hunting and gathering are highly uncertain activities—one day somebody might score a big find or kill, followed by many days of failure.[22] A system of many groups heading out separately to maximize the overall chance of success, who then share the proceeds in common, is a highly *rational* way to organize such resource-gathering expeditions. The behavioral system proposed by neoliberalism, by contrast, is better suited to solitary predators or scavengers than it is to primates living in large groups.

Basically all studies of premodern societies have produced similar results. There was tremendous variety among those societies, of course, but though markets have existed for thousands of years, scholars have not discovered markets or personal profit playing a *dominant* social role in any societies until the advent of capitalism.[23] Moreover, unlike our close cousins the gorillas, whose communities revolve around a single dominant male, or chimpanzees, whose communities are broader but extremely violent and hierarchical, humans appear to naturally sort themselves into relatively equal groupings.[24]

However, it would also be a mistake to claim that socialist egalitarianism is the "true" bedrock reality of human consciousness. Any of dozens of dictatorships today or in history disprove that notion. Nearly all humans certainly have some egalitarian instincts, like the sympathy pain most people experience when they watch someone else suffering and are unable to help; some fashion of sympathy is always built into any group-based society. But it is more accurate to say that group dynamics and politics can influence human groups to behave in many different ways.

At bottom, there are simply *no such things* as "microfoundations." It speaks to the airless culture of economics that such an argument could come to be accepted without so much as an attempt to study premodern societies—or *any* societies, for that matter—to see if its assumptions held true. The Keynesian view of the 1940s through the 1960s would have been a lot stronger, more realistic, and more useful if the bastard Keynesians hadn't stripped out most of Keynes's more radical arguments so they could resurrect the sterile methods of classical economics. So for the policymaker, there is simply no comprehensive escape from having to make decisions about where to deploy state power, whether those decisions are based on empirical models, ideological claptrap, or just muddling through on guesses and instinct. There is no escaping policy choice, and claiming otherwise is always a way to disguise a policy agenda.

This sort of intellectual evasiveness was a signature characteristic of the American neoliberal school. It's an important lesson in ideological combat—through careful selection of which problems to consider, delimiting the space of possible explanations, and scornful contempt of outsider critics, neoliberals created a powerful, hermetically sealed narrative about political economy. The Chicago School won not through argument but by making the hegemonic ideology one that automatically produced their favored conclusion. This wasn't always a cynical enterprise, either—on the contrary, many people who internalized this neoliberal framework, which eventually included the elite of both American political parties, came to believe once again that markets were simply unalterable natural features of society. This kind of indoctrination influenced not just policy-makers but practically the entire American business and political elite—even today, you can find it in nearly all "nonpartisan" coverage of the budget deficit from outlets such as NPR.

However, there was another school of neoliberal economists, centered around Friedrich von Hayek and the Mont Pelerin Society in Switzerland (often called "the Geneva School"). They were not nearly as influential in the American political discourse as the Chicago School, but they were a lot more honest in their argumentation. As historian Quinn Slobo-dian writes in his excellent book *Globalists*, these neoliberals did not bother much with impossible self-regulating market ideology. Instead they were fixated on the problem of democracy, as popular governments took root in former monarchies after World War I. If a democratic government has full powers over the economy, and its legitimacy is based on the consent of the majority of the population, then what is to stop that government from expropriating the wealth of the rich? The Geneva School wanted to avoid that at any cost. They frankly admitted the centrality of state power in any economic system—and then argued for a state structure that could place the market and property rights outside the reach of democratic governments. It was, in other words, overt propertarianism.

Ludwig von Mises was inspired by the example of the police violently putting down a strike in Vienna in 1907, killing dozens of union members. "Friday's putsch has cleansed the atmosphere like a thunderstorm," he wrote.[25] He and other Mont Pelerin Society thinkers began developing ways of limiting the reach of democracy. The basic idea was to make redistribution of or otherwise infringing on property rights illegal—ensuring that violent state authority was deployed only to protect property. As Geneva School economist (and fervent racist) Wilhelm Röpke concluded, "If we desire a free market, the framework of conditions, rules and institutions must be all the stronger and more inflexible. Laissez-faire yes, but within a framework laid down by a permanent and clear-sighted market police."[26]

This kind of thinking underlies many of the structures of the European Union, especially the euro currency area. Originally, eurozone members were obliged to adhere to the Stability and Growth Pact, which theoretically required a maximum budget deficit of 3 percent of GDP and a maximum national debt of 60 percent of GDP—and, should the latter target be exceeded, a plan to reduce debt levels. (This was updated to the European Fiscal Compact in 2012, which is even stricter.)[27]

The authoritarian aspects of this system are not subtle. France and Germany could and did break those rules several times, but less powerful eurozone states have been laid to waste by these budget strictures. After the 2008 crisis, eurozone authorities forced stupendous budget cuts and tax hikes on Greece, supposedly to help cut its budget deficit—which pushed Greek unemployment past 27 percent, worse than it ever got in the United States during the Great Depression.[28] (In reality, the primary purpose was to bail out French and German banks, which had invested heavily in Greek government debt; the austerity ultimately made the debt problem even worse.)

As economist Yanis Varoufakis writes about his brief term as Greece's finance minister in the leftist Syriza government in 2015, eurozone authorities were utterly contemptuous of his efforts to partly roll back the austerity and get some jobs and growth going.[29] With a partial debt write-down and some good old Keynesian stimulus, Greece could have gotten its people back to work, fixed its infrastructure, and *improved* its ability to pay back its debt by boosting tax revenue. Instead, eurozone elites drained Syriza's time and momentum with Kafkaesque bureaucratic wrangling, while the European Central Bank caused a deliberate bank run within the country by withdrawing support for Greek banks, further squeezing the government. In the pinch, Prime Minister Alexis Tsipras blinked, the party gave up on halting austerity, and Varoufakis resigned. As German finance minister Wolfgang Schäuble said during the negotiations, "Elections cannot be allowed to change economic policy."[30] You couldn't ask for a balder statement of propertarian politics.

Just as in the nineteenth century, this resurrected version of propertarianism was straight-up tyrannical. Markets and property rights, under this system, must be protected from democratic control. However, even the crushing of Greece doesn't hold a candle to other stories.

Many Geneva School neoliberals were also fond of Chilean dictator Augusto Pinochet, who overthrew the democratic government of Salvador Allende in a military coup in 1973 (with help from the CIA). Hayek visited Pinochet many times, publicly defended his regime, and organized a meeting of the Mont Pelerin Society in the Chilean city of Viña del Mar in 1981. As he told the Chilean newspaper *El Mercurio* that same year:

> Well, I would say that, as long-term institutions, I am totally against dictatorships. But a dictatorship may be a necessary system for a transitional period. At times it

is necessary for a country to have, for a time, some form or other of dictatorial power. As you will understand, it is possible for a dictator to govern in a liberal way. And it is also possible for a democracy to govern with a total lack of liberalism. Personally I prefer a liberal dictator to democratic government lacking liberalism. My personal impression—and this is valid for South America—is that in Chile, for example, we will witness a transition from a dictatorial government to a liberal government. And during this transition it may be necessary to maintain certain dictatorial powers, not as something permanent, but as a temporary arrangement.[31]

Chile would remain a dictatorship until 1990. While in power, Pinochet's forces murdered at least 3,197 people, and tortured some 29,000, as he personally amassed a $28 million fortune.[32] But hey, at least there was economic "freedom."

That brings me back to Keynes, who is worth exploring in more detail because his economics was quite different from its conventional portrayal, and was fundamentally collectivist (despite his being something of a moderate squish in his personal politics). Again, it was not Keynesianism as advocated by Keynes himself that failed in the 1970s; it was the bastard offspring of it.

For instance, one of the foundational concepts of classical, New Keynesian, and neoliberal economics is the idea of general equilibrium. The economy is pictured as having a sort of ideal state in which all workers are employed, all products are sold, and all prices are in harmony with all others. More important, in these models the economy always trends toward equilibrium—if hit with some shock, it will always self-correct eventually. Thus in Samuelson's New Keynesian model, you could have high unemployment for a time because prices cannot adjust downward fast enough in response to a shock, but it will all shake out eventually, and prosperity will return.

Keynes himself rejected the notion of general equilibrium entirely. In his thinking, there are always *many* possible conditions that the economy could trend toward, and these in turn are always moving as time passes and conditions change on the ground. Where the economy ends up at any point over the short term depends not on individuals and firms thinking rationally about their long-term incomes but mainly on the mindset of the business class and upon the state. In a typical capitalist economy, overall output depends partly on the level of private investment, which is heavily influenced by the attitude of the rich. Keynes observed what anyone who has paid attention to the stock market for five minutes can figure out: that the business and investing classes often pay less than rapt attention to long-term profitability in their investing decisions. Instead there are cycles of often-irrational optimism and pessimism, or what he called "animal spirits." When the monied class is feeling happy and good about the future, they tend to overestimate the likely profitability of investments—and during a serious boom they fling money about with reckless abandon. Conversely, when they are feeling dour and anxious (after, say, a stock market crash), they view practically any investment prospect with suspicion. As he writes in the *General Theory*, the result is wild economic swings between boom and bust. Wishful thinking creates a boom, and when the boom subsides, irrational pessimism ironically creates a self-fulfilling prophecy of depression:

It is an essential characteristic of the boom that investments which will in fact yield, say, 2 per cent. in conditions of full employment are made in the expectation of a yield of, say, 6 per cent., and are valued accordingly. When the disillusion comes, this expectation is replaced by a contrary "error of pessimism," with the result that the investments, which would in fact yield 2 per cent. in conditions of full employment, are expected to yield less than nothing; and the resulting collapse of new investment then leads to a state of unemployment in which the investments, which would have yielded 2 per cent. in conditions of full employment, in fact yield less than nothing. We reach a condition where there is a shortage of houses, but where nevertheless no one can afford to live in the houses that there are.[33]

That leads to the second factor, which is the behavior of the state. Keynes's thought experiment here, which was based on the lived experience of many nations, demonstrates that economies can and do land in a place well short of full employment and production. There is no self-correcting mechanism that will fix a depression—on the contrary, mass unemployment and idle capacity can persist indefinitely. However, the state can act to fix this problem. By subsidizing consumption or investing itself, it can make full employment and production a permanent state of affairs: "The right remedy for the trade cycle is not to be found in abolishing booms and thus keeping us permanently in a semi-slump; but in abolishing slumps and thus keeping us permanently in a quasi-boom."[34] There is no full employment "equilibrium" that happens by itself, but the state can act to create that situation.

One could easily construct a genuinely Keynesian analysis that explained the problems of the 1970s. Economist Steve Randy Waldman, for instance, argues that the major root of the stagflation problem was simple demographics.[35] In the 1970s, the huge baby boom generation came of age right as women started to enter the workforce en masse, creating a spectacular increase in the labor force—which in turn created a big headwind for productivity, which is calculated by dividing production by hours worked. This combined with war, welfare spending, and oil price shocks (which occurred when assertive oil-exporting countries jacked up the price of oil to punish the West for supporting Israel in the Yom Kippur War in 1973) to add further upward pressure on prices.

Keynes never would have said that a nation always has the exact same trade-off between inflation and unemployment—it depends on the circumstances of the time. In the 1970s, the U.S. economy simply couldn't swallow that number of new workers under those conditions without creating significant inflation—especially not when wages were much better relative to today. And even despite the surge in total output and employment, many workers still could not find jobs—thus leading to high unemployment. It's a perfectly plausible explanation, to say the least.

At any rate, these possibilities went unexplored. Instead, the increasingly dominant neoliberals advocated an updated set of policies strongly resembling those of the 1920s. They argued that workers should be easier to fire, government enterprises should be privatized, budgets needed to be balanced (especially by cutting social welfare programs), and industry had to be deregulated (especially finance); if public goals must be achieved, it should be done with market mechanisms.

They asserted these policies would increase growth and get

the economy out of its difficulties. The unions, regulatory state, and welfare programs built during the New Deal and Great Society were simply too much of a drag, they said, and some would have to be sacrificed to return to fast economic growth.

By the late 1970s, these ideas were taken as conventional wisdom among political elites in most political parties. It had left- and right-inflected versions, but the "neoliberal turn" (as it came to be known) was bipartisan at its core. Conservative parties were the most fervent advocates—like the Tories under Margaret Thatcher and the Republicans under Ronald Reagan. But Democrats actually got the trend moving in the United States: it was President Carter and Senator Ted Kennedy of Massachusetts, advised by neoliberal economist Alfred Kahn, who shepherded the first big wave of deregulation, of trucking and airlines. Trucking had been regulated as part of transportation controls going back to the nineteenth century, while the New Dealers had subsidized airlines as the infant industry took shape in the 1930s, and then folded the industry into the regulatory state. The basic strategy for both industries was to try to balance competing priorities: the incomes of the workers, the price for consumers, and the need for national infrastructure. Truck drivers and flight attendants deserve a decent wage, the thinking went, but consumers also need reasonable prices and quality service. A single nation should have unifying infrastructure—all parts of the country (within reason) should have flight and truck service. Therefore the Civil Aeronautics Board (CAB) and Interstate Commerce Commission (ICC) regulated prices, rates, routes, destinations, and other parts of the airline and trucking industries in keeping with these goals.[36]

To 1970s policymakers coming under the neoliberals' sway, this kind of thinking seemed like incomprehensible

Egyptian hieroglyphics, or had simply been forgotten entirely. Consumer advocacy groups added to the attack by portraying the CAB and ICC—often with some justice, to be fair—as in bed with the industries they regulated.[37] Clearly regulation was some kind of anachronistic garbage, doing untold damage to America's transportation system and standing in the way of the free market, which would automatically make the system work without the government having to do anything. The CAB was thus killed entirely, while the ICC was drastically scaled back. "The Motor Carrier Act of 1980 will eliminate the red tape and the senseless overregulation that have hampered the free growth and the development of the American trucking industry," said President Carter announcing trucking deregulation.[38]

The results were terrible.[39] Neoliberal triumphalists later seized on evidence of declining prices as evidence their theory worked, but the price declines only followed the preexisting trend under regulation—indeed, deregulation may have led to increased prices now that both trucking and airlines are dominated by a handful of huge firms with large market power. The clearest effects were massive job losses (particularly among unionized firms), income declines for workers, market monopolization, and decreased service quality. Employee pensions and benefit packages were repeatedly raided in search of higher profits or during bankruptcy proceedings. Now with the individual profit on any one trip the only important metric for success, many small and even medium-sized cities lost most of their flight service. Airline companies began shoving more and more seats onto their planes and adding more and more fees. Many jobs that had been solidly middle-class, in particular truck driving, became grimly exploitative.

One notable casualty of this turn against workers was the

Professional Air Traffic Controllers Organization (PATCO). This union had a poor relationship with President Carter and therefore supported Ronald Reagan in the 1980 presidential election. Reagan promised PATCO he would support their needs, but when the union struck for better pay and benefits in 1981, he made an example of it. The strike was technically illegal, but unions had pushed legal boundaries before without being annihilated outright. But Reagan slapped both PATCO and workers with massive fines, decertified the union from legal recognition, and eventually fired 11,345 air traffic controllers, who were permanently banned from federal employment (many ended up in poverty as a result). It took a decade to restore the air traffic controller workforce, but private companies learned well from Reagan's example. Strikebreaking, union-busting, and suppression of both wages and workers' legal rights all increased dramatically after 1981.[40] So the deregulatory trend continued under Reagan, and actually accelerated under Clinton, as most of the last non-neoliberal holdouts were rooted out of the Democratic Party.

We'll see in the following chapters how all the prophecies of neoliberals turned to dust. Growth in fact slowed, and the self-regulating market turned out to have all the same problems it had back in the 1920s. Making property sacrosanct is simply no way to run an advanced international economy.

CASTING THE FALSE PROPHETS OF GROWTH OUT OF THE ECONOMIC TEMPLE

TINSTAAFL: THERE IS NO SUCH THING AS A FREE LUNCH. This is a common bumper sticker slogan among people who consider themselves economically educated. The implication is that there are always trade-offs—to get anything you want, lunch or otherwise, that thing must be paid for somehow.

This sounds like commonsense truth—after all, for someone to eat a lunch, someone must make that lunch. But propertarian economics takes this sort of general thinking to an extreme conclusion about what makes the economy grow and become more efficient and productive. Business owners must not have any interference from democratic states in piling up as much wealth as possible, they argue, and people must be forced to work for those business owners. The market must rule society, not the other way around.

Neoliberals implanted this autocratic ideology in America and across the world, claiming that by drastically cutting democratic controls over economic policy, growth and riches would follow. But as we've already seen, that prosperity was not guaranteed—on the contrary, such measures often harmed growth, and in the process ushered in a wildly more unequal, unstable economy.

In the neoliberal worldview, constant economic growth is the top priority of any society, and so incentives are taken to be the only kind of motivation that matters—the incentive of the business owner to earn a profit, and the incentive of the worker to get a job. This view emerges quite naturally from the traditional neoliberal models of the economy mentioned above, in which capital and labor are the only direct inputs to production (and technology is basically folded in with capital). It follows that anything that reduces the incentive to invest (such as a tax on corporate profits, or on personal incomes) or the incentive to work (such as unemployment benefits) must reduce the rate of growth.

The bulk of studies "find a negative effect of taxes on growth," William McBride wrote in a 2012 report for the Tax Foundation.[1] "These results support the Neo-classical view that . . . that taxes on the factors of production, i.e., capital and labor, are particularly disruptive of wealth creation." Welfare programs "may threaten financial solvency" in developed countries, wrote the Brookings Institution's Ron Haskins in 2010, arguing that countries should add work requirements so that welfare recipients are forced to look for jobs.[2]

Incidentally, we can already see the strong political slant in this treatment of incentives. On the one hand, it would be harmful to place any barriers to the already wealthy accumulating yet more riches. On the other, it would also be bad for poor people to be able to get income in any way aside from working. Basically the same thing.

We can also see the basic worldview of old classical liberalism coming through again. The economy is once more pictured as something existing outside of politics—a machine that more or less runs itself—and any meddlesome tinkering from politicians can only screw it up. The people should bend themselves to fit the needs of the self-regulating market, not the other way around.

For instance, neoliberals consistently hold that almost any social benefit must come at the expense of broader prosperity—with the exception of certain public goods such as education and basic infrastructure, which some neoliberals will grudgingly admit markets will not provide adequately. Nations might be wise to invest in education and roads, but they can enjoy a comfortable welfare state only at the expense of sandbagging growth and prosperity. Conversely, if growth is coming up short, then we can bring it back by cutting the social programs that do exist. It's as if the economy is a ship, and any welfare benefits are like barnacles clogging up the hull and slowing it down.

As discussed in chapter 3, the 1970s provided the perfect opening for neoliberals to jump in and start tearing down collective controls over the economy. As neoliberals gradually took control of both parties, endorsements of this perspective began to be seen among left-leaning journalists such as Charlie Peters, who wrote "A Neo-Liberal's Manifesto" in *Washington Monthly* in 1982.[3] In that influential essay, he advocated "freeing the entrepreneur from the kind of economic regulation that discourages healthy competition," stopping automatic raises for unions, making it easier to fire teachers, and means-testing Social Security so that it helps only the poor.

Why? Because "economic growth is most important now. . . . Our hero is the risk-taking entrepreneur who creates new jobs and better products," Peters wrote. Social Security must be cut because "the country can't afford to spend money on people who don't need it." (To be fair, he also attacked excessive bonuses for management, and supported environmental regulation and public works.)

This would be the key rhetorical trope and policy argument of the neoliberal turn. Ditch the stifling regulations and burdensome spending programs, and rapid growth will follow. There is a trade-off between equality and growth, and America for too long had erred on the side of the former. That was the mantra chanted by thousands of economists, bureaucrats, and intellectuals working their way up the career ladder.

One good encapsulation of what became a hegemonic ideology can be found in Thomas Friedman's 1999 book *The Lexus and the Olive Tree*. Here is the neoliberal policy platform that was then sweeping the globe, which he aptly depicts as a "Golden Straitjacket":

> To fit into the Golden Straitjacket a country must either adopt, or be seen as moving toward, the following golden rules: making the private sector the primary engine of its economic growth, maintaining a low rate of inflation and price stability, shrinking the size of its state bureaucracy, maintaining as close to a balanced budget as possible, if not a surplus, eliminating and lowering tariffs on imported goods, removing restrictions on foreign investment, getting rid of quotas and domestic monopolies, increasing exports, privatizing state-owned industries and utilities, deregulating capital markets, making its currency convertible, opening its industries, stock and bond markets to direct foreign ownership and investment, deregulating its economy to promote as much domestic competition as possible, eliminating government corruption, subsidies and kickbacks as much as possible,

opening its banking and telecommunications systems to private ownership and competition and allowing its citizens to choose from an array of competing pension options and foreign-run pension and mutual funds.[4]

This straitjacket will tend to strangle democratic politics, says Friedman (listen to the clear echoes of the Geneva School):

> As your country puts on the Golden Straitjacket, two things tend to happen: your economy grows and your politics shrinks. That is, on the economic front the Golden Straitjacket usually fosters more growth and higher average incomes—through more trade, foreign investment, privatization and more efficient use of resources under the pressure of global competition. But on the political front, the Golden Straitjacket narrows the political and economic policy choices of those in power to relatively tight parameters. That is why it is increasingly difficult these days to find any real differences between ruling and opposition parties in those countries that have put on the Golden Straitjacket. Once your country puts it on, its political choices get reduced to Pepsi or Coke—to slight nuances of taste, slight nuances of policy, slight alterations in design to account for local traditions, some loosening here or there, but never any major deviation from the core golden rules.[5]

However, in return, surrendering one's policy control over the economy will pay dividends in the form of faster growth and greater wealth. Prosperity will compensate: "The only way to get more room to maneuver in the Golden Straitjacket is by enlarging it, and the only way to enlarge it is by keeping it on tight. That's its one virtue: the tighter you wear it, the more gold it produces and the more padding you can then put into it for your society."[6]

Friedman is usefully stark about the tyrannical basis of his model of political economy. In his world, elected representative governments will have very little space to make their own economic policy choices. The self-regulating market will not permit "major deviations"; nations can make only tiny adjustments here and there. But, Friedman promises, surrendering economic sovereignty will pay dividends in the form of fast growth and prosperity.

Unfortunately, this turns out to be 100 percent bullshit.

The first big test of propertarian economics came about twenty years earlier, from the "Volcker shock"—the actions of President Carter's appointee Paul Volcker as chairman of the Federal Reserve. Neoliberal "monetarist" economists, following the aforementioned logic of rational expectations, predicted that the runaway inflation we discussed in chapter 3 could be solved quickly and easily with a sharp rap on the knuckles, so to speak. With inflation high for many years, expectations of price increases had become baked into the thinking of workers and firms, they argued, leading to a self-fueling upward price spiral. But if the central bank were to make a powerful demonstration that inflation would be crushed at any cost, then people's expectations would be reset, their behavior would change, and inflation would come down quickly.[7]

In early 1980, Volcker thus jacked interest rates through the roof, which rose from 10.25 percent to 20 percent.[8] ("The standard of living of the average American has to decline," he said.)[9] This sucked credit out of the economy by paying banks that much to park their money at the Fed. Anyone wanting, say, a home or car loan would have to beat that interest rate. Of course, few borrowers could afford to do so, and consequently credit-dependent sectors of the economy (especially home-building) collapsed. The ensuing recession was sharp but only moderately bad.

One side effect was the election of Ronald Reagan, as the economic downturn came directly before the 1980 election, thus dooming Carter to defeat. This would not be the first time that Democrats would sacrifice their own political success on the altar of propertarianism.

However, the monetarist prediction turned out to be totally incorrect: inflation only came down with grinding slowness. At first the strategy seemed like it was working, and Volcker lowered rates down to 16 percent, but prices started rising again. He was thus forced to jack rates back up near 20 percent and lower them only gradually starting in July 1981 as inflation slowly descended. Ruined home-builders mailed Volcker two-by-fours and bricks in protest, while auto dealers sent him the keys of unsold cars.[10] (Suggestions from John Kenneth Galbraith that the government could directly control prices, as it had done during the red-hot war economy of the 1940s, were ignored.)[11]

The second half of the Volcker recession lasted sixteen months and was the worst downturn since the Great Depression at that point. Unemployment reached 10.8 percent, and labor unions were devastated—doubly so by Reagan's direct destruction of the air traffic controllers' union when they went on strike, as we saw in chapter 3.[12] It took a vicious economic pummeling of ordinary people to bring down prices by this mechanism, not some automatic adjustment of expectations by wholly rational actors. (The monetarists, naturally, were not even slightly bothered.)

As the 1980s progressed, it turned out the structure of the American economy had changed for good. Whereas before the mid-1970s worker pay had risen in line with productivity, now it stagnated while productivity kept chugging along. The Economic Policy Institute calculates that while productivity (that is, output per hour worked) has increased 77.0 percent since 1973, hourly compensation has increased by only 12.4 percent.[13]

The gap between wages and productivity

Source: Economic Policy Institute

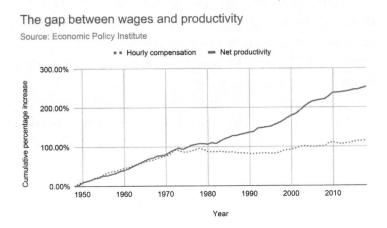

The mechanical consequence was a steady rise in inequality, as income that was once spread throughout society accumulated at the very top. The top 1 percent of income earners went from taking in about 10 percent of total income in the mid-1970s to nearly 20 percent by the 2000s—while the top 0.1 percent went from 3 percent of total income to over 10 percent.[14]

Top 1 percent share of income, 1928–2019

Source: World Inequality Database

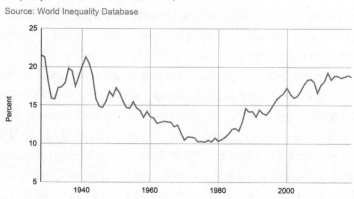

At first, neoliberal reforms still ran into opposition from powerful constituencies, which limited their reach in wealthy countries. Democrats controlled Congress for most of the 1980s, and President Reagan was forced to accept compromises to his utopian vision.

It was developing countries who got the full-strength dose of reform with the "Washington Consensus," which contained a sort of Ten Commandments of Neoliberalism for countries needing help from the International Monetary Fund (IMF).

In the 1980s and 1990s, nations such as Mexico and Thailand got into economic difficulties for a variety of reasons. The IMF would sweep in and demand the same cookie-cutter "structural adjustment" package in every circumstance: austerity (that is, spending cuts—especially to welfare programs—and tax increases), deregulation, labor market reforms (that is, union-busting, wage cuts, and other attacks on workers), and high interest rates.[15]

In many cases the "rescues" made the problem worse than it had been before, even according to the IMF's own criteria for success. Economists Robert Barro (a neoliberal, mind you) and Jong-Wha Lee studied all IMF programs from 1970 to 2000 and found that they decreased growth, eroded democracy and the rule of law, and did not improve debt burdens. "We conclude that the typical country would be better off economically if it committed itself not to be involved with IMF loan programs," they wrote.[16]

A Center for Economic Policy Research paper by Robert Naiman and Neil Watkins studying IMF programs in sub-Saharan Africa also found lower growth, increased debt burdens, and nations forced to reduce spending on education and healthcare to service external debt. "Efforts to reduce Africa's debt burden should be coupled with efforts to reduce the role of the IMF," they argued.[17] Many developing countries took to building up massive hoards of dollar-denominated assets in part to forestall the need for any such "assistance."

Despite the shoddy track record of early forays into proper-tarian economics, there was one period in which it seemed like the promises of its adherents were working out, at least in the United States: the 1990s. By the late 1980s, neoliber-als had mostly rooted the old New Deal attitudes out of the Democratic Party, and in 1992 one of their own won the pres-idency. Bill Clinton set about passing free trade agreements (most notably the North American Free Trade Agreement, or NAFTA, in 1992, and the permanent normalization of trade relations with China in 2000), deregulating finance (two big packages in 1994 and 2000), and "reforming" welfare. Aid to Families with Dependent Children—a program from 1935 that doled out checks to very poor mothers—was replaced with Temporary Assistance for Needy Families (TANF). Un-der TANF, benefits were capped, thus eroding their value by the rate of inflation every year; states got more control over the program (some of the more conservative ones took to spending the money on "crisis pregnancy centers," which often lie to women about the risks of abortion); and work requirements were added. To be fair, Clinton did also pass a boost to the Earned Income Tax Credit, which helped many low-income workers, but they still needed a job to be able to claim the benefit. People with no labor income—that is, the very poorest—get nothing from the EITC.

This was classic neoliberal economic reasoning. (It was also a neat piece of political triangulation. His Republican opponent in 1996, Bob Dole, "had nothing, really, to run on," as Michael Tomasky writes in his biography of Clinton.)[18] Conditioning benefits based on work would increase the supply of labor and hence boost growth. Horsewhipping poor women into the labor market would be better for them than welfare even if they got the same money, because working at a job is morally praiseworthy. The people should serve the market, not the reverse. (The fact that the design of the EITC allowed employers to capture a substantial slice of the benefit, by paying workers less than they otherwise would have, went largely unnoticed until later.)[19]

Still, all this seemed to be paying economic dividends. In Clinton's first term, the economy did fairly well, but it really got going in the late 1990s, generating a major boom in output, plus wage increases, all without excessive inflation. It seemed that propertarianism was working as advertised! Neoliberal Democrats pointed to Clinton's record, his two presidential election victories, and the failed candidacy of George McGovern in 1972 as definitive proof that the New Deal order was dead. (McGovern, who died in 2012 and whose epic loss is now closer in time to the presidency of Warren Harding than to the present day, has since become a sort of bogeyman to scare Democratic base voters away from voting for any leftist candidate, no matter how popular.)

However, economic historians generally agree that Clinton was mainly lucky. His chair of the Council of Economic Advisers, Joe Stiglitz, later concluded that "we in the Clinton Administration took office at the right time."[20] The rapid growth was fueled by the fortuitous coincidence of very cheap oil, the rise of computing technology and the internet (the bones of which had been built with public financing long before, incidentally), and most important, Fed chair Alan Greenspan's correct hunch that this new information sector might provide a productivity boost. He thus chose not to strangle the boom with high interest rates, *disregarding* neoliberal conventional wisdom that the central bank is supposed to start hiking rates before the economy gets hot, to avoid the dreaded self-fulfilling expectations of rising prices.[21] If productivity is booming, then one can have fast growth without price increases, because total production will be running ahead of new spending power.

The result was indeed the best economic performance since the 1970s (though it still wasn't nearly as good as the spectacular boom of the late 1960s). In 2000, unemployment got down to 4 percent—and this time without so much as a whiff of excessive inflation.[22] It was indeed a relatively great time for average Americans—so long as you weren't a poor mother, or thrown in jail because of Clinton's war-on-drugs policies.

However, there were serious problems under the hood of the U.S. economy. Under Clinton's rule, the economy became increasingly dominated by finance. Released from their New

Deal chains, banks got enormous, and raked in even greater profits. Finance went from accounting for about 10 percent of corporate profits to providing about 25 percent—hitting a high of 35 percent in the early 2000s (see below). Meanwhile, thanks to new free trade policies, manufacturing fell from over half of corporate profits to about 20 percent, and total manufacturing employment plunged by 20 percent in the four years after 2000, as China and other poorer countries gobbled up much of the U.S. manufacturing sector, and remaining manufacturers packed up their factories and shipped them overseas en masse.[23]

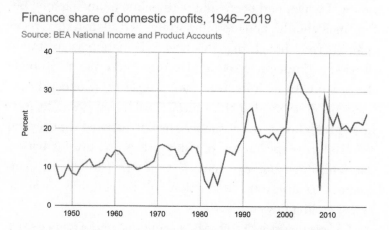

Finance share of domestic profits, 1946–2019
Source: BEA National Income and Product Accounts

(By the way, China, like all the successful East Asian economies, never subscribed to free trade nostrums. Instead it carefully managed its economy to keep production happening domestically, especially by controlling the value of its currency to keep exports competitive.)[24]

And it turned out that the Wall Street wizards had not eliminated any of the old dangers of finance. Immediately after that prosperous year of 2000, disaster struck in the form of a financial crisis centered in tech stocks. The ensuing recovery was slow in both growth and job creation terms, with

George W. Bush turning in the worst economic performance of any president since Herbert Hoover up to that point.

Elsewhere, financial buccaneers took to sandbagging functional enterprises for profit, loading them up with debt and then stripping their assets for a quick personal payout. Sometimes this would destroy the company—as when Carl Icahn bought Trans World Airlines in 1988 and took it private, awarding himself $469 million but loading up the company with $540 million in debt, which would eventually drive it into bankruptcy.[25]

Setting up a productive business and keeping it going over time is a difficult proposition. Milton Friedman famously wrote an article titled "The Social Responsibility of Business Is to Increase Its Profits," but failed to seriously consider the obvious fact that looting and fraud are very profitable. As the Mafia could tell you, it's much easier to strip profits out of a business somebody else already set up—especially if it's carried out through legal financial mechanisms.

It turns out that deregulating finance had some enormous downsides—and that was nothing compared with what was coming. As we'll see in chapter 5, financial crises produce problems that are even broader and worse, which is what happened in 1987 and 2001 (and of course 2008). Even when not sucking the life from productive businesses, a bloated and crisis-prone financial sector that routinely folds in on itself can harm the broader economy by causing bank failures, bankruptcies, and recessions.

When judged according to its stated objective of improving growth, the turn to neoliberal economics must be reckoned a failure overall. The late 1990s were the first *and last* time the

United States got a real full employment boom under neoliberalism. On the whole, everything got worse compared with the postwar years—growth and productivity slowed, wages stagnated, and inequality skyrocketed.

Averaged over time, the differences were substantial. Robert Skidelsky, a biographer of John Maynard Keynes, calculated in 2010 that "the average American would have been 10 percent richer had the US GDP per capita grown as fast between 1980 and 2007 as it did between 1951 and 1973."[26] And after the 2008 financial crisis, things got much worse. Following the lead of economist J. W. Mason, in the figure that follows I calculate that the rate of growth per person slowed by about half compared with the 1945–2007 trend.[27] As of 2019, economic output was something like 15 percent below the pre-crisis trend—an amount greater than the outputs of California and Virginia put together.

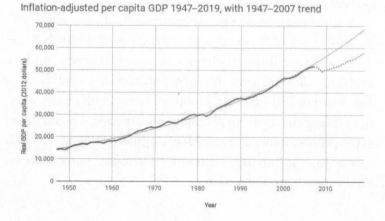

Inflation-adjusted per capita GDP 1947–2019, with 1947–2007 trend

We have seen that instead of producing fast growth, offering ourselves up as blood sacrifices to the gods of the free market did the opposite. But this raises the question of why. It could just be a coincidence—perhaps the postwar turbo-boom was a single peculiar event that couldn't be repeated, and the still relatively decent performance of the 1980s and 1990s was realistically as good as it could get.

But this doesn't jibe with the facts. After the 2001 recession, the economy was *obviously* well short of full capacity. Inflation was below the Fed's 2 percent target for almost all of President Bush's first term, and both job growth and output growth were distinctly weak. The economy was noticeably struggling to stay barely above stall speed—and when the 2008 crash hit, it got much worse.

So what was dragging down the American economy?

One answer is inequality. Neoliberal "reforms" had the effect of funneling money up the income ladder, as taxes on the rich were lowered steadily, unions were slowly strangled by offshoring and legal harassment, the minimum wage failed to keep up with productivity, and rules against monopolies were taken apart.

Chester Bowles, an advertising executive and head of the Office of Price Administration during the Second World War, made this argument about the 1920s and the Great Depression in a remarkable 1946 book called *Tomorrow Without Fear*, which was recently republished. As mentioned before, as income becomes more and more unequally distributed, it becomes harder and harder to sustain domestic consumption, because wealthy people save a greater fraction of their income instead of spending it. In turn, the wealthy have fewer and fewer places to invest the money they save, because cash-strapped consumers don't have the disposable income that would justify investment in new businesses.

Bowles marshals statistics demonstrating that while

productivity had increased by 24 percent in manufacturing and 39 percent in the electric power industry during the 1920s, pay to workers in those sectors had increased by only 10 and 6 percent, respectively. In mining, meanwhile, productivity had increased 27 percent, but pay had actually *decreased* by 10 percent. "All across the nation the purchasing power being distributed to our wage earners, who with their families constitute the great majority of the nation, was falling further and further behind the incomes that were necessary to buy the steadily increasing amount of goods we were capable of producing," Bowles wrote.[28]

So instead of going into the pockets of ordinary citizens, as the 1920s progressed the national income increasingly went into speculative frenzies in real estate, dubious business propositions, and finally the enormous stock market bubble of 1929. Bowles concluded:

> If ever it has been demonstrated that prosperity cannot continue unless enough income is being distributed to all of us—farmers and workers as well as businessmen—to buy the increasing products of our increasingly efficient system, it was demonstrated in the twenties. If we need any demonstration of the fact that our economy can choke itself to death on too many profits, the twenties provide that demonstration.
>
> Even with the most business-minded administration in our history, even with falling taxes and a government surplus, even with everything that businessmen thought they needed to insure continued prosperity, we could not duck that basic issue for more than a few short tinsel-decorated years.[29]

In other words, inequality is a drag on growth. The smaller the fraction of income going to the broad mass of the population, the more the economy will bog down. Marriner Eccles, FDR's Federal Reserve chair, made a similar argument:

> As mass production has to be accompanied by mass consumption, mass consumption, in turn, implies a distribution of wealth—not of existing wealth, but of wealth as it is currently produced—to provide men with buying power equal to the amount of goods and services offered by the nation's economic machinery. Instead of achieving that kind of distribution, a giant suction pump had by 1929–30 drawn into a few hands an increasing portion of currently produced wealth. This served them as capital accumulations. But by taking purchasing power out of the hands of mass consumers, the savers denied to themselves the kind of effective demand for their products that would justify a reinvestment of their capital accumulations in new plants. In consequence, as in a poker game where the chips were concentrated in fewer and fewer hands, the other fellows could stay in the game only by borrowing. When their credit ran out, the game stopped.[30]

These two perspectives are interesting not only for their content but also for how they prove that argument and evidence really did have a powerful effect on the thinking of political elites and policymakers. In the 1990s one never, ever heard this sort of reasoning coming from top advertising executives or the chair of the Federal Reserve.

Economist John Kenneth Galbraith (who worked at the

Office of Price Administration as well) also pinpointed in-equality as a prime cause of the 1929 crash. With the top 5 percent of households taking up about a third of the national income, luxury goods and investment became predominant sectors of the economy:

> This highly unequal income distribution meant that the economy was dependent on a high level of invest-ment or a high level of luxury consumer spending or both. The rich cannot buy great quantities of bread. If they are to dispose of what they receive it must be on luxuries or by way of investment in new plants and new projects. Both investment and luxury spending are subject, inevitably, to more erratic influences and to wider fluctuations than the bread and rent outlays of the $25-week workman.[31]

Steve Randy Waldman has updated this argument for modern times. Since the 1970s, household borrowing has increased along with inequality, while interest rates have declined—showing that "growing inequality required ever greater inducement of ever less solvent households to borrow in order to sustain adequate demand."[32]

Neoliberal propertarians dealt with the inequality argu-ment not by refuting it empirically but (as usual) by evasion. Milton Friedman came up with a "permanent income hy-pothesis" thought experiment, which imagined a society in which income is statistically equal, but fluctuates at random, and everyone knows perfectly what their lifetime income is go-ing to be.[33] Therefore disproportionate saving among the rich measured as a cross section in time *could* be a statistical illusion, as people making more would save more only temporarily to insulate against future drops in income. Hey presto, excess saving by the wealthy doesn't exist—and therefore inequality doesn't matter for growth.

This is another good window into the sociology of the economics profession, which takes great delight in contrarian arguments that deflate traditional moral values. As economist Noah Smith writes, "A clear-thinking, rational, but somewhat Asperger-y economist flouting social norms with an analysis that is insensitive but correct on technical grounds . . . is a narrative that, in my experience, is central to economists' image of their profession's social worth."[34] A whole generation of economics grad students were trained like circus seals to guffaw on cue at arguments like Bowles's. The idea that inequality might sandbag growth was regarded as a quaint anachronism, something only weak-minded bleeding-heart liberals could possibly believe. Even liberals like Paul Krugman dismiss Bowles-style arguments out of hand.[35]

Friedman's supposition combined with the dogmatic culture of economics meant that few even bothered to look at whether the permanent income hypothesis was actually true. However, some have done just such studies and found indeed that rich people do save dramatically more than the poor, and not in any way that would be explained by a desire to smooth their consumption over time.[36]

The permanent income hypothesis is also just, you know, *flagrantly preposterous.* We very obviously do not live in a world in which income is statistically equal. Moreover, as Waldman argues, the hypothesis implies that there should be no difference in inheritance between rich and poor, because everyone would spend and save in equal proportions over their lives. Any nine-year-old who can read a newspaper would correctly laugh that idea out of the room. Indeed, there are wealthy people alive today who are still passing down Gilded Age fortunes from the 1880s—according to *Forbes*, for instance, the Hearst dynasty is the twelfth-richest family in the country thanks to inheriting a media empire that William Randolph Hearst founded in 1887.[37]

But inequality is only part of the story of how growth slowed. Another characteristic aspect of neoliberal economics is financialization. We have already seen how finance has swallowed up a greater and greater share of corporate profits. A side effect of this domination was weak corporate investment, which was obvious by the mid-2000s. As J. W. Mason demonstrates, in the 1950s and 1960s firms typically borrowed for investment, spending about 40 percent of loans on factories, equipment, and so on. But that changed after the 1970s, with the proportion of borrowing spent on investment plunging to about 10 percent. Instead, corporations borrowed to "disgorge the cash"—spending money on stock buybacks (legalized by Reagan's Securities and Exchange Commission in 1982) and dividends. "If the corporate sector lacks funds for investment, it appears to be because too much money is flowing out, not because too little money is flowing in," he writes.[38]

A side effect of ruthless financiers with a laser focus on short-term profit taking command of productive business is a sharp increase in incompetence and corruption. Investigative reporter Maureen Tkacik wrote a sweeping article for *The New Republic* detailing how finance logic infected the airplane manufacturer Boeing, leading to the infamous crashes of the 737 MAX.[39] Finance dweebs overruled Boeing's expert engineers and insisted that they could get better margins by cutting corners and outsourcing as much as possible; the result was an automatic system that crashed the plane into the ground if it malfunctioned—"the world's first self-hijacking plane," she writes. This "airplane is designed by clowns, who in turn are supervised by monkeys," one Boeing employee wrote to another in 2017.[40] That does its part to harm business performance—who wants to buy a self-crashing airplane?

But fundamentally, if businesses skimp on research, development, and investment so that they can disgorge profits into the mouth of Wall Street, they obviously are going to become less innovative. One big source of growth—increases in labor productivity—will be harmed.

Another classic characteristic of neoliberalism is business concentration—the construction of monopolies (where one business wholly controls a market) and oligopolies (where a few businesses do, often in tacit coordination). In a free market, there is supposed to be competition between businesses. Customers will buy only the goods and services that are a good value for money, and therefore businesses will compete on price and quality. But if one business becomes very large, it can leverage its market power to buy up competitors, or run them out of business by temporarily dumping its products below cost. Customers are left with no choice but to take whatever the monopolist offers.

Gilded Age "robber barons" famously rolled up key industrial markets in this way starting in the 1870s. Andrew Carnegie took command of steel, Cornelius Vanderbilt railroads, William Clark copper, J. P. Morgan finance, and so on (though most such were involved in several lines of business, and all relied on relationships with financiers).

Meanwhile, other businesses operating economic choke points can leverage them to dominate a market. John D. Rockefeller used his control of railroads to drive independent oil producers out of business by charging higher prices to transport their product to market, eventually rolling up most of a fragmented oil market into one company, Standard Oil—and in the process becoming probably the richest person since the advent of capitalism.[41]

If a business does not have to compete, it will logically tend to spend less on innovation. It is much easier to sit back and collect monopoly profits than it is to be constantly trying to push back the technological frontier. Therefore, if monopolists and oligopolists come to dominate a country—that is, under a propertarian regime—growth will slow and the economy will stagnate.

This isn't just a historical consideration—the modern economy is once more dominated by robber barons. The Open Markets Institute has collected data on dozens of different markets that show a stark increase in the market share of the largest companies over the last few decades. Ninety-one percent of online search is controlled by Alphabet (the parent company of Google), while Amazon alone accounts for about half of online retail. The three biggest social networking companies make up 85 percent of that market.

Outside of tech, three companies now control 75 percent of the American beer market; four companies make 97 percent of America's dry cat food; the four largest service providers control 98 percent of the American cellphone market; the two largest cell phone operating systems (Android, made by Google, and iOS, made by Apple) run on 99 percent of American mobile phones; and the four largest appliance manufactures construct fully 100 percent of American washers and dryers.[42]

In a monopolized market economy, both political power and money flow up to the top. Citizens who need goods or services are forced to accept whatever the monopolist is offering. In the late nineteenth century, if you needed oil, and almost everyone did, you paid what Rockefeller was asking. Then those same companies end up in a monopsony position regarding their workers and suppliers—that is, they are the sole purchaser of labor and supply goods—allowing them to squeeze those groups as well. For instance, back in 1980, 37 cents of every food dollar spent by Americans went to farmers. Today, thanks to monopolist agricultural middlemen, only 15 cents does.[43] All this also does its part to sandbag growth.

Their extreme wealth also gives oligarchs enormous control over the political system, both directly, in the form of political contributions and lobbying spending, and indirectly, in terms of subsidizing think tanks and advocacy organizations that shape political discourse—which oligarchs often spend creating propaganda to slow the economy even more. The late Wall Street baron Pete Peterson, for instance, spent over half a billion dollars between 2007 and 2011 funding a slew of pro-austerity think tanks and publications.[44] His money is a big reason much mainstream media coverage continues to consider the budget deficit a fearsome problem by definition.

In addition to distorting press coverage, monopolists have also strangled journalism directly. Historically, the business model of journalism has been based on advertising, but Google, Facebook, and Amazon had gobbled up about 80 percent of the digital advertising market as of 2019. That share increased to 90 percent thanks to the pandemic, and indeed those three companies raked in more than half of *all* ad spending in 2020.[45] This has devastated journalism across the country, as publications can't survive on the remaining scraps. Meanwhile, other Wall Street barons have bought up hundreds of local papers and gutted them for a quick buck.[46] Google in particular also has enormous structural power over the online advertising market, as it owns the biggest single marketplace for ads (its subsidiary DoubleClick), and the biggest single purchaser of ads (Ad Exchange, another subsidiary), putting everyone else in the market at a disadvantage. More importantly still, Google also gets first crack at all the data produced though all those transactions, which is immensely valuable. It could put hundreds of publications out of business at a stroke if it chose to. As *Talking Points Memo* publisher Josh Marshall has written, "Google's monopoly control is almost comically great."[47] (A great part of the so-called innovation in the tech sector is actually just bleeding other productive sectors to death.)

In other words, an unregulated market supposedly free of government regulation will quickly end up controlled by unelected and unaccountable business titans. Under monopoly capitalism, it is wealthy oligarchs who decide which businesses will succeed and which will fail; what workers shall be paid, and under what conditions; where goods will be transported, and what they shall cost; and so forth. They often make poor decisions, to be sure, but they still rule—and their decisions have manifestly strangled the forward progress of the economy.

So once again the promises of neoliberalism turn out to be wildly at odds with actual results. The movement misdiagnosed the problem it was supposed to solve, failed to produce the economic goods it promised, placed vast swaths of American life under the control of ruthless business and financial barons, and set the stage for the worst economic collapse since the 1930s. The supposed trade-off between equality and growth was a false dichotomy. It was never the case that social welfare programs or regulations were an anchor chain around the neck of the economy. On the contrary, such programs provided the key restraining and channeling mechanisms that allowed society as a whole to take advantage of advances in economic production. When they were removed, the whole system slowed, sagged, and fell into crisis, dragged down by parasitic finance and ponderously huge fortunes.

But this raises another question: Should we be so focused on growth as such? That thorny problem will be the focus of chapter 5.

SOCIAL GROWTH

IN MAY 2016, the billionaire Bill Koch raked in one of the biggest sums ever for a single wine collection, pulling in a cool $21.9 million for 20,000 bottles at a Sotheby's New York auction.[1] But that $1,095 average per-bottle price was easily bested in March 2019, when an anonymous owner netted $29.8 million, also at Sotheby's, for a collection of just under 17,000 bottles—or an average of roughly $1,750 each.[2]

Meanwhile, a Federal Reserve survey conducted in 2018 found that 39 percent of Americans at the time did not have enough savings or credit to cover an unexpected $400 expense out of pocket, and a quarter skipped needed medical treatment that year over cost worries.[3] Mysterious!

In chapter 4, we saw how the last generation of policymakers drastically slowed the rate of economic growth in the United States. But this howling abyss between the fortunes of the billionaire class and average schlubs who can't afford to go to the doctor raises a deeper question—just what is the point of growth, anyway?

We shall see that the *character* of growth matters at least as much as raw growth per se, and much more for a country that is already rich, such as America. As a country becomes wealthier and wealthier, there is less and less of a point to compulsively pile up more total riches. Instead, *distribution* and *control* of growth take priority. Once there is plenty of economic production, the main task of government becomes harnessing that production to the benefit of all. In a rich country, managed wisely, every citizen should be able to enjoy a reasonably comfortable lifestyle. On the other hand, if the ultra-rich are allowed to gobble up most economic production, growth quickly becomes socially and literally toxic.

As we've learned, a propertarian economic order does not produce fast growth, as advertised; instead, the whole economy becomes geared around monopolist abuses and Wall Street asset-stripping. This illustrates part of a broader truth: as inequality and financialization take hold in an economy, growth is not just slowed but also *done poorly*. A top-heavy income distribution acts like a giant tumor on the body of the economy; it diverts investment that otherwise would have built enterprises or infrastructure to serve the whole citizenry into, at best, ridiculous luxury markets, or at worst, pollution-spewing industries and catastrophic financial bubbles.

Of course, people paying over $1,000 for a single bottle of wine—or indeed over half a million dollars, which is the current record—are just the tip of the iceberg of wretched excess that now fuels a major global economic sector.[4] Billions are spent today on paintings, ultra-premium watches, mansions, personal yachts, and other silly toys. This reaches preposterous proportions in Middle Eastern petro-dictatorships, where vast oil wealth is at the personal disposal of ruling families. In 2013, for instance, a German shipbuilder delivered the *Azzam*—at 590 feet long (about the size of a smallish cruise ship) the largest motor yacht in history up to that point, equipped with a missile defense system and a submarine—to Khalifa bin Zayed bin

Sultan Al Nahyan, the president of the United Arab Emirates. It cost a reported $605 million, with daily operations running a further $60 million per year.[5]

More ridiculous still, such incomprehensibly pricey goods are often barely used by their purchasers. Randall D. Smith, head of the notorious hedge fund Alden Global Capital, has made a king's ransom looting local newspapers across the country, and accumulated sixteen Palm Beach mansions between 2013 and 2017 with the proceeds.[6] If those are his only houses (they are not) and he does not travel at all (he definitely does, a lot), he could spend a maximum of just under twenty-three days in each house per year.[7] In other news, the Department of Housing and Urban Development counted the American homeless population in 2019, and found 567,715 people without a place to live.[8]

But it gets far worse than ridiculous waste on wine and yachts. When capitalists dominate the growth process, it becomes socially cancerous. This phenomenon was most obvious in American history during the second half of the nineteenth century, when the state became dominated by capitalist barons. In *Railroaded*, the historian Richard White argues that the entire period was fueled by "dumb growth," as Wall Street buccaneers drove rapid growth, building far more railroad infrastructure than any business calculation could have possibly justified. Failing railroad firms routinely required state bailouts or simply collapsed, and thousands of miles of track rusted away to nothing—yet the rail barons still became enormously rich by siphoning short-term corporate profits into their protected personal accounts and repeatedly securing state subsidies. The new railroads also transported countless white hunters, who exterminated millions of native bison in a frenzy of mindless slaughter, with little of the resulting meat or hides even making it to market—part and parcel of a genocide that largely erased the Native American communities wherever whites were established. The bison were replaced by cows in a business that made nearly as little sense as the railroads, despite the cattle barons running most of their herds on public land, much of which was straight-up stolen from those same Native Americans.

"The railroad corporations that I have examined here were unsuccessful and powerful. My guys could be ruthless, but their corporations were failures constantly in need of subsidy and rescue," White writes. "The issue is not whether railroads should have been built. The issue is whether they should have been built when and where they were built. And to those questions the answer seems no."[9]

In another book, *The Republic for Which It Stands*, White cites research showing that the height and life expectancy of Americans (a reasonable proxy for nutrition and quality of life) steadily declined for almost the entire nineteenth century, only bottoming out in the 1890s.[10] As full-blown capitalism took hold across the country, cities were poisoned by industrial effluent, factory farms produced contaminated and low-quality food, poor sanitation led to regular outbreaks of disease, workers were constantly maimed or killed in dangerous factories and railroads, and with the capitalist class hoovering up the lion's share of income, the citizenry struggled to afford basic necessities. Attempts to regulate working conditions or raise taxes to provide for things such as public sanitation were, of course, ferociously opposed by business. It's always cheaper for a firm to just dump its pollution into the nearest river instead of cleaning it up properly, and as a rule business owners hate meddling bureaucrats telling them how to run their operations, even if it's to prevent children from being torn apart by spinning machinery. An industrial oligarchy treats its workers as disposable, the public commons as a waste dump, and any possible restraint on their activities as an intolerable threat to their power and profits.

The final quarter of the nineteenth century was when capitalists achieved near-total domination over the U.S political system. It's often called the Gilded Age, after a satirical Mark Twain novel. (A gilded product is something cheap covered with a thin layer of gold to make it look expensive.) It's critical to realize once again that this was not an era free of government regulation. On the contrary, the robber barons colonized state power and turned it to their own uses. Financier Jay Gould, for instance, lost a railroad strike to the Knights of Labor in 1885, and faced another in 1886. To beat his workers into submission, Gould decided to sue his own railroad into bankruptcy with another part of his business empire. That drove it into federal receivership, transforming railroad workers into government employees under the control of a court-appointed receiver, who was naturally a Gould crony, named John C. Brown. Brown quickly declared any strike an attack on the federal government, allowing him to call in federal marshals or even the army in case of a labor dispute. The Knights indeed lost the ensuing strike.[11]

When legal chicanery didn't work, oligarchs would sometimes resort to extreme state-backed violence. In 1914, Colorado mine workers went on strike and constructed a large encampment near the town of Ludlow. Colorado National Guard and private security forces broke the strike by setting the camp ablaze and opening fire with machine guns. An estimated twenty-one people died, including eleven children who were suffocated under one of the burning tents.[12] Under a system of propertarianism, political domination is usually rather subtle, coming in the form of slanted contracts, chronic unemployment, political corruption, and so on. But sometimes it means a bullet through the head or being burned alive.

But legal tricks like Gould's were just part of a broader strategy among robber barons to turn the legal system into their own private government. As White explains, their legal toadies developed a preposterous reinterpretation of constitutional civil rights as protecting corporations from regulations of the labor market, which eventually received constitutional sanction from the Supreme Court. Their reasoning was so slapdash that in the case that granted corporations Fourteenth Amendment protections, *Santa Clara County v. Southern Pacific Railroad*, the justices *did not even explain* how they came to the decision, or what it would mean. By this logic, "the courts potentially made licensing laws, strikes, boycotts, the closed shop, and even some public health regulations the legal equivalent of slavery," White writes.[13]

As I noted in chapter 2, there is *no such thing* as deregulation (unless we consider a country that simply collapses into violent anarchy). All markets are created and sustained by the legal system, and the way they operate varies tremendously based on the rules the state enforces. Corporations themselves are *entirely* a legal construct. All important political choices are about *how* to deploy the state's authority, not whether to reduce it; indeed, as we have seen, capitalist-style regulation often means calling forth the most nakedly coercive state power—namely, armed police and soldiers.

Capitalist domination also makes the economy unstable. As we saw in chapter 4, when the economy is severely unequal, rich people have fewer places to stash their money away, because the masses don't have the income that would justify investment in new businesses, houses, and so on. Financial assets such as stocks can become more valuable if the underlying enterprise becomes more profitable, but they can also become more valuable if lots of people simply bid the price up. And when there is an ocean of money chasing a limited number of assets, that possibility becomes more and more likely.

In other words, severely unequal economies are prone to financial panics—especially if controls on the financial sector are weak, or get removed. The nineteenth century suffered repeated financial crises: in 1837, 1873, and 1893.[14] There was yet another panic in 1907, and the worst one of all occurred in 1929 (which I will discuss shortly).

New Deal regulations abolished financial crises for about fifty years, but they started happening again almost immediately after President Reagan began cutting away at those regulations in the 1980s. The end of that decade saw a huge collapse of savings and loan businesses (a type of small-scale bank that accepts deposits and makes loans). S&Ls were hit hard by the high interest rates of the early 1980s, and Reagan allowed them to invest in risky corporate debt. The collapse destroyed about a third of the S&Ls, and the resulting bailout cost about $800 billion (adjusted for inflation), though the broader damage to the economy was relatively limited.[15]

The next bubble came just a decade later, in tech stocks. In the late 1990s, a frenzy of speculation inflated the stock prices of start-up companies without a prayer of ever turning a profit, like the notorious Pets.com. Hundreds of businesses went belly-up, and the NASDAQ stock index lost 78 percent of its value between 2000 and 2002.[16] This time the collapse touched off a mild recession, in which recovery both of jobs and growth was sluggish.[17]

The next bubble deserves closer scrutiny, as the memory is still fresh and the history is instructive. It started inflating almost immediately after the dot-com bust, as Wall Street turned away from tech and started investing in the housing market. Simultaneously, foreign demand for dollars (as other countries needed them to settle their international accounts, to protect themselves against speculative attack, and to ward off IMF "help") stimulated the production of all kinds of dollar-denominated assets—and housing debt was one of the biggest untapped markets. Financiers created all manner of new investment products on the back of home mortgages, which fueled a housing construction boom and a steep run-up in real estate prices.

The key mechanism was the mortgage-backed security, which is basically just a big pile of mortgages. The original idea behind such securities (which have existed for decades) was to free up bank capital and thereby encourage more home loans. But in the 2000s, their purpose became deception. Mortgage lenders figured out that they could make risky loans to unqualified borrowers (that is, people who would likely default) and then quickly sell the loans off to a third party on Wall Street, who would package them into securities deliberately designed to be nearly impossible to understand, thus hiding the bad loan. These securities would often be sliced and diced into yet more securities—eventually traders developed the "synthetic collateralized debt obligation," with which they could effectively bet on a housing security without actually owning it (and thus make an unlimited number of gambles on the same asset).[18] Trillions of dollars in financial assets grew on the back of the U.S. housing market. Through the magic of complicated, obscurantist math and models, Wall Street wizards "proved" that these securities were as safe as U.S. government bonds. Suborned ratings agencies, who were paid by the banks to rate these products, stamped most of them as investment-grade—and almost nobody actually read the documents to see what kind of loans they were made of.[19]

It seemed Wall Street had created a virtually risk-free asset where investors around the world could park their money. That further stoked demand for more home loans to feed into the securitization machine. But there was a problem: virtually everyone who could actually afford to buy a home had already done so. Lenders solved this by dropping their standards to nothing. The worst ones took to giving out so-called NINJA loans to people with no income, no job, and no assets. These typically had a low initial "teaser" rate, which skyrocketed after a few months. Others took to tricking ordinary buyers—especially African Americans—into these awful loans because they were more profitable. A whistleblower from Wells Fargo testified that management had pushed sales teams to steer "mud people" into dangerous "ghetto loans," because they carried greater fees.[20]

All of this bid up home prices across the country—by the early 2000s average home prices had clearly diverged from their previously strong relationship with rent prices, indicating a bubble inflated by speculation—and fueled a gigantic surge of house-building, especially in the sprawling suburbs of the Sun Belt. In strictly zoned cities such as New York or San Francisco that didn't have anywhere to expand, the price increases were particularly dramatic. Private residential investment as a fraction of the economy surged to its highest level since 1950, when millions of World War II veterans and workers were all buying homes at the same time.[21]

This, of course, eventually touched off the 2008 recession—the worst financial crisis since 1929. Most of the biggest financial players around the world had invested heavily in toxic mortgage assets. Meanwhile, over the previous decades a "shadow banking sector" (basically a collection of financial companies and systems that provide bank-like services, mostly for other banks and large corporations) had grown up outside the control or protection of any regulator.[22] When Wall Street finally ran out of suckers to trick into doomed mortgage loans, housing prices stopped going up, people were unable to refinance, and the securities started to fail.

That in turn sparked galloping panic in the unregulated funding markets that big financial firms relied on to meet their daily obligations. Smaller investment banks started to burn through their cash reserves and teeter on the edge of collapse. Eventually even the biggest companies were threatened— especially AIG, the world's largest insurer, which had made billions in subprime bets. If it had failed, it would have knocked down even the biggest Wall Street players like ninepins.

The rest of the story is reasonably well known. The Bush Treasury Department stepped in with a gigantic cash bailout for the rest of Wall Street, while the Federal Reserve straight-up nationalized AIG and stabilized the rest of Wall Street with trillions in credit. The Fed also saved the banking systems of Japan, the United Kingdom, Switzerland, and the eurozone—all of which had enormous exposure to dollar-denominated toxic assets but, unlike Russia and China, had not accumulated much dollar reserves—by allowing them to exchange their currencies for dollars, effectively allowing them to print dollars at will. Effectively, it was as if the Fed had become the lender of last resort for the entire planet.[23]

Global finance was saved—but the rest of the economy was not so lucky. Half of the middle class's wealth (mostly tied up in homes) evaporated. The Obama administration passed a stimulus that was less than half as big as it needed to be, which stopped the recession, but then quickly pivoted to austerity to reduce the budget deficit. This locked in an inadequate recovery, especially when Democrats lost the House in the 2010 midterms, largely because unemployment was 10 percent on Election Day.[24]

Meanwhile, rescuing the financial system without drastically restructuring it proved to have devastating side effects. The Obama administration was so fixated on financial instability that it quietly used a homeowner assistance fund to give the banks another backdoor bailout.[25] The reasoning was that the banks would be harmed by reducing the outstanding amount on underwater mortgages or by letting people erase their mortgage debt in bankruptcy. There was "$750 billion of negative equity in housing—the amount that mortgages exceeded the value of the houses," Obama economic adviser Austan Goolsbee told the writer Reed Hundt.[26] "For sure the banks couldn't take $750 billion of losses and for sure the government wasn't willing to give $750 billion in subsidies to underwater homeowners, to say nothing of the anger it would engender among non-underwater homeowners." As a result, homeowners ate the loss, and about 10 million of them lost their homes.[27]

These foreclosures were often illegal. As journalist David Dayen writes in his book *Chain of Title*, during the bubble years, banks were often extremely careless with their paperwork when they were slicing and dicing mortgages into all those securities. So when it came time to foreclose, they often simply forged the necessary documents. This was the "robo-signing" scandal—it turned out that the banks had whole floors of people committing document fraud on an industrial scale, where people paid $13 per hour would falsely attest to "personal knowledge" of complicated mortgage files hundreds of times per day.[28]

And that was only part of an ongoing epidemic of financial crime that stretches back into the bubble years. Wall Street banks rigged municipal bond markets, tricked their customers, and lied to investors—indeed, Goldman Sachs famously built a subprime mortgage asset stuffed with toxic waste, sold it to other investors, and then bet against it. The Securities and Exchange Commission sued Goldman Sachs for misleading its clients, but the company escaped with a wrist-slap fine of $500 million and an admission that their marketing materials "contained incomplete information."[29] HSBC laundered money for drug cartels and other criminals.[30]

Yet the Obama Department of Justice did almost nothing about this epidemic of crime, as journalist Jesse Eisinger writes in his book *The Chickenshit Club*. Only one midlevel bank executive was put in prison over financial crisis–related crimes, and again and again the banks got away with minor fines paid by their shareholders. The reason, again, was that if Wall Street was truly held to account, the economy might collapse. "I am concerned that the size of some of these institutions becomes so large that it does become difficult for us to prosecute them when we are hit with indications that if you do prosecute, if you do bring a criminal charge, it will have a negative impact on the national economy, perhaps even the world economy," Attorney General Eric Holder told the Senate Judiciary Committee in 2013.[31] (He later walked back his comments.)

Unsurprisingly, the crime spree continues to this day. In February 2020, Wells Fargo got yet another wrist-slap fine for a fourteen-year history of rigging their sales numbers and illegally inflating their stock price by adding new accounts to their existing customers without asking, or just making up false identities to create fake accounts.[32]

The point of going over all of this history is to emphasize how *grotesquely* these free financial markets failed at their appointed task. According to neoliberal theory, banks are supposed to "intermediate" between savers and borrowers, channeling capital to its most productive use. Instead, they first directed trillions upon trillions of dollars in capital directly into the incinerator, and were saved from self-immolation only by trillions more in cash and credit from Uncle Sam. That crisis in turn touched off the worst economic downturn in eighty years, strangling overall growth to this day. The bubble didn't even create a surplus of housing—after the crisis, residential investment collapsed to its lowest level as a share of the economy since 1947, and stayed there until 2014.[33] Even today, thirteen years later, it is just returning to the 1945–2007 average (thanks in part to the enormous pandemic rescue packages). A brief glut of McMansions in the suburbs turned into a severe housing shortage in many cities, caused by the years of low investment and many of the foreclosed homes becoming blighted.

Unless tightly controlled by the state, a financial sector first sucks the life out of the rest of the economy, and then uses the proceeds to take control of the political system. And it wasn't just fear that motivated the Obama administration's decisions; there were plenty of financial motivations as well. Obama himself is now giving regular paid speeches before Wall Street banks at $400,000 apiece, while his former treasury secretary, Tim Geithner, is running a hedge fund.[34]

So let's return to the Great Depression. The stock market frenzy of the 1920s was a similarly two-sided disaster. During the bubble years, ordinary business logic went out the window, and billions of dollars were directed into what amounted to fraud schemes. As Chester Bowles wrote in *Tomorrow Without Fear*:

> The important thing to remember is that much of the investment of those years in new factories and equipment was not made with a rational eye on the long-range profitable market for the product which the new factory was to produce. Many businessmen had long since quit asking questions of this sort. Almost any project, no matter how farfetched, no matter how impractical, found a backer. In fact, it often found ten backers where one was sufficient.
>
> Let there be a rumor that a real-estate boom was in the making, as in Florida, and thousands of speculators with hundreds of millions of dollars were on their way to Florida to get in on a good thing. Let there be a rumor of a corporate merger, and stocks skyrocketed on the assumption that this was simply the first move toward bigger and better profits.[35]

When the bubble collapsed, it sparked the biggest economic disaster in world history. Thousands of U.S. banks failed, GDP fell by nearly a third, industrial production fell by almost half, and unemployment rose to 25 percent. It seemed as though American democracy was about to fold in on itself.

People have written whole books on the Depression, of course, but what is most interesting for our purposes is that the response from the political leadership in the 1930s was radically different from that in the 2010s.

In contrast to President Obama, President Roosevelt and New Dealers totally overhauled American society. Instead of spending most of their political capital on saving the corrupt, dysfunctional finance system, they rebuilt it from the ground up, and clapped the fresh banks with ironclad regulations to prevent a recurrence of the crisis, which worked. Financial criminals were relentlessly hounded by law enforcement and congressional investigators; even President Hoover's treasury secretary, Andrew Mellon, was investigated.[36] Instead of panicking about the budget deficit after only two years, the administration pushed a *gigantic* fiscal stimulus—amounting to 40 percent of the size of the 1929 economy (or about seven times larger than Obama's stimulus).[37]

These reforms and projects radically transformed the lives of ordinary American citizens. Laws and regulations cleaned up America's food and water, ended child labor, reduced working hours and made workplaces dramatically safer, provided electricity to the cities and the countryside, eradicated diseases such as malaria and hookworm (both were once endemic in the South), connected communities across the country with highways, bridges, and airports, protected cities and towns from floods with dams, and provided the start of a pension system for the old and disabled.[38] New protections for unions sparked a spectacular surge in labor organizing—by the late 1940s about a third of American workers were union members, and received higher wages and many employment protections as a result.[39]

The New Deal was hesitant and incomplete in many areas (especially because the swing voters in its coalition were racist southern Democrats, who demanded many grim compromises with white supremacy), but its ambition was still staggering. A single agency, the Public Works Administration (PWA), was in 1934 consuming 74 percent of the cement production of the entire country, and 40 percent of the steel.[40] The PWA built some 34,500 projects across the country, from rural roads and post offices to the Lincoln Tunnel and Grand Coulee Dam—to this day the largest single electricity-generating station in the country (though that required later upgrades, and some nuclear plants exceed it in overall production).[41]

The Works Progress Administration worked mainly on smaller projects, but employed more people: some 8.5 million.[42] It mainly built roads, airports, bridges, and the like, but also the Tennessee Valley Authority (TVA), a gigantic power-generation and flood-management system that covers parts of seven states. That in turn was part of an overall New Deal effort to bring the American South—which had been an economic laggard since the end of the Civil War—up to par with the rest of the country. To this day the TVA is a major source of electric power and employment in the region.

The Roosevelt administration also crafted a suite of agricultural programs to address the farming crisis specifically, because back then about a quarter of Americans lived on farms.[43] The strategy was a mixture of planting restrictions to reduce supply (and hence increase prices) and direct subsidies so that farmers could enjoy an income roughly on par with that of workers in cities.[44]

Again, much of this was somewhat haphazard and incomplete. Roosevelt briefly turned to austerity in 1937, which caused another recession; genuine full employment would not come until World War II. But at bottom, the New Deal changed a country that was falling to pieces into one that was basically functional. As a result, life expectancy—which had started to rise because of the limited reforms of the Progressive Era, only to fall during the Depression—began a steep upward climb.[45] Incomes rose for the working class, and inequality fell dramatically. A big reason the United States was able to fight both Nazi Germany and imperial Japan simultaneously was the New Deal's projects—indeed, many of the biggest ones were repurposed for war production in the late 1930s and early 1940s.[46]

The destruction and excess of uncontrolled capitalism is not just a waste of resources; it is politically poisonous. All governments require legitimacy. This is obtained in democracies through a social contract that produces broad buy-in from a critical mass of the citizenry—a widely shared belief that if people behave according to traditional norms, then they can expect a decent life. Obviously this has never been achieved perfectly in the United States—even during the peak of the post–New Deal golden years, African Americans were largely excluded from the social contract—but comprehensively shattering that bargain risks extremism or revolution.

When millions are living hand to mouth while a tiny elite flies around in private jets, piles up dozens of homes, and spends millions of dollars on fancy baubles, it produces disillusionment and resentment. A severely unequal, dysfunctional economy is a breeding ground for demagogues and charlatans, who blame the problems on despised out-groups, stirring up xenophobic fury. It is no coincidence that Adolf Hitler came to power when unemployment in Germany was about 30 percent.

The tremendous danger of economic dysfunction was not lost on Franklin D. Roosevelt, who viewed the New Deal as an urgently necessary remedy to stave off extremism and preserve American democracy. As historian Eric Rauchway writes in his book *Winter War*, only a couple of months after the November 1932 election, "Adolf Hitler had become chancellor of Germany by rallying citizens to a violent, racist vision of national greatness, and Roosevelt worried that a similar movement could arise in the United States if Americans did not find reason to renew their trust in the institutions that governed them."[47]

And Roosevelt succeeded. An entire generation of Americans was turned away from revolutionary extremism or simple despair, instead becoming committed democratic citizens. Conservatives howled that the New Deal was creeping communism, but in fact Roosevelt was explicitly trying to forestall that possibility. For a democratic government to avoid being toppled by a revolution, he figured, the citizenry must be cut in on a share of prosperity. Modern conservatives can indulge their antigovernment fantasies only if there is a foundation of functioning government and a modicum of equality; if these disappear, then the society will quickly crumble. The post-2008 era has been called a Second Gilded Age, and just like in the first one, American life expectancy has fallen steadily for years.[48]

All this leads to a general conclusion: to get a high-performance economy that actually delivers the goods to the citizenry (both literally and figuratively), nations must manage their economic affairs carefully. Letting Wall Street speculators direct national investment based on whatever bubble happens to be inflating, or whoever has the best political connections, does not create broad prosperity. Social growth requires regulations.

Even the most selfish businesspeople are often led to this conclusion in their own affairs. In the book *Nature's Metropolis*, historian William Cronon tells the story of how Chicago became a center of wheat trade in the nineteenth century. When the wheat business was first getting going, farmers would load their crops into sacks and sell them individually. Then grain traders figured out that it would be a lot more efficient to simply load all the grain into train cars, store it in steam-powered grain elevators, and then both buy and sell wheat by weight. No laborious fussing about with sacks needed.

But this posed a problem, because not all wheat is the same. The traders came together in the Chicago Board of Trade (a private association that would later become one of the biggest financial markets in the world) and devised a system of wheat grades based on quality and harvest dates. That in turn created a cheating problem, as farmers or traders could get better money by passing off dirty wheat as the good stuff, or grading their wheat higher than it really was. The traders had to institute random inspections to ensure quality and consistency, lest the whole market be undermined by fraud and Chicago loses market share to another city. Anybody who cheated risked being locked out of the entire market.[49]

In other words, the Chicago Board of Trade had to invent *regulations* to make their market work at all. Of course, because the authorities here were not accountable to anyone but rich merchants, the regulations were slanted and often broke down. Financiers routinely cornered the Chicago market on one or another commodity and caused disastrous price gyrations, but were not punished because they were too well connected. But the fact that ruthless businesspeople could not avoid the logic of market rules even in their own private domains is telling.

All that said, the United States is still rich today. In a country like this one, growth should be viewed with a pragmatic and somewhat skeptical eye. Boosting productivity so a country can have more output for less work and fewer raw materials is generally good, but if we're just talking about working more or fueling socially toxic business, it is not. (Indeed, as we will see in chapter 6, in some areas there is certainly too much output.)

At bottom, increased productive efficiency—*real* efficiency, in the form of more output for the same amount of work, not some accounting trick from Wall Street—can and should be a broadly positive thing. It means more potential time off, more potential income for both workers and nonworkers, and a smaller potential uptake of raw materials.

It makes sense for a poor nation to focus mainly on growth. Impoverished people live shorter, sicker lives, and a decent standard of material comfort hugely improves people's well-being. Everyone is better off when they have enough to eat and a roof over their head. Then as national income grows, a nation can purchase better infrastructure, medical and sanitation services, and other items that make places nice to live in.

But the United States is not a poor nation. On the contrary, even after a generation of neoliberal disasters it is still at the cutting edge of world economic productivity, roughly tied with Germany and France. We have *way* more than enough income to provide the whole American citizenry with a decent standard of living. We must simply choose to provide it.

PART II

MAKING AMERICA GREAT FOR THE FIRST TIME

THE BROKEN AMERICAN LABOR SYSTEM

AMERICANS ARE HARDWORKING PEOPLE: in 2019, we collectively worked 257 billion hours, or 1,779 hours for every worker.[1] That is far, far more than in comparable rich countries. Sometimes Americans take pride in their supposed workaholism as a demonstration of our national grit, but the reality is that not long ago American work time was about average compared to other rich countries. It is *recent policy choices* (or the lack thereof) that force Americans to work that much.

Far too many Americans have few or no vacation days, or not enough pay to enjoy them properly; or work hundreds of hours of unpaid overtime; or are forced to choose between parenthood and a job; or spend their old age hunched over a cash register for lack of income or insurance—or spend years fruitlessly searching for work that does not appear. Time off is good for workers, but one must have a job to be able to enjoy it.

It is even more senseless when one considers how rich the United States is. A poor nation might need to work hard just to produce enough to survive, but America is swimming in wealth. Those 257 billion hours are a gruesome excess of toil, a huge nation of people pouring out their precious, irreplaceable lives in pointlessly enormous quantities of work—while at the same time, a smaller number of people are destitute for lack of employment.

However, it doesn't have to be this way. The United States could be a vacationer's paradise, with weeks of paid vacation for every worker, while at the same time providing jobs to nearly all those who currently lack them. America has long since solved the hard problems of economic production. This is a very rich country—all that is lacking is a sensible and moral ordering of the labor system.

HOW OTHER COUNTRIES WORK

Let me start with some international comparisons to explore how awful the American labor system is. First, we work far, far more than our counterparts in rich European nations. The OECD collects national statistics on labor, which are shown in the following figure. Among peer nations, the United States is tied with New Zealand for the most working hours.

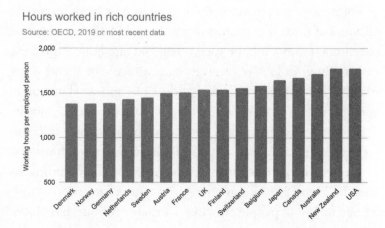

Hours worked in rich countries
Source: OECD, 2019 or most recent data

If we worked as much as the Danes, Americans would have about *ten weeks* of extra free time every year. But it gets even worse, because we must account for differences in wealth. Across almost all countries, there is a clear trend: the richer the nation is, the less time its workers spend on the job. It makes intuitive sense—the more production a nation's economy is throwing off per unit labor, the more free time workers can have. European countries have typically chosen a mix of greater wealth and greater free time.

But not so much in the United States. In the following figure I have plotted hours worked against GDP per hour worked for all OECD countries (except Luxembourg and Ireland, which have inflated GDP figures due to corporate tax dodging, and Turkey, which does not have recent working hours data). We see that the richer countries get, the fewer hours they tend to work—but we also see America's outlier position:

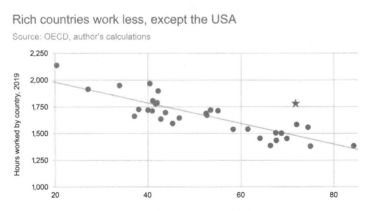

Rich countries work less, except the USA

Source: OECD, author's calculations

Hours worked by country, 2019

GDP per hour worked (PPP)

If we measure the distance from the trend line in hours, we find that workers in the United States work 299 more hours than its enormously wealthy economy would predict—making it by this measure the most overworked country in the world by far.

Most under- and overworked nations
Source: OECD, author's calculations

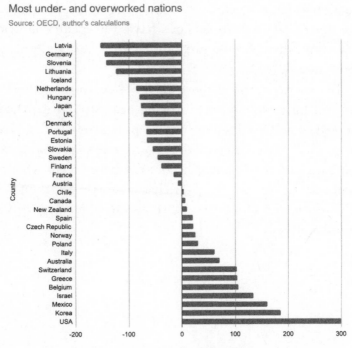

Distance from OECD trend in hours

Again, this is a relatively recent development. As noted, almost all rich nations have reduced their work hours as they have become richer. But this is not true of the United States. Among wealthy OECD nations with data going back that far, the United States was in the middle of the pack in 1970 (shown in the thick black line). But unlike every rich nation except Sweden, we have barely cut working hours at all since then (and Swedes were already ahead of the leisure curve in the 1970s):

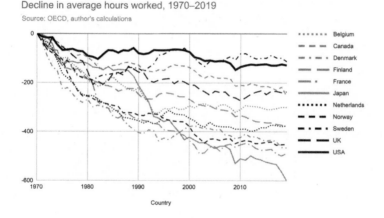

Decline in average hours worked, 1970–2019
Source: OECD, author's calculations

In addition to sheer overwork, Americans are also trapped in a brutal labor system. There is only meager support for the unemployed and disabled, and virtually nothing for people who have dropped out of the labor market. We have no mandatory paid family or sick leave, and hardly anything to help workers transition between jobs.

Take unemployment insurance—payments to workers who lose their job. This varies considerably across countries, both in funding and in institutional structure, but we can take a quick glance to see how much income drops during a period of unemployment.

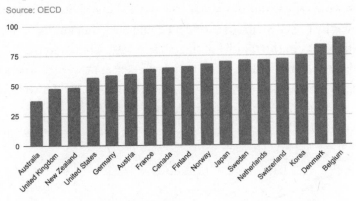

Net replacement rate of short-term unemployment benefits for a single person at 67% of the average wage, 2019
Source: OECD

Now, this changed a lot during the coronavirus pandemic. The CARES Act contained a huge boost to unemployment benefits—a flat $600 per week—that made American unemployment the most generous in the world by far. Some very low-income people who got laid off were paid double or more what they had made working. However, this was a temporary boost. At the time of writing, a more modest addition of $300 is set to expire in September 2021.

Additionally, the United States scores much worse on another employment-maintenance metric. Almost all wealthy nations have a sizable complex of institutions to catch workers who lose their jobs and slot them into new ones—active labor market policies (ALMPs). That includes things such as worker retraining, job placement centers, subsidies for employers who hire the long-term unemployed, and so forth. The idea is both to help keep people employed and to keep the economy productive by avoiding waste of human potential.

The next chart shows the fraction of GDP dedicated to ALMPs as of 2015 (the data are somewhat out of date but there haven't been large changes since then). Denmark spends fully 2.1 percent of GDP on ALMPs, while Norway spends only 0.5 percent. But the US is not just dead last among rich nations, it's nearly in last place among *all* OECD nations, spending just 0.1 percent of GDP on these programs (only Mexico is stingier).

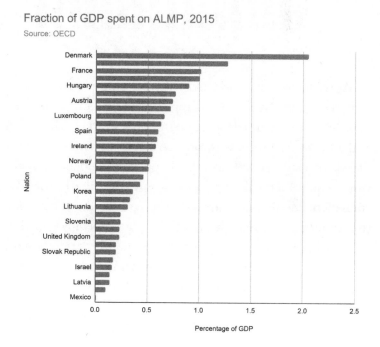

Fraction of GDP spent on ALMP, 2015
Source: OECD

This near-total lack of ALMPs helps explain why while *employed* Americans work a great many hours, the fraction of the population *participating* in the labor market (that is, the employed population plus unemployed job-seekers) is relatively low. Here we see the percentage of the prime working-age population (ages twenty-five through sixty-four) in the labor market across rich OECD countries:

Labor force participation rate (ages 25–64), 2019
Source: OECD

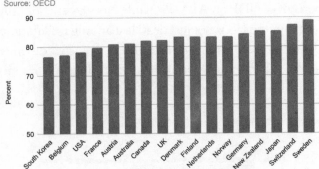

As we have seen in previous chapters, a propertarian labor system deliberately makes unemployment brutally unpleasant in order to horsewhip people into the labor market, where they make profit for business owners. All Republicans and many Democrats still try to make this happen, as evidenced by the work requirements built into welfare reform, the Earned Income Tax Credit, and many other programs. But the result is that instead of getting jobs, many people simply give up. The most successful labor systems in the world today are rationally managed—*helping* people into work rather than bluntly coercing them—to avoid a pointless waste of human lives.

Another labor problem America has failed to address is bearing children. Parenthood presents a problem for a worker, for three reasons. First is that raising a child takes a tremendous amount of time, energy, and money—thus conflicting with work. Second, even when a child is old enough to be placed with a nanny or daycare, such care can be prohibitively expensive. Third, compounding both other problems, is the fact that the prime childbearing years are in young adulthood—when people are starting their careers and their salaries are usually at their lowest point.

These obstacles were more manageable in previous eras

when it was feasible to support a family on one middle-class salary. But since the 1970s, both parents generally must work if a family is to remain solvent—even quite far up into the upper middle class. Additionally, of course, many women quite rightly want an equal chance at jobs and career success.

That's why other countries have built out the welfare state to help parents. The usual approach is paid family leave, in which new parents have their salary paid by the government while they take time off work to care for an infant, plus some sort of daycare subsidy to cover the time between infancy and school age.

The United States is virtually alone among all nations in providing no paid leave policy at the national level (in April 2021, President Biden proposed a modest paid leave proposal, but at the time of writing Congress had not passed it). Table 1 shows a selected comparison of a range of wealthy

TABLE 1

PAID MATERNITY LEAVE SYSTEMS, 2014			
Country	Duration	Size of benefits (% of previous earnings)	Source of funding
Australia	18 weeks (either parent)	Federal minimum wage	Social insurance
Austria	16 weeks	100%	Social insurance
Belgium	15 weeks	82% for the first 30 days; 75% for the remainder (up to a ceiling)	Social insurance
Canada	17 weeks (federal)	55% for 15 weeks up to a ceiling	Social insurance

PAID MATERNITY LEAVE SYSTEMS, 2014

Country	Duration	Size of benefits (% of previous earnings)	Source of funding
Czech Rep.	28 weeks	70%	Social insurance
Denmark	18 weeks	100%	Mixed public and employer funds
France	16 weeks	100% up to a ceiling	Social insurance
Germany	14 weeks	100%	Mixed public and employer funds
Greece	17 weeks	100%	Social insurance and public funds
Japan	14 weeks	67%	Social insurance and public funds for 1/8 of the total cost
Latvia	16 weeks	80%	Social insurance
Norway	35 (or 45) weeks	100% (or 80% for 45 weeks)	Social insurance
Poland	26 weeks	100%	Social insurance
UK	40 weeks	6 weeks paid at 90%; lower of 90%/flat rate for weeks 7–39	Mixed (employers reimbursed up to 92% by public funds)
USA	0 weeks	N/A	N/A

and middle-income countries (with some institutional details omitted for the sake of brevity).[2]

It's important to realize that these subsidies are not just about handing money to parents. Paid leave also helps maintain the national workforce by allowing parents—especially women—to reconcile parenthood with their careers. That helps explain the especially low labor force participation among American women. Lack of family benefits tends to push women out of the labor force, as women end up having to choose between families and a job. That in turn worsens the gender wage gap, because even when they can work, women often get passed over for jobs or promotions because employers worry they will have children and leave, or they get forced off their career track for a time and lose out on raises.

Second, family benefits are also aimed at maintaining a stable population. Many European and East Asian countries have struggled for decades with below-replacement birthrates. Declining population strains government budgets, as fewer productive workers must shoulder the burden of caring for a greater retired population. For many years, it appeared as though the United States was immune to such effects, but its birthrate has fallen sharply since 2008, driven down by declining teen pregnancy and falling fertility among immigrant populations. Some of that is no doubt due to changing cultural norms, but much is certainly also due to not being able to afford children.

At any rate, the point of family benefits is not to try to shove people into parenthood. If individuals choose to forgo having children, that is of course their right. Instead the point is to create national institutions that allow people to make that choice *one way or the other*. Surveys show a large gap between the number of children women report wanting to have and the number that they actually end up having.[3] Full reproductive freedom requires more than access to contraception—it also requires a welfare state that can allow people to have whatever kind of family they want. A propertarian labor system such as exists in the United States is anti-family.

When people become old, they often lose the ability or inclination to work. Thus retirement—the idea that past a certain age (typically sixty-five), people should have the ability to relax for the rest of their lives. Retirement in the United States has traditionally rested on three pillars: Social Security, pensions, and private savings. The last of these got special attention starting in 1978 with the partly accidental creation of the 401(k) tax benefit, which incentivizes workers to save and invest by allowing them to defer taxes in those accounts until after they retire.[4]

All three of these pillars are in trouble. Social Security is the strongest by far, but it was cut as part of a 1983 reform bill, which trimmed benefits and slowly advanced the age at which full benefits can be claimed. Here we see that American Social Security payments relative to previous incomes are considerably below the average in wealthy nations.

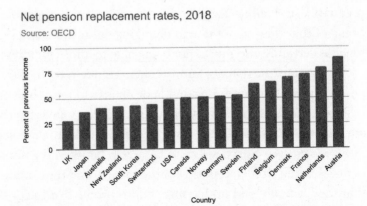

Net pension replacement rates, 2018
Source: OECD

Additionally, the average figure here tends to overstate the generosity of Social Security for poorer retirees. Where many OECD countries have a flat baseline pension that all retirees get, U.S. benefits are calculated based on earnings, so seniors with a low earning history receive lower benefits.[5]

Meanwhile, defined-benefit pensions have largely vanished, and 401(k) accounts have proved to be an awesome policy disaster. Instead of enabling middle-class savers to build up their nest eggs, the vast bulk of 401(k) assets are accounted for by the wealthy.

Using the Survey of Consumer Finances from the Federal Reserve, I calculated that 40 percent of households headed by people aged fifty to sixty-four have nothing at all in a personal retirement account. Two-thirds in that age group have less than one year of income saved up in retirement accounts.

Retirement assets to income ratio by percentile for ages 50–64, 2016
Source: Author's calculation of Survey of Consumer Finances data

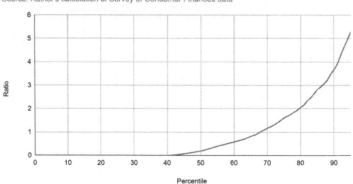

A similar conclusion holds if we consider total net worth (that is, including all assets, not just retirement accounts). I find that around 30 percent of households headed by people between the ages of fifty and sixty-four have a net worth that is less than one year of income. Three-quarters of these households have a net worth less than seven times their income, which is the amount retirement advisors commonly say fifty-five-year-olds need to have achieved to secure their retirement.

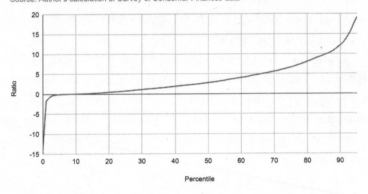

Net worth to income ratio by percentile for ages 50–64, 2016

Source: Author's calculation of Survey of Consumer Finances data

Meanwhile, a 401(k) account is generally complicated and burdensome to navigate. As journalist Helaine Olen writes in her book *Pound Foolish*, many eligible workers do not enroll, whether because of procrastination or out of fear of the vast industry of financial swindlers, spawned by these tax benefits, whose business model is tricking people into high-fee plans. Those who do enroll often make horrible decisions or end up getting rooked by financial companies.

Finally, there is evidence that large swaths of the population simply cannot afford to save more than they currently are. Early withdrawals from 401(k) accounts mean steep tax penalties, but many have done it anyway, especially when times are hard. A Federal Reserve study found that at the bottom of the Great Recession in 2010, early withdrawals from people under fifty-five were nearly half the size of contributions.[6]

Taken together, America's retirement institutions are failing U.S. seniors. A huge fraction of the population over age sixty-five simply cannot afford to retire—the rate of participating in the labor market (that is, people either employed or looking for a job) among this group has increased sharply recently, rising from 12.9 percent in 2000 to 20.2 percent in 2019.[7] Bankruptcies are also skyrocketing among this cohort, more than doubling in number between 1991 and 2016.[8]

We saw previously that the American employment rate among prime working-age people is considerably below the developed-world standard. But its employment rate among people *over* age sixty-five is the opposite—as we see in the following figure, it is dramatically above the wealthy-country average. Not only does America fail to provide jobs to most people who could take them and need them, it fails to allow a significant proportion of its senior population to retire.

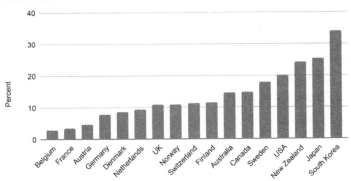

Senior labor force participation among rich countries, 2019
Source: OECD

"Senior labor force participation among rich countries, 2019" Illness often limits our ability to work, and virtually everyone gets sick occasionally. To prevent such routine occurrences leading to the loss of a job—and employees from coming to work sick and infecting their coworkers, such as during a viral pandemic—sensible countries require some paid sick leave for most workers.

But not the United States, which lags well behind even middle-income countries in this arena. As a WORLD Policy Analysis Center meta-analysis details, the United States and South Korea are the only OECD countries without any national sick leave program.[9]

Today, a handful of individual U.S. states do have a sick leave program—but most are pathetically meager, and even the most generous are still not as good as those in the most advanced nations. Table 2, for example, compares the California system, the new Massachusetts system (which was hugely upgraded in late 2018), and Norway's system.[10]

TABLE 2: PAID SICK LEAVE COMPARISON

Location	Paid sick leave base period	Accrual method/ requirement	Wage replacement rate
California	3 days	1 hour per 30 hours worked, starting after 30 days employed, usable after 90 days employed	100 percent of prior average non-overtime wage

Location	Paid sick leave base period	Accrual method/ requirement	Wage replacement rate
Massachusetts	26 weeks for family member's illness, 20 weeks for own illness	None	80 percent of wages up to half of the average weekly wage, 50 percent beyond that up to a cap of $850 per week ($42,000/ year)
Norway	1 year	1 month worked at same job	100 percent of previous average wages up to 608,106 kroner per year (about $69,700)

Supposedly liberal California is about 5 percent of the way to a first-class system, even setting aside its onerous qualification procedure. Massachusetts will be in the same league as the most advanced nations when its system is fully implemented (it did not start collecting revenue until mid-2019, and benefits were not disbursed until 2021). But even then, Massachusetts comprises only about 2 percent of the U.S. population (again, President Biden has proposed a fairly meager national sick leave program, but at the time of writing Congress had not passed it).

Similarly, disability often limits people's ability to work. That is the motivation for Social Security Disability Insurance (SSDI) and Supplemental Security Income (SSI), programs that provide welfare income to the disabled.

The disability system is quite stingy, with an average monthly payment of $1,277 in 2021—barely more than the poverty level for individuals.[11] But perhaps more important, the qualification process for SSDI is extremely onerous. To qualify, one must have worked previously and earned enough "work credits." The enrollment process is notoriously slow, and enrollees have to undergo regular reviews that often amount to finding excuses to kick people off the program instead of determining if they are actually disabled.[12]

The meagerness of SSDI can be seen in the poverty rate among disabled people, which is the highest among all economic categories both in terms of income earned through the market and in terms of total disposable income (that is, including welfare payments). In 2017, disabled people had a market poverty rate (that is, measuring whether their labor and ownership incomes alone kept them out of poverty) of 50.1 percent, as compared with a market poverty of 49.4 percent for the elderly. But while the more generous Social Security old-age pension knocks down elderly poverty to only 14.1 percent as measured by disposable income (still too much, but certainly a vast improvement), the disabled population remains at a sky-high 26.6 percent.[13]

Finally, there is just plain old time off work. Most countries have holidays of some kind to commemorate religious (or quasi-religious) celebrations, important historical events, or seasonal markers. Then, following the usual pattern of nations purchasing better lives for their citizenry as they become wealthier, most rich nations have added a paid leave requirement for workers.

The details, eligibility requirements, and funding systems vary enormously between countries. But the general trend is clear: as usual, the United States is far, far behind peer nations. It does at least have some public holidays, but unlike every other wealthy nation, it has no statutory leave whatsoever.

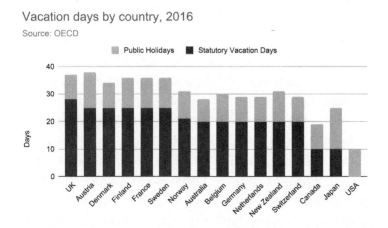

Vacation days by country, 2016

Source: OECD

Not shown in this chart is whether the public holidays are required to be paid, which varies quite a lot between (and even within) countries. But the United States has no such standard, thus making it the only OECD country with no required paid time off whatsoever. Even if we assumed that all American workers got the private-sector average of eleven days of paid vacation (in fact, only 75 percent do), that would still put the United States in second-to-last place.[14]

All told, America is about two generations behind the curve with its labor time institutions. Americans as a whole are swimming in wealth, but they have little free time in which to enjoy it. Luckily, all these problems are easily fixable. Reforming the American job market to reduce working hours, spread jobs more widely throughout the working-age population, help ensure employment, and enable parenthood and retirement would be quite straightforward. We can simply follow the model of cutting-edge European countries, adapted where necessary for an American context.

PROPOSED COLLECTIVIST SOLUTIONS

The simplest way to cut back on working hours is to add multiple new federal holidays. Currently there are ten, spread somewhat unevenly throughout the year. March, April, June, and August have none at all, while November and January both have two. If we add one to each of the months missing a holiday, and then one more at some point, that will make for an even fifteen, or three weeks total.

These holidays should generally be stipulated either to always fall on a Monday or Friday (so as to maximize three-day weekends) or, if a fixed date is chosen, to have the actual vacation day honored fall on the nearest Friday or Monday.

Many employers have a policy of following the federal government practices on holidays, so these should take partial effect just through that channel. However, employers could be incentivized to honor the holidays by requiring 50 percent extra pay for work performed on those federal holidays.

The second-simplest strategy for reducing working hours is legally mandating paid vacation time for all workers. One excellent example is that of Denmark, which mandates five weeks of paid vacation per year for most employees (vacation days accrue at the rate of 2.08 days per month). All workers are eligible for the full five weeks, even if they have only worked at a job for a short time. Unfortunately, self-employed or unemployed people are not included in the Danish scheme (though they are eligible for a sick leave benefit), but there's no reason in principle why America couldn't set up a fund for such folks.[15]

To ease the adjustment process, a United States Vacation Act could start with a mandatory two weeks of paid vacation for all workers, with an additional week added every year until four weeks is reached. Meanwhile, vacation days would add up at whatever rate would accumulate a year's worth of vacation over one year of work (1.17 days per month for a two-week vacation period, 1.75 days per month for three weeks, and so on).

Next, the United States should construct a paid leave program for new parents, as Matt Bruenig suggests in his Family Fun Pack proposal, increasing the current baseline of twelve weeks of unpaid leave for some workers to thirty-six weeks of publicly funded paid leave for every newborn or adoption.[16] Where there is one custodial parent, that person will receive the full thirty-six weeks. Where there are two custodial parents, each will be entitled to eighteen weeks, but each will also be permitted to transfer up to fourteen of their eighteen weeks to the other parent. The point would be to build in flexibility to account for the fact that some parents may have better jobs or may simply want to spend time at home, but also encourage both parents to spend at least some time bonding with their new child.

Individuals on leave will receive a benefit equal to 100 percent of their earnings up to the minimum wage and 66 percent of their earnings beyond the minimum wage up to a maximum. The minimum benefit, which everyone will be eligible for even if they do not have prior earnings, will be the minimum wage and the maximum benefit will be the national average wage.

Meanwhile, the federal government should stand up a new sick leave program. All employees who have worked for at least one month will be eligible for up to twelve months of sick leave at the same income replacement rate as the paid leave program, conditional on a doctor's signed confirmation that the employee is too ill to work. The first month will be paid by the employer, with the government picking up the rest. Just as in Denmark, the unemployed and self-employed will also be eligible for a government benefit. (People who are still sick after twelve months will be considered disabled and folded into the Social Security Disability Insurance system.)

That brings me to retirement pensions. Currently the average monthly Social Security benefit is $1,543.[17] This is typically calculated based on a formula applied to an inflation-adjusted average of one's thirty-five highest-earning years up to the payroll tax cap ($142,800 in 2021), though the calculation varies depending on when you retire. At the time of writing, for someone retiring at sixty-five, the figures are 90 percent of the first $996 in previous monthly earnings, 32 percent of earnings between $996 and $6,002, and 15 percent of earnings above that, up to the cap.[18]

To compensate for the retirement problems noted earlier, the eligibility age for full Social Security should be returned to sixty-five, and benefits should be reformed and increased. The phase-in structure should be eliminated, with a flat moderate benefit for all people who have maintained U.S. residency for at least thirty years prior to turning sixty-five (people with less residency time would be eligible for reduced benefits on a prorated basis). Then additional benefits will be added based on retirees' work history, similar to the existing system.

Fully calculating the benefit schedule would be hard to do in advance. But the overall objectives are simple. First, eliminate poverty among the elderly, so every senior citizen can retire with dignity. Second, provide a substantial boost to Social Security benefits for the nonwealthy retired population, aiming to get the overall labor participation rate for those over sixty-five in line with peer nations.

For instance, we might start with a flat $1,200 per month for all residency-qualified Americans over sixty-five. Then we might add 25 percent of previous monthly earnings up to $1,000, 15 percent of earnings between $1,000 and $2,000, and 5 percent of earnings above that, up to a maximum of $3,200 per month (which is just a bit above the current theoretical maximum benefit of $3,148 for those who retire at sixty-five). If after a few years that doesn't get the retirement rate up to where we want, we could nudge it up some more.

For SSDI, the application process should be streamlined and simplified, and benefits should be topped up. The prior work requirement should be abolished, as it adds needless complexity and is nonsensical on its face. If someone deserves an income because they cannot work now, it is ludicrous to base that on whether they have worked before. A simple certification from a doctor that one cannot work should be the only requirement. Once again, the major objective should be to eradicate poverty among the disabled. Since there is no reason to worry about work incentives, the benefit should be a simple flat payment—say, the poverty rate for individuals, plus 20 percent (though anyone whose benefits would be cut under that new system should be grandfathered in under the old calculation).

It's worth mentioning that one of the reasons SSDI is so stingy is conservative and liberal fears that shiftless workers will fake disability to get free money. Centrist reporters, for instance, stirred up much worry over the fact that after the Great Recession disability applications increased sharply.[19]

In reality, attempting to get disability when one might *theoretically* work is overwhelmingly the result of poor macroeconomic policy creating high unemployment and stingy benefits elsewhere in the welfare system. During the recession, some small minority may have faked disability, but many more almost certainly claimed legitimate benefits when they couldn't find appropriate work (e.g., a paralyzed person in an area with only heavy construction jobs nearby) and their unemployment ran out.

As the economy improved after 2010, disability applications peaked and fell to below their pre-recession level, while the overall number of beneficiaries peaked in 2014 and has declined steadily ever since.[20] A healthy, sensible labor market *entices* those who are able to work into good jobs, and freely hands out benefits to those who can't. The Nordic countries have both cushy welfare states *and* super-high rates of employment.

Once the welfare state is completed, we can think about more direct management of the labor pool. To the extent that all of America's huge volume of work time is actually spent on productive activities and not just goofing off at the office, employers would have to hire additional staff to cover for vacation time and shorter days. America should develop active labor market structures to help meet this need; more important, it should channel labor demand generally into the most underemployed demographics.

In peer nations, these programs generally fall into one of four categories. First, there is job brokering to match unemployed workers with job openings, done with job placement centers, online search tools, or other similar mechanisms. Second, there is education—retraining unemployed workers in some way to make them a better fit for existing jobs. Third, there are private wage subsidies—attempting to convince employers to hire the long-term unemployed by shouldering some of their wage burden for a time. Finally, there is direct job creation through public employment.

A large meta-analysis of ALMP studies across multiple European and Anglophone countries found considerable variation in program success, in terms of the effects on future unemployment and wages.[21] In general, job placement programs tend to show short-term positive effects, while retraining programs take somewhat longer to bear fruit. This makes sense, as it takes time for people to learn new things. Private employment subsidies took the longest to show a positive effect, but the effect was substantial.

Direct public employment, alas, was the least effective, and even showed a negative effect in some studies. However, there are few studies on these sorts of programs, which are rare in any case, and they clearly get less attention and money from national governments.

Taking those and other findings into consideration, I suggest the following sketch of an American ALMP structure. First, the state-level unemployment systems will be centralized into one federal program, which will provide twenty-six weeks of coverage at a 90 percent income replacement level, up to a cap of $1,000 per week, with the federal government shouldering 90 percent of the total cost. The requirement that unemployment must not be caused by the worker will be removed; all unemployed people save those fired for gross negligence or crimes will be eligible. The super-unemployment benefits during the pandemic were a godsend to many Americans because of our crummy welfare state and extreme inequality, but in general it shouldn't be necessary to pay people *more* when they become unemployed.

Meanwhile, states that accept federal subsidies will be freed from any contribution or administrative duties. Instead the administration of this portion of the unemployment insurance scheme will be turned over to unions, who will have to raise the remaining 10 percent of the costs from their members, as will be discussed in chapter 9 (so that workers will have a strong incentive to join the union).

Then the federal government will create a Bureau of Employment that will open a Job Office in every city of at least modest size. The current unemployment insurance extended benefits program (restricted to states experiencing high unemployment) will be made permanent across all states for an additional forty weeks of benefits, funded and administered by the federal government. Unemployed people who exhaust their traditional benefits will be automatically enrolled in this program. They will then become eligible for a period of wage subsidies for a private-sector job, or could choose to enroll in a job training program available for free at the Job Office, or enroll in traditional educational institutions, or take a public-sector job if one is available.

In addition to regular unemployment benefits, the government should set up a job-seeker allowance for people who wish to work but have no work history or otherwise do not qualify for unemployment insurance. This would be similar to the Finnish system: a flat, modest benefit with minimal activation requirements.

Finally, direct public employment should be expanded, but primarily with the goal of building productive state sectors. We don't want large, permanent make-work programs for exclusively low-skill workers, to avoid the demonstrated stigma and ineffectiveness of traditional public ALMP programs. Instead the Bureau of Employment should encourage operations such as Amtrak, the U.S. Postal Service, the various government departments, and other state enterprises to take up the long-term unemployed where their skills are appropriate or can be trained up.

During the Great Depression, the Roosevelt administration set up the Public Works Administration to both hire the unemployed and construct needed public infrastructure—including many projects, such as dams and tunnels, that are still in use today. This should be resurrected and made permanent, both to carry out public infrastructure construction and maintenance projects on an ongoing basis as well as to build elastic capacity to expand its operations very rapidly when a recession strikes and millions are thrown out of work.

When the Obama administration was writing up the Recovery Act stimulus package in early 2009, there was great emphasis on "shovel-ready" projects. The thinking was that to deal with an immediate recession, America needed to spend immediately, and big infrastructure takes a long time to plan and get going. It was thought that it would be wasteful to spend a lot on projects that wouldn't even be started before the recession was over. This turned out to be a drastic miscalculation, as the Great Recession lasted much longer than anticipated, and furthermore, there are many public works projects—such as replacing water systems, many of which are literally poisoning the citizenry (as we all have learned in the case of Flint, Michigan) or falling apart—that could be spun up in a short time. But it is true in general that public works, if begun from a standing start, are not ideal for immediate, short-term stimulus.

But a new PWA could get around this problem with proper planning. It would develop and maintain a large engineering library of needed potential projects around the nation, both on its own and through consultation with local governments and other agencies (perhaps also hiring private construction firms if necessary). This would include very large projects, as done under the original PWA, and smaller projects such as schools, hospitals, roads, and renovations, as done under the Works Progress Administration. Second, it would develop crash education programs that would be ready at any time to train up mass numbers of unskilled or inexperienced workers in such work. During good economic times, it would chip away at the most urgently needed projects using its permanent staff, so as to preserve skills and develop best practices. During a recession, it would quickly expand (the extent depending on the scale of the downturn) and build out as much of its library as practicable. Then as conditions improved, it would scale back and transition back to its original state. The problem of not having shovel-ready projects would thus be sidestepped.

Obviously, not every unemployed person will be suitable to work construction or maintenance projects (though these projects would require some administrative staff as well). But when a recession happens, typically younger, low- and medium-skilled workers are first to lose their jobs—and nowhere more than in the construction sector. Construction was hit worst out of all major industries during the 2008 recession, and continued to shrink for nearly two years after the recession was officially over.[22] All told, construction employment shrank by 30 percent from 2006 to 2011, a loss of about 2.3 million jobs.[23] The majority of cyclically unemployed people should be ready for PWA work with only minor training, if any.

Taken together, this new PWA would solve several problems simultaneously. It would build up permanent state

capacity and institutional knowledge for infrastructure construction and maintenance—and preserve private-sector
skills by preventing routine mass unemployment in construction and associated skill losses. (This might even push against
stagnant construction productivity, which has been a problem for decades.)[24] The bulk of its building would happen
when interest rates and commodity prices were low, making
necessary spending considerably more efficient.

Most important, it would catch millions of unemployed
people who might otherwise not be able to find a job in hard
times. But it would also avoid the stigma of traditional public
ALMP programs by making work productive and at least
moderately skill-boosting. In the 1930s, working for the PWA
or WPA was often considered a point of pride.

HOW ARE YOU GOING TO
PAY FOR THAT?

That brings me finally to the question of financing. Many of
the above programs, such as mandatory paid vacation, will
be basically free (aside from employers having to deal with
some staffing issues). But others require a lot of money—so
where's it coming from, you dirty commie?

Some things can be paid for by borrowing and printing
money—remember from chapter 2 that so long as the United
States is short of full employment, we can borrow and print
without limit. But in a well-run country, that should happen
as rarely as possible. We want full employment and full production to be the norm, not the exception, and when that is
the case funding huge new programs through printing would
create massive inflation. Therefore, to fund our comfy welfare

state in a *technical* sense we are going to have to raise taxes. Of course, I am not qualified to specify exactly which taxes should be raised, but the United States has a ton of running room in this department. In this country taxation only makes up 24.5 percent of GDP, as compared with 45.4 percent in France and 46.3 percent in Denmark—neither of which has the world reserve currency, or the biggest consumer market, or control of global financial pipelines that would make it trivial to chase down rich tax cheats.[25]

However, we must also consider the fact of inequality when discussing taxes. As noted previously, the richer people are, the more of their income they tend to save. Therefore, if we were bumping up against an inflationary constraint, imposing a tax on the rich specifically might not do much of anything to keep prices down. Indeed, a policy that taxed the rich and transferred that money down the income ladder to people much more likely to spend it would likely be powerfully inflationary even if it did nothing to the budget deficit. Ultimately, any big expansion of the welfare state is going to require taxes on the working class.

So in the broadest sense, we should think of tax payments not as some burdensome imposition but simply as the way we collectively care for ourselves and each other. All the things we don't fund collectively end up being shouldered by individuals, whether it's childcare (average costs range from $5,436 per year in Mississippi to $24,243 in Washington, D.C.), an increasing fraction of medical expenses (about a quarter of Americans between eighteen and twenty-four report that they or someone in their household has struggled to pay a medical bill), or a college education (the outstanding total of student debt now tops $1.7 trillion)—or people simply go without those things.[26]

The "How are you going to pay for that?" question implies that the cost is going to be painful. But the real pain comes from failing to set up the kind of welfare programs and protections outlined in this and the following chapters. We all pay in the form of more stressful, shorter, less healthy lives that are devoured by pointlessly huge amounts of work.

BOTTOM LINE

Status quo apologists such as Steven Pinker argue that liberal capitalism more or less automatically produces broad quality-of-life improvements.[27] But as we've seen, the productive resources developed by economic advancement provide only the *potential* for improvement—they must be actively harnessed by state policy to actually benefit the broad population.

But in a sense, America's current pathetically backward labor system is a blessing. It is not necessary to innovate new institutional forms or experiment in untested policy areas, as it was back in the early 1900s. Copying and pasting proven models from wiser nations, plus learning from America's own history, is mostly all that is needed. With just a few such reforms, the American worker could be living a life of nearly incomprehensible luxury.

This would provide an important ancillary benefit: reduced resource use. As we'll see in chapter 8, it should be possible to maintain a high standard of living without destroying the biosphere. Nevertheless, no matter how hard we work on renewable energy, recycling, and so on, more wealth and production will always tend to use up more resources. Cutting back on work time should be only the start of a gradual evolution away from growth for its own sake and toward a more steady-state economy in which work becomes progressively a smaller and smaller part of one's daily life. One of the first major union demands was for shorter hours, as expressed by the slogan "Eight hours for work, eight hours for rest, eight hours for what we will." In the future the final term should come to dominate more and more, with the official working day shrinking to just a few hours, and even the working class having most of their lives free to do whatever they feel like doing.

At a certain level of economic development—roughly when the entire world has a luxurious standard of living—there is little point to piling up more and more wealth and production. The economy should serve human needs, not the other way around. Once we have enough economic production to more than satisfy everyone materially, then we can gradually forget about increasing total output, and simply enjoy life for its own sake. (Perhaps we might want to keep things going to explore the stars, but that's rather far down the road.)

In a 1930 essay called "The Economic Possibilities for Our Grandchildren," Keynes predicted this would happen over the next century. He thought that by 2030 the "economic problem" would be solved, and human beings could ascend to a higher moral plane:

> When the accumulation of wealth is no longer of high social importance, there will be great changes in the code of morals. We shall be able to rid ourselves of many of the pseudo-moral principles which have hag-ridden us for two hundred years, by which we have exalted some of the most distasteful of human qualities into the position of the highest virtues. We shall be able to afford to dare to assess the money-motive at its true value. The love of money as a possession—as

distinguished from the love of money as a means to the enjoyments and realities of life—will be recognised for what it is, a somewhat disgusting morbidity, one of those semi-criminal, semi-pathological propensities which one hands over with a shudder to the specialists in mental disease.

He envisioned a new utopia based around freedom and luxury:

I see us free, therefore, to return to some of the most sure and certain principles of religion and traditional virtue—that avarice is a vice, that the exaction of usury is a misdemeanour, and the love of money is detestable, that those walk most truly in the paths of virtue and sane wisdom who take least thought for the morrow. We shall once more value ends above means and prefer the good to the useful. We shall honour those who can teach us how to pluck the hour and the day virtuously and well, the delightful people who are capable of taking direct enjoyment in things, the lilies of the field who toil not, neither do they spin.[28]

Keynes was basically correct about advances in economic productivity over the past ninety years. But he was wrong about the utopia—we are today stuck in almost exactly the same pit as his society was back in 1930. A minority of wealthy business owners dominate the world, and they have made a mess of things. The economic problem *has* been largely solved; there are just huge political obstacles to taking advantage of all the last century of progress. One of the bigger ones is the American healthcare system, the subject of chapter 7.

THE HELL OF AMERICAN HEALTHCARE

ITEM: SEVERAL YEARS BACK, Monica Smith of Indiana was on Medicaid, and when she got in a serious car accident she assumed that her insurance would cover her injuries. Medicaid *would* have paid the bills, but the Parkview Regional Medical Center in Fort Wayne refused to send the agency the bills. Instead the hospital placed a lien on the insurance settlement that she had gotten from the driver who caused the accident, at a price five times higher than the charges Medicaid would have allowed for her treatment. Basically, the hospital was trying to steal her accident money through the legal system. She did eventually get her settlement, but not for four more years. "It felt like, what is even the point of having health insurance if you won't bill it?" she told *The New York Times*.[1]

Item: Tom Saputo had good private insurance. When he developed a rare lung disease and suddenly stopped breathing in 2016, his wife sent him to the emergency room. He ended up in intensive care and was eventually airlifted to another hospital, where he luckily got a double lung transplant. This extraordinarily difficult surgery cost $40,575, which his insurance did cover. But the twenty-seven-mile helicopter ride was billed at over $51,282—and because the air ambulance company was out of his insurance network, he was on the hook for $11,525. As he recovered from the brutally invasive surgical procedure, the helicopter firm (which was owned by private equity investors on Wall Street) harassed him and his family for months, trying to get as much money as possible. Eventually the company dropped the bill when *Kaiser Health News* and *Good Morning America* started asking questions.[2]

Item: Veteran Shannon Harness came down with sudden appendicitis in 2019. Despite being uninsured (Obamacare coverage cost $350 per month, which he could not afford), he rushed to the nearest hospital, where he underwent an appendectomy. But it later turned out the procedure had gone wrong, and he had a large blood clot in the appendix area, necessitating another surgery. After several days in intensive care, he was sent home, where he was eventually slapped with a bill for $80,232. After lengthy disputes with the hospital, that was reduced to $56,162, and then again to $22,304.[3]

I could easily fill an entire book with accounts like these just by reading the stories from reporters such as Sarah Kliff of *The New York Times*. Roughly two-thirds of people filing for bankruptcy cite medical expenses as a contributing factor.[4] It's a window into the profound dysfunction of the American healthcare system, which is both a kludgy mess and strangled by propertarianism. We spend far more than any other country on our medical system, yet do not even provide universal access to healthcare. Spending more for less—it's the American way!

COMPARING THE AMERICAN SYSTEM TO THE REST OF THE DEVELOPED WORLD

Fixing the medical system so that people are at least not bankrupted when they get sick is conceptually trivial. It would be a monster political lift, but the resources are already there. It's just a matter of sweeping the policy decks clear of a lot of crap, overcoming the propertarian ideology that both defends the status quo and is causing the healthcare system to devour the American economy, and setting up new payment and access systems that will allow anyone to receive good care whenever they need it.

Let me start by exploring exactly why American healthcare costs so much. The OECD reports that in 2018 (the most recent year for which good data are available), the United States spent 16.9 percent of GDP on healthcare—which is $10,586 per person, or about $3.5 trillion in total.[5] Switzerland, whose system is somewhat similar to the American one, was in second place, but it spent just 12.2 percent of GDP. Other countries with radically more generous healthcare spent even less: France spent 11.2 percent, Norway 10.2 percent, New Zealand 9.3 percent, and Finland 9.1 percent. If we brought down American healthcare costs to the Swiss level in 2018, we would have saved about $967 billion. If we brought it down to the OECD average, we would have saved *$1.67 trillion.*

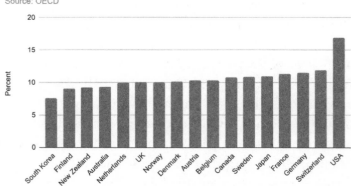

Percentage of GDP spent on healthcare, 2018
Source: OECD

The direct government share of that spending, through Medicare, Medicaid, child insurance programs, military healthcare, and so on, is a bit less than half: 45 percent for the state versus 55 percent for private spending.[6] That means that just the government side of our healthcare system cost about 7.6 percent of GDP in 2018—which is actually a bigger share of the economy than most peer nations spent on their far more generous universal government programs. Canada, for instance, spent just 7.5 percent of GDP on its single-payer system—meaning if we were to transplant our northern neighbor's Medicare-for-all program into the United States, taxes would actually go *down*. Furthermore, as we shall see, even the huge pile of private healthcare money—which is easily enough to pay for a *second* high-quality healthcare system—depends on government subsidies and regulations to function at all.

What gives? Now, it's natural for a country to spend more on healthcare as it becomes richer, and the United States is the richest large country. High income means more money to spend on expensive medical equipment, surgeries, drugs, and so forth. With more resources, by rights a country's citizens should be able to live longer and healthier lives.

But that is not remotely the case in the United States. A 2018 *Journal of the American Medical Association* (*JAMA*) study examined healthcare spending and health outcomes for America and several peer nations, and found we are getting *massively* ripped off.[7] On the one hand, we actually go to the doctor rather less than people in peer nations. We rank low in both physician and hospital visits, and in both hospital overnight stays and the length of those stays. That enormous mountain range of money is not buying us much access to care when we need it—indeed, *43 percent* of Americans with income below the median reported they had skipped recommended care of some kind, and even 32 percent of those with above-median income said they had done so.[8]

On the other hand, most of America's health outcomes are poor to middling, and some of them are downright atrocious. We have a decent rate of survival for strokes, cancer, and heart attacks, but the worst overall life expectancy among rich countries—about six years less than Japan, five years less than Switzerland, and four years less than Norway or Iceland.[9] Indeed, American life expectancy has declined for five years straight and counting beginning in 2016, which has not happened since the double crisis of World War I and the 1918 influenza pandemic.[10] Our infant mortality rate is also the worst in the developed world, and our maternal mortality rate (26.4 deaths per 100,000 live births) is *appalling*—almost three times higher than Germany's and more than six times higher than Denmark's.[11]

So what the hell are we spending all this money on? The

JAMA study provides some answers. First, administrative costs are dramatically higher: 8 percent of spending as compared to 5 percent in Germany, 3 percent in Canada, and 1 percent in France. That is obviously because our system is so fragmented and complex. Pretty much anyone who has ever used American healthcare is familiar with the bureaucratic nightmare created by our hodgepodge of different government programs and subsidies, plus the slew of private insurance companies, all with their own separate bureaucracies. That's about $280 billion per year spent on people pushing paper, emails, and faxes (still a central method of communication in medicine, for incredibly stupid reasons) around in circles.[12]

Second, American spending on drugs is radically higher than in other countries. The *JAMA* study found that 15.3 percent of health spending went to drugs, which is both a larger proportion than any other country studied and *much* larger in dollar terms, since overall U.S. health spending is so high. We spent about half again as much on drugs as Switzerland, twice as much as the United Kingdom, and three times as much as the Netherlands. (The figures are from 2015, but we can safely assume the proportions haven't changed much.) Once again the reason for this is obvious: drug prices are *massively* higher here. For instance, pharmaceutical companies charge Americans more than twice the British price for the arthritis medication Humira, over three times the German price for the diabetes medication Lantus, and more than four times the French price for the asthma treatment Advair.

The most important factor of all is the prices medical providers charge. American medical personnel are the best-paid in the world—nurses by a modest margin, general practitioners by a larger one, and specialists by a huge amount. That is definitely a contributing factor (if doctors made what they do in peer countries, we would save $100 billion), but the bigger culprit is enormous medical cost bloat.[13] Data from the Kaiser Family Foundation show that compared with peer countries, Americans' deliveries and C-sections cost about 50 percent more, angioplasties and bypass surgeries cost two to three times as much, MRI scans two to four times more, and appendectomies two to five times more.[14]

Indeed, many providers do not have a clue what their procedures actually cost in overhead. A 2018 *Wall Street Journal* report told the story of one hospital in Wisconsin that got curious and decided to figure out their expenses for a typical knee replacement.[15] They had been setting their list price according to market logic—that is, as high as they possibly could—which had steadily pushed the price up to over $50,000 (though the list price is often changed in negotiations with insurers, which are confidential). After an eighteen-month investigation where productivity experts measured the overhead cost for the use of all the various types of equipment and followed the doctors and nurses around with timers, the hospital found an overhead cost of just $10,550 at most.

Knee replacements are one of the most common surgical procedures in the country, and this hospital—whose price was close to the median for the procedure—was clearing roughly an *80 percent profit margin*, at least according to its list price. And that margin was after the hospital paid all the enormous doctor salaries mentioned earlier, as well as other inflated costs. Now that massive pile of useless spending starts to make more sense.

So we see the fundamental reason American healthcare costs are so high: just as in higher education, propertarian thinking has come to dominate the medical sector. Care has taken a backseat to money for all the big players in the medical sector—drug companies, insurance companies, and providers. Indeed, this Wisconsin hospital is far from the worst-behaved. One *Health Affairs* study in 2015 found the fifty most expensive hospitals in the country charged uninsured patients *ten times* the Medicare-allowed rate for the treatment, which itself is high by developed-world standards.[16]

PROPOSED PROPERTARIAN REFORMS AND THEIR INADEQUACIES

Just how the United States saddled itself with such a dysfunctional nightmare of a healthcare system is a complicated question. But three factors are definitely important: the goofy American Constitution, racism, and propertarian ideology. In the first instance, America's system of legislation is riddled with veto points—the House of Representatives, the Senate, the president, or the Supreme Court can effectively block any new law—making it very hard to pass or change anything. Employer-based insurance, for example, got its start during World War II. At the time, pay increases were tightly controlled to forestall inflation, and so companies began offering health insurance benefits to attract then-scarce workers. This was codified in 1943 when the IRS ruled that money paid into employer insurance plans was exempt from taxation.[17] Once that was locked in, it became very difficult to change—and that tax break has become very pricey, costing the government $272 billion in 2018 (including a few other similar tax breaks), according to the Congressional Budget Office.[18]

In the 1930s and 1940s, several attempts to set up a universal Medicare-style system were blocked, mainly by various combinations of the American Medical Association, who feared it would mean salary cuts; propertarians, who hated the idea of socialized medicine; and southern racists, who feared it would mean integrated hospitals.

The majority of Americans did indeed get insurance in the two decades after World War II, mostly through a job. (Generosity and family inclusion for insurance programs was a major objective of unions, which were strong at this time.) However, the poor and elderly still struggled to get coverage, because markets are an atrocious way to deliver healthcare. For other forms of insurance, such as for your car or your home, your insurer charges you exactly what you are statistically expected to claim, plus some profit margin. An *individual* might be lucky and receive more than she paid in, but across demographic categories, it all nets out. This is why young men have to pay more in car insurance premiums than older ones—they are more likely to crash.

This is classic propertarian logic—everyone should pay for their *individual* needs through the market. But in the case of health insurance, for many people it is obvious they have healthcare conditions that cost more to treat than they can afford. Poor people have little disposable income, and therefore basically any treatment is out of reach. People with serious chronic conditions (such as diabetes) can easily pile up bills beyond their ability to pay, even if they have a good job. And even healthy people generally get sicker as they get older, and as doctors learned to treat previously deadly conditions such as cancer, healthcare for elderly people became radically more expensive. Thus in 1960 about half of people aged sixty-five to seventy-four had some coverage, but only a third of those over seventy-five did.[19]

In other words, any reasonable system of healthcare financing *must* have systematic transfers from the healthy and the well-off to the sick and the poor. Any health insurance plan set up along typical market lines will immediately price out people who need care the most, and likely collapse in an "adverse selection" death spiral, where the healthy population opts out and only the people who cannot finance their treatment remain. Even private insurance groups had to set up increasingly elaborate regulations to keep themselves whole, with rules such as requiring every employee to participate in a plan or charging everyone the same premium regardless of their healthcare use.[20]

This is partly why President Lyndon Johnson could get Medicare and Medicaid passed in 1965—because those programs included only the old and the poor, two increasingly impossible-to-insure populations. Indeed, though they were a godsend to the populations who were covered, they were also a giveaway to insurance companies and medical providers. Private insurers no longer had to shoulder the cost of expensive care for older people, and providers could rake in money treating people who, thanks to the programs, could now go to the doctor. This has been a consistent feature of American healthcare policy: expending enormous effort to protect and preserve a private, quasi-market healthcare system that doesn't work all that well even in the best of times.

In 2010, after several failed attempts to extend coverage to the remaining 15–20 percent of the population without insurance, we got Obamacare, which was supposed to be the final puzzle piece in the American healthcare system. It consisted of two major parts: a big expansion of Medicaid (paid for almost entirely by the federal government) and new healthcare exchanges where anyone could shop for coverage. The exchanges were the centerpiece of the law, and naturally had a labyrinth of regulations to forestall the market problems mentioned earlier. The basic idea was a three-legged policy stool: an individual mandate that everyone must buy insurance (to avoid the adverse selection problem), means-tested subsidies so that people could afford the coverage, and "community rating" so that insurance companies had to offer the same price to everyone whether they were sick or healthy (though it did allow some price differences based on age). To that Democrats added caps on out-of-pocket costs, a provision allowing children to stay on their parents' insurance until they turned twenty-six, and a variety of other regulations. It all seemed so *smart*, and some liberals predicted that it would begin to erode the employer-based system.[21]

Unfortunately, the design of the exchanges was slapdash and incompetent. The subsidies were too modest and began to be phased out at income levels that were far too low. Furthermore, they halted abruptly at 400 percent of the poverty line (about $51,000 in income for an individual in 2019, or $105,000 for a family of four in 2019), in what came to be called the "subsidy cliff." Make one dollar too much, and you could lose hundreds or thousands of dollars in tax credits—effectively imposing a stupendous marginal tax hike at that particular point.[22] For even modestly comfortable middle-class people above the 400 percent of the poverty line, the premiums and deductibles (that is, the amount that must be paid before insurance will cover anything aside from preventative care) were quite expensive. Most insurers dropped out of the exchange marketplaces in the following years, leaving many regions with only one insurer, and hence no market competition, which raised prices further.[23]

Ironically, this turned out to make the exchanges work *better* for low-income people, because insurers could game the marketplace rules to get their population the best possible subsidies. This is worth explaining for the sheer insanity it reveals. Under the original law, Obamacare exchange subsidies were calculated based on the cost of the second-cheapest silver-level plan (the system was changed under President Biden, which I will discuss below). If you made between 100 and 400 percent of the poverty line, then you got a federal subsidy to make the premium of that *particular* plan a set percentage of your income (varying depending on how much income you made), no matter what the sticker price was.

If there were lots of insurers on the marketplace, then the second-cheapest silver plan was competed down to a low price. But if there was only one, then the insurer set up dummy silver plans to make the second-place one as expensive as possible. That means anyone buying anything but a second-place silver plan would get a bigger subsidy, allowing the insurer to cut the net cost to policyholders who were eligible for subsidies. So for instance, in 2018, Los Angeles had several insurers in its exchange, while Crockett County, Tennessee, had just one. For an individual making $35,000 that year, Los Angeles had bronze plan headline premiums of $258 per month, while in Crockett County they cost $460. But larger subsidies more than canceled out the difference—the net cost to the policyholder in L.A. was $188 per month, while in Crockett County premiums were zero.[24]

This is an example of market logic backfiring once again. Los Angeles, run by earnest liberals trying to make Obamacare work as designed, ended up harming its worst-off citizens, while Tennessee, which tried to hamstring the law at every turn, ended up helping them by accident. However, that decent outcome for the lower middle class came at the cost of making the nonsubsidized insurance even more ridiculously expensive, and soaking the government for inflated premiums. What was supposed to be a smoothly operating insurance marketplace quickly evolved into an expensive, jerry-rigged, and markedly worse version of Medicaid for the near-poor and lower middle class.

It turns out the relatively simple Medicaid expansion was by far the most effective part of Obamacare. In 2012, the Congressional Budget Office predicted that by 2016, 23 million people would have exchange coverage, but in reality only about 10 million did. Conversely, the CBO predicted that 10 million people would get Medicaid coverage, but 14.4 million actually did by 2016 (likely because the rollout effort notified a lot of people who had previously been eligible but didn't know it).[25] That was doubly remarkable given a conservative 2012 Supreme Court decision that rewrote the law through judicial rule-by-decree and made the Medicaid expansion optional for states. Most conservative ones promptly refused to participate, which left out more than 2 million people.[26]

Ironically, this outcome was the result of incompetent negotiating by liberal justices Stephen Breyer and Elena Kagan, who traded Chief Justice John Roberts's support for the individual mandate for the Medicaid requirement.[27] To add insult to injury, later under President Trump Republicans deleted the individual mandate penalty, and the exchanges were barely affected. It seems the mandate wasn't all that necessary after all—and it definitely was not worth trading the Medicaid expansion for it.

Now, all this changed dramatically thanks to President Biden's American Rescue Plan (ARP), a giant pandemic relief bill passed in March 2021 that contained healthcare reform provisions almost as big as Obamacare itself. Most notably, the government will pay 100 percent of the cost of COBRA coverage (which previously allowed laid-off individuals to keep their insurance if they paid both their prior contribution *and* the employer contribution, which was incredibly expensive for people without a job); the aforementioned subsidy cliff was eliminated, so no person on the exchanges will pay more than 8.5 percent of their income in premiums (which will effectively end the subsidy-gaming madness mentioned earlier); and states got more money to entice them to expand Medicaid.[28] It's a big step forward. But these provisions are set to expire in two years, and they will accomplish little on cost bloat on their own—on the contrary, most of the provisions involve flinging money at inefficient private insurers. It remains to be seen whether Democrats will make this change permanent, much less start dealing with the janky employer-based system that is at the root of most of our problems.

There is simply no getting around the fact that private insurance in this country is the biggest thing standing in the way of a more decent healthcare system. It's the largest source of coverage—about half of Americans get their insurance through a job somehow—but this coverage has been getting steadily worse for the last several decades, and is a huge political obstacle to reform.

The Kaiser Family Foundation keeps numbers on private coverage, and they find that between 1999 and 2019 the fraction of firms offering coverage has fallen from 66 percent to 56 percent. The average annual premium of an employer-based family plan has increased from $5,791 to $21,342 over that twenty-one-year period. The average portion of that taken out of workers' paychecks has increased from $1,543 to $5,588 over the same time frame.[29] That isn't adjusted for inflation, mind, but it's still a huge jump. Increases in premium prices have far outstripped both overall inflation and wage increases for this entire period. Moreover, because healthcare is such a large portion of overall spending and inflation calculations are based on a "basket" of goods that includes healthcare spending, adjusting for inflation will tend to obscure the magnitude of the price rise—akin to saying that because healthcare prices have gone up so much, they must not have gone up so much.

Meanwhile, more and more costs have been shifted to individuals. The percentage of employer-sponsored plans for a single person that had a deductible increased from 55 percent in 2006 to 83 percent in 2020, and the average size of that deductible increased from $584 to $1,644. Over the same period, the fraction of employer-based plans with a deductible over $1,000 has increased from 22 percent to 57 percent, and the fraction with a deductible over $2,000 has increased from 7 percent to 26 percent.[30]

Indeed, the private insurance system has become so incredibly expensive that many providers will offer people a substantial discount not to use their insurance—if they pay up front.[31] But if they are uninsured and don't prepay, as mentioned previously, they often get slammed with inflated predatory bills. The whole thing is starting to crack apart.

Still, people who are insured tend to be somewhat leery of proposals to replace their coverage, and propertarians of all stripes have exploited this hesitancy in their effort to defend the status quo. The first rhetorical strategy, often seen among moderate liberals, is to stoke loss aversion by raising fears about people losing their coverage. "A lot of people love having their employer-based insurance," Nancy Pelosi told the *Washington Post* in 2019.[32] Democrats should worry about "minimizing disruption . . . to people who currently get insurance through their employers, and are largely satisfied with their coverage. Moving to single-payer would mean taking away this coverage," Paul Krugman wrote in 2017.[33] Most "people who have employer-based coverage like it and don't want to change," Jonathan Chait wrote the same year.[34]

A key premise of this talking point is that people currently have the power to keep their present coverage. As a factual matter, this is the opposite of truth. In reality, people are kicked off their private coverage by the millions every month. Whenever people lose their job or quit, or if their employer changes or drops their plan, or if they fail some means test, they typically lose their insurance. A University of Michigan study examined people in that state with employer-based coverage (nationwide, that is about half the population, for a total of about 153 million people) between 2014 and 2015, and found that after a year just 72 percent of those people were on the same plan. It was even worse for people on Medicaid: only 62 percent of people enrolled in the program were still on it a year later, and fully 30 percent had experienced a period of being uninsured.[35]

We can safely assume that Michigan is roughly representative of the nation as a whole. That means during normal times something like 43 million people are forced off their employer-based insurance plan each year (either into another plan or to no plan), and perhaps 27 million are forced off Medicaid.[36] By comparison, Bernie Sanders's Medicare-for-all bill would be implemented over four years, each year adding a new age cohort to the program. Starting from the above figures, that means it would switch an average of 38 million people off their employer-based coverage every year—astonishingly, fewer than are forced to switch during normal times!

In other words, if universal Medicare was rolled out over four years, *even during the period when it was rolling the entire employer-based insurance population into the program, it would cause fewer insurance switching events than the internal functioning of the system it was replacing.* After that, of course, nobody would lose their insurance ever again.

But these are not normal times. The nation was beaten over the head with the reality of private insurance when mass layoffs hit as a result of the coronavirus pandemic. (A preliminary Kaiser Family Foundation study found that something like 2–3 million people lost their employer-based coverage—which was actually less bad than expected because layoffs were concentrated in professions that did not offer coverage.)[37] Under the status quo, if you like your employer-backed insurance, sorry, you do *not* get to keep it. You can and probably will get kicked off it sooner or later—if you lose your job, change jobs, or your boss decides to change your coverage. The only way to *actually* solve the problem of people constantly being forced to switch their insurance plan, or losing it entirely, is to enroll all people in a permanent universal program. (Indeed, a poll on the question of whether employers should be allowed to change insurance plans whenever they want found 77 percent of Americans in opposition.)[38]

The pandemic has also hammered hospitals, because almost all of them are set up as businesses instead of public services. By early May 2020, more than a million healthcare workers had lost their jobs, because people stopped coming in for the elective procedures that had been most providers' bread and butter.[39] It is quite the irony that during a once-in-a-century global pandemic, in which many hospitals were swamped with demand for treatment, healthcare providers should be threatened with bankruptcy. Yet that is what happens when one gears a healthcare system around propertarian thinking.

At any rate, the second strategy for status quo defenders is the rhetoric of choice, which is a key trope for propertarians in many contexts. During the 2020 Democratic presidential primary, Pete Buttigieg advocated a "Medicare-for-all-who-want-it" plan that supposedly would not force people off their existing coverage. (It actually would have, but never mind.)[40] By this view, instituting a Sanders-style Medicare-for-all system would be wrong because it would not allow people to choose the insurance that is best for them. In contrast, Buttigieg's plan "[wouldn't] require you to take it," the candidate said in an NPR interview, "because I think people should be able to choose."[41]

As a factual matter, this is once again not at all true of the status quo. Aside from millions of people being forced off their coverage every month, even when people can choose under the status quo there are no good options. Those on employer plans sometimes can choose between different varieties of coverage, as can people on the Obamacare exchanges. But this is less of a free choice than a gamble with your health, because the only options are between plans that are cheaper up front but cover less care (a choice I made most recently in my employer plan, incidentally, as the price had gone up by more than half over the preceding two years) and more expensive ones that cover more. That requires you to guess how much care you might need—perhaps possible in the case of chronic conditions such as diabetes, but not so much in the case of a random disaster that can strike anyone at any time. If you are young and healthy and go with the cheap option only to be hit by a car as you're crossing the street, that could prove to be a disastrous miscalculation.

On the Obamacare exchanges at present, this gamble between plans is even worse, because the correct decision depends on a bewildering maze of fine print and regulations. As with cheaper employer plans, bronze-level insurance is supposed to be cheaper up front but have more cost-sharing, while gold or platinum plans are more expensive in premiums but better for people who need a lot of care. However, thanks both to the law's design and to rules from the Trump administration, in some states it is actually cheaper for older people with chronic conditions to go with the bronze option—while the opposite is true for younger and healthier people.[42] Making a correct purchase on the exchanges means you basically have to take a second job as an amateur insurance claims adjuster, and a third one as an amateur legislative expert. (Again, all this will probably change for the better under the Biden administration, but as of the time of writing new regulations had not yet been released.)

Most important, any system that is based on a variety of healthcare options necessarily precludes the possibility of everyone, without exception, being enrolled in the same high-quality plan. Personally, I *do not want* to choose which of forty-seven different insurance plans is best for me, and even when I try I probably am not correctly calculating which of the fifty-page insurance contracts is "best" for me—and I pay fairly close attention to this stuff. I look at the horrifying tangle of options (none of which are very good), get increasingly frustrated, and make a rough guess. All I want is to be able to go to the doctor when I am sick or injured, for God's sake. Indeed, I would pay a considerable sum simply to not have to bother with the rotten insurance paperwork.

A system that ostensibly increases my choice in fact *forbids* me from choosing the thing I want the most by far, and *forces* me into a situation I fear and hate—an extremely common result of propertarian systems. If I were shoved onto a Medicare-for-all plan that was accompanied by a sharp tax increase, I would feel profoundly relieved. My lived experience of freedom would be drastically improved. No longer would my insurance be chained to my job, no longer would I have to worry about gargantuan balance bills, and no longer would I have to fret over a mountain of insurance paperwork every stinking year.

PROPOSED COLLECTIVIST SOLUTION

It should be clear by now what should be done here. The Obamacare exchange strategy was a dismal failure, and the employer-based system is slowly falling apart. Medicare and Medicaid, by contrast, are by a large margin the most effective insurance systems in the country. They have their problems, of course—Medicaid is too stingy and hard to qualify for, while Medicare has become more annoyingly complicated over the years as more benefits have been tacked on. It is a huge pain to get enrolled in all the various parts when one turns sixty-five, and the prescription drug benefit (Part D) is ludicrously expensive for taxpayers because Medicare is not allowed to bargain over prices. Medicare Advantage (Part C) is just a way to allow private insurers to administer the program that costs considerably more than traditional Medicare, in part because the insurers routinely defraud the government by rigging the payment metrics.[43] Finally, neither program covers all medical needs, particularly vision and dental. Medicaid has some coverage for long-term care, but Medicare does not.

However, all these problems are easily solved. Simply sweep everyone onto Medicare, combine all its various parts into one, and add new benefits for vision, dental, and long-term care. The coverage would be so good that supplementary private insurance would be basically unnecessary. It really is that simple.

HOW ARE YOU GOING TO PAY FOR THAT?

That brings me finally to the question of financing. During the 2020 Democratic presidential primary, "How are you going to pay for that?" was the single most common question asked about Medicare-for-all—one so emblematic of faulty propertarian logic that I chose to use it as the title of this book. Bernie Sanders had a reasonably effective answer, which was to say that new taxes would be imposed that would still be considerably less than what people are already paying for their insurance, leaving just about everyone ahead in terms of money.

But we're now in a position to really dig into the ludicrousness of this question. We have seen how this line is wrong or misleading in most circumstances, and we will see more examples in future chapters. Applied to healthcare, it is simply preposterous. Americans are *already* paying through the nose for their healthcare, which is in most important respects the worst in the rich world. Indeed, not only would Medicare-for-all be cheaper, but done properly it would halt the cancerous healthcare cost bloat that is devouring the American economy from the inside. We can't afford *not* to have Medicare-for-all, or something like it.

Here's how it could work. How much a Medicare-for-all system would cost depends largely on the policy design of the program, because it would be effectively setting prices for all medical services across the board—we can save as much or as little as we like. So let's aim for spending 12 percent of GDP (or $2.5 trillion in 2018), roughly equivalent to Switzerland, and funding the spending with taxes (in keeping with the logic outlined at the end of chapter 6). That still gives us about the most expensive healthcare system in the world, but most people will end up saving money compared to what they spend now, and the luxuriousness and quality of care will be world-class. To get there from our current position, we need to find about $1 trillion in savings.

Starting from the insurance side, let's assume Medicare-for-all would have administrative costs of 3 percent of spending—the same as Canada or Australia, countries that have similar programs. That gives us administrative costs of $80 billion, or a savings of $200 billion. For drugs, let's stipulate a budget of $800 per person, which is toward the high end of comparable countries. This would be reasonably straightforward. Instead of drug patent holders charging the profit-maximizing price to individuals (leading to things like a new cure for hepatitis C costing $84,000), the medical price regulator, as the sole purchaser of pharmaceuticals, would set prices commensurate with the costs of drug development and the social utility of each treatment.[44] (This is how countries such as Japan do it.)

Alternatively, or in addition, we could set up a prize system instead of patents for drugs. For obvious reasons, the patent monopoly system incentivizes development of drugs that can be taken for long periods, such as statins and antidepressants, while pushing pharma companies away from developing treatments that are only taken once. This is particularly bad with respect to new antibiotics, which are critically needed because some strains of bacteria have evolved resistance to every available antibiotic. If that resistance becomes endemic among all common bacteria and no replacement drugs are developed, medicine will be set back half a century—organ transplants will become impossible, any moderate surgery will again become hugely hazardous, and pneumonia and tuberculosis will again kill millions every year.[45]

Drug companies are reluctant to invest in antibiotic research because doctors will naturally resist prescribing new antibiotics in order to stave off resistance (which means the drug companies won't see the large sales they are hoping for); on the other hand, when they *do* develop new ones, they push doctors to overprescribe so as to jack up profits, increasing the risk of resistance developing to the new drugs. Indeed, much of the resistance to classic antibiotics such as penicillin is because drug companies in the past conducted big marketing campaigns hawking them as miracle cures for just about anything.[46] But if the government set up a prize of, say, $20 billion for a new antibiotic (proved to work by outside studies not funded by the drug company), after which it would pass into the public domain, then incentives would be straightened out. All this would of course be supplemented by the existing complex of publicly funded research at institutions such as the National Institutes of Health and the Centers for Disease Control. Incidentally, an NIH scientist named Barney Graham has been a central figure in the development of advanced vaccine technology for the last twenty years—and, as a fortuitous capstone of that career, designed the Moderna coronavirus vaccine all but single-handedly over a single weekend. Since he is a government employee, the American state will own some of the patents on the treatment, but Graham told *The New Yorker* he has no regrets whatsoever. "Almost every aspect of my life has come together in this outbreak," he said.[47] Apparently monetary incentives are not the only ones that matter!

In any case, our drug budget is thus $260 billion per year, which is more than enough to make sure all Americans can get the treatments they need. That gives us further savings of roughly $275 billion, for a total of $475 billion.

The rest of the savings must of necessity come out of providers. Here it is impossible to even guess at the details of where the money might come from, because there is no complete set of price data for all medical procedures. Indeed, investigations into this question have found gigantic discrepancies among different providers for the same treatment.[48]

But it simply must be the case that we could wring out enough savings for providers to get by with "only" the remaining $2.36 trillion—requiring a savings of about $525 billion. (I'm sweeping together all remaining categories of spending into "providers" here, which is not strictly accurate, but close enough for our purposes.) The first order of business for a Medicare price regulator would be to conduct a nationwide audit of medical pricing to root out cost bloat, waste, and outright fraud, which, as we have seen, saturate the entire medical sector. Once the government has a grasp of the actual overhead structure for average hospitals, clinics, medical device manufacturers, and so on, it can adjust prices just as it would do for drugs.

Finally, there is the question of revenue. As noted previously, at the present time the healthcare programs directly supported by taxes cost 7.6 percent of GDP. That means we need to find another 4.4 percent of GDP in revenue. (Again, it is not always necessary to fully fund new programs with taxes, but in the case of something permanent and this large, it is sensible.) That's about $820 billion in 2018—or $2,500 per person, though obviously we would want that cost to be levied in a progressive fashion. That is a pretty considerable tax, but *far* short of what most people are already paying in premiums, as seen earlier. Indeed, if we count premiums as a tax, which they basically are, then American workers are already the second most highly taxed in the developed world (just behind workers in the Netherlands).[49]

Now, so long as we are nationalizing the insurance industry, there's no reason in principle why we shouldn't nationalize hospitals as well. That is what the United Kingdom did with its National Health Service (NHS) back in the 1940s, and it worked out well. The major problem with the NHS of late is underfunding, but that will not be a problem under our vastly more generous scheme. But whether a reform program leaves hospitals in private hands or not, the main point here would be to overhaul providers so that they are oriented around providing care, not making profits. Being the only purchaser of medical services would give the state enormous leverage over how providers operate.

That said, the state may be forced to take certain hospitals into public ownership if they turn out to be too fraud-riddled, or serve too few people, to operate profitably. Even if it requires some modest subsidies, there is every reason to ensure that every poor and rural community has a minimum standard of care available. Indeed, the government currently owns and operates many hospitals under the Department of Veterans Affairs, where, despite some problems, surveys report a generally high standard of care.[50]

Make no mistake, this would be a difficult task— essentially requiring a major build-out of state capacity at a level that hasn't been seen since the 1930s. But there is simply no alternative to competent bureaucracy when it comes to healthcare. That's how it works in every other country with a decent medical system, no matter its design. And on the other hand, while the *size* of government-run health programs would be vastly larger than they currently are, the necessary regulations would be in many ways much simpler. No longer would governments have to fiddle around with hundreds of rules on private insurers to prevent them from ripping off their enrollees, or conduct all the complicated eligibility tests for Obamacare or Medicaid. America currently has by far the most complicated healthcare system in the world, and it is run by a state that is exceptionally bad at detailed regulations. A healthcare program that was *really big* but had simpler, clearer rules would be much better suited to our national strengths.

BOTTOM LINE

A national healthcare system is best when everyone is included in the same program. It allows us to harness our collective resources and direct them toward the people most in need. That will include just about all of us at some point, since we all become ill or are injured at some time in our lives. Medicare-for-all would let us live far less anxious lives, safe in the knowledge that whatever happens to us, at least we can go to the doctor if we need to.

THE SOCIAL CLIMATE

FOR SOME YEARS NOW, there has been a refrain on the left that climate change is directly the fault of capitalism. Naomi Klein made this argument in her 2015 book *This Changes Everything: Capitalism vs. the Climate*. It's an intuitive idea, and there is definitely something to it—historically, as countries have adopted capitalism, become more wealthy, and used more resources and energy, they have increased their greenhouse gas emissions.

Capitalism is also responsible for the single largest obstacle to attacking climate change: the wealth and power of the fossil fuel industry. Capitalism's ravenous need for energy has delivered gigantic profits to companies such as ExxonMobil, which has spent vast sums both lobbying directly against any kind of climate policy and sowing doubt about the reality of what was happening. By 1977 the company knew (as was already clear in the scientific community) that burning carbon fuels warmed the planet, yet it spent decades and billions of dollars on a disinformation campaign to trick the public, with considerable success.[1]

A further obstacle emerging from capitalism is propertarian ideology. As we shall see, the most prominent economists working on climate change do indeed accept the science, but have advanced extraordinarily dangerous policy recommendations based on neoliberal models that downplay or ignore the biggest risks of climate change.

So for the most part, we really can lay responsibility for climate change at the door of capitalism. But we must add a few caveats. Noncapitalist countries have also been big emitters—especially the Soviet Union, which was fixated on a heavy industry–led growth model that involved *enormous* use of coal, steel, and concrete. Indeed, not only was the USSR a considerably heavier emitter than comparably wealthy countries, it created multiple environmental catastrophes through carelessness and poor planning.[2] Most notoriously, Soviet irrigation projects nearly dried up the Aral Sea, previously the fourth-largest lake in the world, destroying a thriving ecosystem (and a fishing industry that had been around for centuries) and creating toxic dust storms that continue to poison nearby communities in Kazakhstan.[3]

This leads to an important conclusion. What causes greenhouse gas emissions is the combustion of fossil fuels for transportation or energy, certain industrial processes such as the smelting of steel or the manufacturing of cement, some forms of agriculture (especially cattle raising), deforestation, and so on. *Any* economy that relies on those processes will necessarily worsen climate change, whether it is capitalist or not.

But by the same token, it is not high production and advanced technology themselves that cause climate change—it is the extent to which those things are based on greenhouse gas–emitting processes. Already many replacements for current production technologies are being developed or rolled out. The world could both be rich and enjoy a stable climate, but first we must overcome Big Carbon and propertarian ideology, and recognize the interdependence of the whole world.

POSSIBLE IMPACTS OF UNCHECKED CLIMATE CHANGE

Let me begin with the basic science of climate change. Molecules such as carbon dioxide are called greenhouse gases because they absorb infrared radiation (thanks to their structure and the way they bend). Sunlight hits the earth's surface, increasing its temperature and causing it to emit more infrared light. Carbon dioxide molecules in the atmosphere then absorb some of those infrared photons and radiate some of them back toward the ground, warming the overall planet. The greater the concentration of carbon dioxide in the atmosphere, the more infrared radiation will be reflected back to the surface, and the more temperatures will rise. There are other greenhouse gases as well—methane (the primary component of natural gas) is eighty-seven times more effective than carbon dioxide at trapping heat over a twenty-year period.[4] Fluoroform, a commercial refrigerant, is *11,700* times more effective.[5]

Now, some level of greenhouse effect is a good thing. Without any greenhouse gases in the atmosphere, the earth would be about 33 degrees Celsius colder than it is today.[6] But further warming of the earth—happening mainly because humans have been digging up carbon fuels and burning them, creating carbon dioxide—is a problem because it will disrupt the delicate ecological balance all living things, including human beings, have adapted themselves to over millions of years. Trying to understand and model the entire planet's climate behavior is of course immensely complicated, but scientists are ever more certain that a hotter planet will have more droughts, more extreme heat waves, more flooding, higher sea levels, more powerful extreme weather events, and so on, which in turn will disrupt biological processes such as bird migration, pollination, and plant growth. The earth has warmed about 1 degree Celsius since preindustrial times, and we are indeed seeing many of the negative effects predicted decades ago.[7]

What's more, the increase in temperature is happening in the blink of an eye relative to the enormous span of geological time. The climate has changed many times in the past, but most of these shifts happened over thousands of years or longer, which gave species time to adapt. Ones that happened very suddenly—such as those caused by massive volcanic eruptions or asteroid strikes—have generally caused mass extinctions.

The higher the temperature, the greater the damage—and at some as yet unclear temperature point, the earth will start hitting feedback loops that will likely make the warming begin to feed on itself. For instance, if the northern ice cap melts, it will release water, which absorbs sunlight much more readily than ice, accelerating warming. Or if the permafrost in the far north of Canada and Russia melts completely (as has already started), it will release billions of tons of methane that are currently locked in ice, accelerating warming further still.

That in turn raises the dire prospect of truly apocalyptic scenarios, such as the rapid collapse of the West Antarctic or Greenland ice sheets, which would raise sea levels by three or seven meters at a stroke.[8] One paper estimated that if the earth warms by 12 degrees Celsius, the majority of the human population would be living in locations where temperatures would regularly reach fatal levels—so hot that if you were outside for very long, you would die of heatstroke even if you were in the shade wrapped in a wet towel.[9] Or if ocean current systems are disrupted (which also already appears to be happening), weather patterns around the world would be radically disrupted—especially in Europe, where the Gulf Stream keeps the continent several degrees warmer than it would be otherwise.[10]

PROPOSED PROPERTARIAN REFORMS AND THEIR INADEQUACIES

Sounds bad. But maybe not, according to economist William Nordhaus, who won the Nobel Memorial Prize in Economics in 2018 and is the most prominent and influential climate economist in the world. He makes a by now familiar argument that modest market mechanisms are all we need to deal with climate change.

The argument is based on a neoliberal model he has constructed: the Dynamic Integrated Model of Climate and the Economy, or DICE. The details are very complicated, but the basic approach isn't hard to understand. He starts by projecting the future path of economic growth (according to orthodox models) and collects the estimated economic cost of warmer temperatures into a "damage function." Then he adds a "discount rate" to account for the fact that people typically value future wealth less than present wealth. Thus he calculates a "social cost of carbon"—that is, the total economic cost of each ton of carbon dioxide—and, after accounting for the cost of climate policy, an optimal carbon tax to cancel out that cost.[11]

In other words, climate change will cause some amount

of economic damage to the economy, and so we should levy a tax on carbon emissions exactly equal to this price in order to compensate—but not too much, lest the cost of the tax outweigh the benefits. The DICE model produces a price of $31 per ton in 2010 dollars, and he reckons that if this level of carbon tax were implemented, greenhouse gas emissions would peak around 2050 and fall slowly afterward.[12] By the end of the twenty-first century carbon dioxide concentrations would be about 650 parts per million (as compared to about 280 ppm in preindustrial times, and about 415 ppm today), and the average atmospheric temperature would be about 3.5 degrees Celsius higher than in preindustrial times.[13]

This is a bewildering conclusion for anyone who has consulted the reports of the Intergovernmental Panel on Climate Change (IPCC), a vast collaborative effort among the world's climate scientists. Their 2014 report predicts that the risk of 4 degrees of warming—just half a degree above Nordhaus's Goldilocks scenario—would "include severe and widespread impacts on unique and threatened systems, substantial species extinction, large risks to global and regional food security, and the combination of high temperature and humidity compromising normal human activities, including growing food or working outdoors in some areas for parts of the year."[14]

It simply doesn't seem right that such dire conditions should cause only slight damage to the global economy—and if we dig into the details, there are a number of serious objections to his model. To start with, Nordhaus's neoliberal growth model simply assumes that growth will keep trundling along of its own volition. As we saw in chapter 4, this is not the case.

Maintaining a steady state of growth requires state policy and international coordination that have not been in evidence since 2008, and there has been a sharp decline in growth rates in both rich and poor countries.

Now, as also noted previously, it would be *possible* to restore a decent level of growth with ordinary stimulus strategies (such as giving out $1,200 checks to the population), but that raises a second objection. One of the reasons growth has been so lousy of late is that nations around the world are starved of investment. Thanks to inequality there is a huge surplus of savings, yet nowhere good for them to go because the working classes do not have the income that would justify businesses investing in new capacity. An easy way to address this problem would be for states to spend hugely on green energy and decarbonization projects. This would both provide a place for investment to flow and put money into the pockets of people who do the necessary work. Nordhaus assumes that climate policy will be a drag on the economy, but if done properly, it would certainly provide at least some boost.

But the biggest problem with the DICE model is the damage function. Nordhaus creates this by collecting a number of papers that provide estimates of the hit to GDP at various temperature levels, plotting a curve that fits the resulting data points, and adding 25 percent to account for damages left out of these estimates.[15] Right off the bat this is a very weird way of making a predictive model. Normally when one is plotting a line measuring some physical phenomenon, one starts with *actual measurements*. This is impossible in the case of future climate damages, because the earth has as yet warmed only 1 degree Celsius—and even then there is tremendous disagreement about how much that warming has harmed the economy. (The 25 percent figure, meanwhile, is completely pulled out of his backside.)

Moreover, the papers he included simply *assumed* there would be no tipping point—that is, a temperature beyond which damages radically accelerate. Indeed, the maximum temperature of any estimate he included was 6 degrees Celsius. That's a very high temperature relative to today, but not even close to some of the dire situations I mentioned earlier. If we plug 12 degrees of warming—the scenario mentioned earlier, where a majority of people will be unable to go outside for much of the year—into his damage function, we get a hit to GDP of just 34 percent. That is frankly preposterous.

We can clearly detect all the pathologies of propertarian thinking here. There is the idea of the self-regulating market, assuming that economic growth will keep chugging along no matter what. There is the assumption that government regulation and spending will always slow down that growth process. And there is the fixation on trying to jam every problem into an economic framework, measured in dollars and cents, no matter how wildly ill-suited that might be.

If we get our heads out of the propertarian septic tank, we can think about the problem of climate change a lot more clearly. At bottom, it is an issue of risk management—the economy is a secondary issue. We can say with high confidence that warming in the range of 3–4 degrees will be *terrible*, regardless of the damage it does to GDP. Indeed, calculating damages in terms of output will necessarily minimize the damage to poorer countries, because they produce very little. The entire continent of Africa, with its 1.3 billion people, produces only about 3 percent of world output.[16] One could easily imagine a climate future where billions perish from various disasters, but because they largely live in poor countries it would not be very "expensive."

That said, the economic damage would also likely be very serious—rich countries cannot consider themselves immune. The extreme possibilities mentioned earlier also need to be taken into consideration even though we have no idea how likely they might be. As the late climate scientist Stephen Schneider wrote, climate change creates an "uncertainty explosion" because all the unknown elements feed into each other.[17] We don't know for sure how much greenhouse gas humans will emit over the coming decades, we don't know for sure how the biosphere will handle all that extra carbon, we don't know for sure how much the planet will warm with a greater carbon dioxide concentration, and we don't know for sure how different regions will respond to higher temperatures (for instance, the Arctic is warming much faster than the rest of the planet). The range of possible overall impacts depends on all of those things together, but because they are both interlocked and have a high degree of uncertainty individually, the range is very wide.

In other words, we can rule out neither surprisingly mild nor apocalyptic climate futures. What matters for policymakers is the latter category, because an apocalypse is a hell of a downside. If we take aggressive action and climate impacts turn out to be milder than anticipated, then we will have *maybe* wasted a lot of money on solar panels, wind turbines, and so on. But if we *don't* take aggressive action and climate change turns out to be very bad, then we will experience unprecedented mass death and economic calamity. If some of the worst-case possibilities come to pass, then it's not hard to imagine a chaotic collapse of advanced societies around the world. It would be worth almost any price to head off that possibility.

ISSUES WITH GREEN AUSTERITY

So what is to be done? To begin, we must understand that wealth as such is not the problem. This conflicts with the analysis of some environmentalists, who advocate a "degrowth" climate strategy. They start by pointing out that increased production has historically meant increased emissions of greenhouse gases. The way to attack climate change, by this view, is *negative* growth—shrinking the economy to reduce emissions.

It should first be noted that while in the twentieth century growth was indeed associated with more carbon emissions, that relationship has broken apart in recent years. Since the mid-2000s, U.S. carbon emissions have fallen by about 10 percent even as inflation-adjusted output has grown by about 8 percent.[18] In other words, growth has increased for a decade and a half, while greenhouse gas emissions have decreased. Even more impressive stories can be found in Europe. France's carbon dioxide emissions per person have fallen about 53 percent from their peak in 1973, while its output per person has about doubled over the same period.[19] Denmark's emissions per person have fallen by about 60 percent since 1996, while its output per person has increased by about 30 percent.[20]

Now, even Denmark's performance is still short of what is necessary to halt climate change, but on the other hand, none of these decarbonization efforts has been maximally aggressive. American efforts have been halfhearted at best—and indeed, much of the decline in U.S. emissions can be chalked up to moving manufacturing to China, particularly of steel, which is actually worse for emissions because Chinese industry is so inefficient. Still, there was some genuine progress. France's emissions fell because it moved most of its electricity production to nuclear, while Denmark's did mainly thanks to a massive build-out of wind power—both meaning absolute emissions reductions not compensated for by increased emissions elsewhere.

This reconciliation of growth with cuts in emissions matters especially because the degrowth school is seldom explicit about what their strategy would mean in practice—namely, a ton of austerity and a prolonged recession. If done bluntly, by simply slashing government spending, this would throw millions of people out of work and almost certainly cause the governing party to lose the next election.

Now, it could be planned better, by spreading the austerity out as evenly as possible—through work-spreading (that is, allocating a smaller amount of work evenly among workers), or even by deliberate adoption of obsolete labor-intensive production methods—but this would still be painful and likely unpopular. Green austerity would mean both reduced income and, if the pain was to be spread around, an intrusive bureaucratic apparatus to ensure use of inefficient methods. This is an inherently difficult hand of cards to play—spreading losses is always a lot less popular than spreading gains. Countries that have been forced to do this during wartime have sometimes collapsed altogether under the strain.

Worse still, green austerity would be a slow and inefficient way of cutting emissions—and to head off catastrophic climate change, greenhouse gas emissions must come down *extremely* fast. For instance, a recent IPCC report estimated that the world must cut its climate emissions by 45 percent of its 2010 levels by 2030 to stay under 1.5 degrees of warming.[21]

Reducing economic activity is one way to cut emissions, but another way is to replace carbon-emitting systems—power generation, transportation, construction, and such—with zero-carbon ones. A planned recession that reduced output by 10 percent would cut emissions by only about 10 percent, whereas replacing coal-fired power plants alone with green power would cut emissions by about 21 percent in the United States. (By way of comparison, during the worst year of the Great Recession, 2009, American emissions fell by about 6.2 percent.)[22] Doing so would require massive new investment, and hence *more* production and growth.

In sum, it is possible to preserve most of our advanced technology and a comfortable standard of living without torching the biosphere. Neither will that depend on keeping poor countries down—on the contrary, if climate policy is done properly, all nations should be able to eventually ascend to a high standard of living without breaking the biosphere. What we need is to attack the problem at the root of our energy, manufacturing, and agricultural systems.

PROPOSED COLLECTIVIST SOLUTIONS

A global climate policy would of course be an immensely complicated endeavor, but it's not hard to draw up a rough sketch of what is necessary. We can break the needed action into five categories: energy, research, efficiency, planning, and international aid.

This chart from Our World in Data gives us a good idea of the global sources of climate emissions:[23]

Where greenhouse gas emissions come from
Source: Our World In Data

Land use
18.4%

Waste
3.2%

Direct industrial processes
5.2%

Agriculture and fishing
1.7%

Fossil fuel leaks
5.8%

Unallocated fuel combustion
7.8%

Energy use in industry
24.2%

Transport
16.2%

Energy use in buildings
17.5%

Electricity, heating and cooling of buildings, and transportation account for nearly half of greenhouse emissions.[24] Tackling these sectors is conceptually simple: decarbonize electricity generation, and replace all carbon-burning transportation and heating with electric versions. It would take a titanic effort, of course, but the needed technology is already ready to go, or nearly so.

Energy

Let's talk sources. Zero-carbon power plants are already being deployed at scale in many countries, including the United States. In 2016, zero-carbon sources outstripped coal in U.S. electricity production for the first time, at 1,415 billion kilowatt-hours for renewables and nuclear as against coal's 1,239 billion kilowatt-hours. In 2020, zero-carbon power increased to 1,582 billion kilowatt-hours—more than twice coal's figure that year.[25] Today, wind and solar make up about half of this zero-carbon power (and production is ramping up very quickly), largely thanks to previous government research and installation subsidies. These are worthy but very modest policies; with a giant increase in funding, wind and solar deployment could be drastically accelerated. That would require big upgrades to the U.S. electricity grid, to accommodate how wind and solar are less steady than a carbon-powered plant that can be switched on or off at will. But by connecting the entire country into one big grid, adding a lot of power storage, building long-distance high-voltage connections across the country, overhauling appliance use, and a variety of other reforms, that problem can be overcome. In general, all power infrastructure will need to be upgraded and ruggedized far beyond what is most profitable. In February 2021, for instance, Texas was struck by a cold snap that knocked out about a third of its power generation capacity, because nobody had wanted to pay for the winterization that would only be useful once a decade or so.[26]

Meanwhile, nuclear power is theoretically promising but practically challenging. It produces no emissions aside from what is needed in construction, and it has a track record of success—as in France, as noted previously. France's current per-person emission figure is less than a third of the current U.S. figure.

However, today traditional nuclear power plants are extremely expensive, and indeed have gotten more so over time. By contrast, the price of solar panels has fallen by 99 percent over the last forty years.[27] The reason is that the usual nuclear plant is a very large and complicated facility that is difficult to build and insure, partly because it requires so many safety mechanisms to lower the risk of disaster.

Now, a serious nuclear accident is a real menace, as seen in Chernobyl and Fukushima, but it's also true that when we consider the total death toll of carbon-based electricity, nuclear is safer by a mile.

Burning carbon fuels necessarily releases toxic byproducts. Coal is especially filthy, producing nitrogen and sulfur oxides, mercury, and particulate pollution that cause all kinds of illnesses. Natural gas is much cleaner to burn, but still not perfectly clean, and it produces significant pollution during production and transport. A 2007 study found a rate of 24.6 deaths caused per terawatt-hour of coal power generated; the comparable figures are 18.4 for oil, 2.8 for natural gas, and 0.074 for nuclear.[28] Nuclear accidents are terrifying and get tons of attention, but the quiet plume of suffocating coal pollution is worse by several orders of magnitude. Nuclear power, like wind and solar, causes virtually no deaths.

At any rate, the typical mega-reactor can probably play no more than a minor part in any climate strategy, if only for cost reasons. Indeed, two new reactor projects in South Carolina and Georgia saw cost overruns so severe that they bankrupted the contractor, Westinghouse; one was abandoned in 2017 and the other's fate is uncertain.[29]

Research

That brings us to research. By way of example, there are many promising alternative reactor designs that could revolutionize nuclear technology, making it both cheaper and safer. In particular, a high-temperature liquid fluoride thorium reactor (LFTR) has enormous theoretical promise. Thorium is a much more abundant fuel than uranium, dissolving it in a fluid makes it easier to manufacture and process in the reactor, and the heat makes it more efficient. This technology would produce far less waste and could be operated at atmospheric pressure instead of the very high pressures required in traditional reactors, reducing both explosion risk and expense (since no enormous pressure vessel would be needed). All told, these should be cheaper, more efficient, and safer—indeed, one prototype reactor was in operation at Oak Ridge National Laboratory in the 1960s for several years.[30]

Of course, that promise comes with some downsides. The liquid high-temperature chemical presents corrosion problems, and radiation might degrade the containment or power generation equipment. These reactors also present a proliferation risk, because in some designs it is easy to create enriched products that would be relatively easy to turn into a nuclear bomb.[31]

Most important, there is no supply chain for producing these reactors. It's not an accident that LFTRs never made it out of the prototype stage—it's because their state funding was cut off in the late 1960s. Nuclear reactors are some of the most challenging engineering problems human beings have ever attempted. It takes tons of money, advanced science, and cutting-edge manufacturing technology to build just *one*. To deploy them at scale, we need a vast complex of specialized supply, construction, and maintenance firms, plus elaborate government regulations to make sure everything is done consistently and safely.

The *science* of LFTRs pencils out, but the only way to determine if they make sense at a large scale is for the state to step in with subsidies and controls to see if mass production can actually happen. This is what happened with light-water reactors in the United States (which were heavily subsidized not just for power reasons but so they could be used in naval vessels and to build nuclear weapons).[32] There will for sure be unforeseen obstacles to producing LFTRs, as there always are when developing a new technology, but only by actually giving it a good solid try can we find out whether our scientists and engineers can tinker their way around them.

LFTRs are just an example of what is needed for climate research. What governments around the world should be doing is flinging gigantic sums at both improvements to existing zero-carbon technologies and any moon-shot idea that shows promise. We should be plowing money into solar-collection generators, new wind turbine designs, geothermal exploration, tide power generation, electric or fuel cell airplanes and cargo ships, airship transport, and so on. Once the design is worked out and a prototype has been constructed, then the state must provide subsidies to get the full industrial supply chain up and running—and it may make sense for the government to simply run the entire system itself.

This was ostensibly the point of President Obama's Advanced Research Projects Agency—Energy (ARPA-E, which was part of the Recovery Act stimulus), but this fund was far too conservative. Most of its loans actually made a profit, with only a few failures—meaning they were sure things, not risky, innovative gambles.[33] Of course we do not want to fund outright boondoggles, but any state-backed climate research fund should have a lot of failures, because then we know we are pushing the envelope of what is possible.

Once we have made the electrical grid carbon-free, the logical second step will be to make electricity the source of all energy needs. This also will require new science and technologies to replace carbon-heavy prevailing methods.

Industry is the area that probably needs the most immediate research attention. Steel and concrete are probably the most important industrial commodities outside of oil, and as yet zero-carbon methods for producing them are uneconomical. Creating steel from iron ore is typically done by burning coke (basically a purified kind of coal) in a blast furnace, which creates enormous emissions. Recycled steel can be smelted with an electric arc furnace, but this is a comparatively small portion of total steel production. There are replacement processes that could smelt iron ore without carbon fuels, but as yet the kinks have not been worked out, and they are more expensive than the traditional method.[34]

Something similar holds for concrete. Concrete requires sand, water, an aggregate of small pebbles, and cement. All these require energy to obtain and transport, but the biggest energy cost is cement, which is usually made by cooking limestone and shale in a carbon-fired kiln at very high temperatures. (Concrete is also often made stronger by laying steel rebar in the wet mix to reinforce it.) Concrete is so common that it accounts for about 7 percent of all greenhouse gas emissions.[35] Just like with steel, materials scientists have been working on various methods to reduce the emissions from cement production (such as using a solar forge) and improved ingredient mixes to make it more durable—but again, most of them are more expensive than the traditional method under current conditions.[36]

Across all areas of industry, the government will have to step in and fund additional research, impose extra costs on carbon-based production so as to accelerate the deployment of zero-carbon methods, and otherwise target emissions sources to wrench them down. However, over the medium term, we will probably need to start taking carbon out of the atmosphere. As Denmark and France show, there is a lot of low-hanging fruit when it comes to emissions—a wasteful country such as the United States or Australia should be able to slash its emissions by, say, three-quarters without too much fuss. But it will likely be a lot harder to iron out the final 5–10 percent or so. It may well be simpler and more economical to spin up a big carbon capture industry to compensate for the emissions that are extremely hard to eradicate. But more important, there have already been so many emissions that significant carbon capture is a practical necessity at this point to head off a calamitous future.

Once again, there are already worked-out methods for pulling carbon dioxide out of the air—where it could be processed into carbon fuels or simply stored—in the prototype stage.[37] But just as with LFTRs, there is no broader supply chain to support building these facilities at scale. State subsidies will have to breathe that into existence.

Efficiency

That brings me to efficiency. We should be looking not only for ways to replace carbon power but also for ways to use less energy, period. When it comes to personal transportation, for instance, electric rail transport is far more efficient than individual cars. Electric cars are of course much better than gas-powered ones, and there will surely be a need for them in the future, but they also consume a lot of electricity and require a great deal of energy and raw materials to create the necessary metal, plastic, and especially batteries.

Individual cars use up a tremendous amount of land as well, because they are among the most inefficient ways of moving people from one place to another. For one typical use of a car, commuting to work, you need a parking space both at home and at work. Then you need a roadway to move between the two points. Under ideal conditions, a lane of traffic can carry up to 1,600 people per hour—while a dedicated two-way bike lane can carry perhaps 5,000, a dedicated bus transit lane 8,000, an on-street rail line 25,000, and a subway line 70,000 (or even more with competent logistics).[38] Worse, when highways are approaching their peak use, capacity tends to *fall* due to traffic jams, which are impossible to avoid because each individual is operating his own machine. Car-dominant cities end up dedicating enormous chunks of prime urban real estate to lane after lane of highway, yet are still clogged with traffic twice a day during rush hour.

Worse still, cars are dangerous. In 2019, 23,744 American car occupants were killed in collisions, along with 5,014 motorcyclists, 6,205 pedestrians, and 846 cyclists.[39] So many people are killed while walking or biking around American cities because the typical urban landscape is violently hostile to people outside their cars—with high speed limits, few protected crosswalks, and few protected bike lanes.

Boosters of electric cars have long promised that self-driving technology will solve these problems, but not only has this proved to be a dramatically harder task than anticipated, it would likely increase driving as well. A clever study that gave a few individuals a chauffeur to simulate the effect of being able to call a robot taxi whenever they wanted found they increased their vehicle miles traveled by 83 percent on average.[40]

Instead, nations should be looking for ways to move away from cars wherever possible. But achieving this will take a revolution in city planning. In the mid-twentieth century the automobile became the dominant form of transportation across the developed world, especially in the United States. America tore up most of its public transit systems, let its passenger rail rot, and went on a bender of freeway and suburb construction that has proved to be an environmental and social disaster.[41] Whole built-up neighborhoods—typically in minority or impoverished communities—were bulldozed for urban freeways, all in service of a dirty, resource-hogging transportation technology that reaps a daily harvest of carnage.

The resulting dominant American urban form, centered around the detached single-family home, is hideously inefficient. The low-density sprawl thus created eats up land and makes public transit, walking, and cycling very difficult. Separating each home makes heating and cooling more energy-intensive, because there are no shared walls.

Now, it would be going too far to outlaw detached single-family homes. But even rowhouses (which are connected on two sides) and modest multiunit apartment buildings *are* outlawed on most American urban land. Central cities could stand more large-scale apartment towers, but there is a huge lack of densely packed homes and medium-sized apartment complexes across the country, and it is probably more important to develop these given what has already been built. Greater density in turn would enable better public transit and make protected pedestrian and bike paths more useful; all of these could be linked with interstate high-speed passenger rail lines that could replace a lot of airplane trips. Indeed, cities such as Paris and Amsterdam have taken great strides to banish private cars from their central districts (with certain exceptions, such as for disabled folks), and the result is a more efficient city that is also a cleaner, healthier, much more pleasant place to live.[42]

The energy efficiency of housing could be further upgraded with better insulation and appliances. In addition to more people living in larger buildings with shared walls, insulation and climate control systems in line with the Passivhaus standard (including techniques such as triple-pane windows, capturing heat from sunlight, heat pumps instead of furnaces and air conditioners, and so on) will drastically lower the energy costs of shelter. Replacing natural gas stoves with inductive electric ones will cut emissions and radically improve the air quality inside the home.[43]

Better recycling is another big potential source of efficiency. Procedures for reusing paper, glass, plastic, and so forth have gotten much better over the years, but there is a great deal of room for improvement. According to the OECD, Germany recycles about 49 percent of its municipal waste, while the U.S. figure is just 25 percent.[44] Improvements in this area could include things like separating paper from the rest of the recycling stream, creating a national reusable glass bottle standard (as it is much more efficient to reuse glass than to remelt it every time), funding safer electronics recycling centers, and so on. Again, this is a very complicated topic, but the amount of sheer waste in the American economy could certainly be cut dramatically by paying it some serious attention.

Summing up so far: The world cannot possibly endure even Americans continuing to live their energy-hogging, wasteful lifestyle, let alone the rest of humanity joining them. There are simply not enough resources for 8 billion people to all live in their own detached single-family McMansion, each with a four-ton SUV that gets ten miles to the gallon parked out front. But conversely, neither would it be some drastic imposition on the American way of life to cut our resource use by, say, 90 percent. On the contrary, living in denser communities, with somewhat more modest dwellings, a great deal more human-powered movement, and a great deal less pollution would make our lives more pleasant, healthier, and longer. (We may have to learn to get by without low-grade plastic, however, as that has proved exceptionally annoying to recycle.)[45]

Planning

At any rate, all this is meant to give just a flavor of the kind of thing nations across the world should be exerting their every sinew to accomplish. There are worked-out models of a post-carbon economy that suggest we could have both continued growth and zero greenhouse emissions, but they have their own questionable assumptions.[46] The only way to actually find out how to make it work is to try as hard as we can. The previous history of spectacularly rapid innovation suggests strongly we should be able to get there, but it will take concentrated effort.

That means planning. All the preceding suggestions will require the government to take up a role in directing the necessary effort and investment. Market-based policies such as a carbon tax or renewable installation subsidies can play a part in changing behaviors, but elsewhere the state will have to directly take the lead. Overhauling American cities will mean changes in rules about zoning, funding for highway reclamation projects, public transit, social housing, bike and pedestrian access, and other things. Developing new technologies will require direct state coordination of both research and the eventual deployment of new technologies—possibly including owning and operating the eventual institutions, as the United States currently does with the Tennessee Valley Authority. The United States went from the theory of nuclear fission to a working nuclear weapons program in just six years, but it took an enormous state investment of money and resources.[47]

So far I have not mentioned agriculture and land use, because this area needs a combination of research and planning. Currently there are many promising plans to reduce the emissions from food production, which should be pursued with all speed.[48] However, there is a greater degree of lifestyle choice with food than there is with renewable power. The plain fact is that we all need to eat a lot less meat, because growing animals for slaughter is an inherently inefficient way to make something to eat.[49] Raising animals requires using land to grow animal feed, and that land could be used for human plant foods instead; furthermore, most of the energy that goes into the animal-raising process ends up supporting the animal's metabolism, when it could be used more directly to support humans' metabolisms. Then, of course, most meat is produced in industrial feedlots and slaughterhouses under appalling conditions for both animals and workers.

In a broader sense, all other life on earth provides incalculable benefits to humanity. Plankton produce the oxygen we breathe, forests clean the air and water we drink, and bacteria help grow the food we eat. Some economists have attempted to quantify these benefits and produced estimates in the trillions of dollars, but in general this planet would not be habitable without the rest of the biosphere providing innumerable ecosystem services, many of which are still poorly understood or impossible to value in dollars and cents.[50] Even simply in terms of recreation dollars, wilderness can often provide more economic benefit than ruthless exploitation (such as blowing up mountains to get at the coal inside them).[51]

But we should of course also make as much room as possible for other plants and animals to live, even if it doesn't narrowly benefit humanity. There is every reason to extend the egalitarian moral umbrella to other living beings as much as we can, especially those with advanced intelligence, such as gorillas and dolphins. Today, and especially once a light-touch renewable economy has been established, we should try to care for all life on the planet as decently as we can. Given the terrific disruption that humans have already imposed on the natural world, it is the only thing that could possibly save a decent chunk of existing species, which are already going extinct at a terrifying rate.

INTERNATIONAL AID

Finally, that leads me to the most underappreciated aspect of climate policy: international aid. There are dozens of poorer countries that are starting to move up the development ladder, and yet more that would do so if not for political dysfunction, oppression, disadvantageous terms of trade, or other problems. The world cannot afford the as yet undeveloped world following in the footsteps of China, which has so far largely developed with carbon power, and as a result now emits *twice as much* greenhouse gas as the United States in total (though much less per person).[52] If India alone (which will soon be the world's most populous country) goes along the China track, the climate is toast.

Developed nations such as the United States simply have no better option than to set up a gigantic international investment program to help poorer nations leapfrog carbon fuels and current inefficient production processes. Future development in the Global South must be zero-carbon because the climate cannot handle the emissions, but it also must be efficient because there are simply not enough resources for everyone to adopt a wasteful American lifestyle.

A paper by Jacob Fawcett for the People's Policy Project proposed a Global Green New Deal wherein the rich world would set up an investment fund doling out $2 trillion per year, with a U.S. share of about $680 billion.[53] Propertarians would no doubt be outraged at this idea, regarding it as some unjustifiable handout to poor people who don't even live in America.

However, properly considered, this is less an act of charity than a sensible move to protect American national security and livelihoods. It would help poorer nations a lot, to be sure, and that is only fair given the history of Western exploitation and colonialism. But it would also help the United States. For one thing, America is not at all immune to climate change—the American Southwest is moving into a semipermanent state of drought, wildfires in California have gotten worse, midwestern farms have seen devastating floods, Alaskan permafrost is melting, and so on.[54] All that will get much worse if we allow warming to spin out of control. Paying a relatively modest sum to stop foreign emissions from destroying the American climate would be well worth it.

Additionally, all that money would not simply vanish from the global trade system. Quite a lot of it would be spent first on American capital imports to get nations up and growing, and then, when they have developed a domestic market, on imports of goods and services—the Democratic Republic of the Congo, for instance, cannot afford many iPhones or movie tickets in its current wretched state. Again, with a balanced trade system (as described in chapter 2) poorer nations can start climbing up the development ladder without causing mass deindustrialization or declining wages in the developed world. Indeed, mass investment into poorer countries, done properly, would be a good place for some of the excess savings in the rich world.

Similar to how the Marshall Plan benefited both Europe and America by helping spin up the whole global economy, a Global Green New Deal would eventually benefit the whole planet on net. No longer would the developed world need to keep the Global South impoverished to maintain their unfair share of the planet's resources. On the contrary, they could enjoy greater export earnings thanks to half the planet no longer having to live hand to mouth.

Climate change is where the interdependence of all human society is most obvious and undeniable. We are all at each other's mercy, and the consequences if we fail to coordinate will be dire in the extreme. But by the same token, the potential benefits of cooperating would be magnificent. We could enjoy a cleaner, healthier, more just world, if we cared to make it so.

INEQUALITY, EXPLAINED

IN THE 1950S, economist Simon Kuznets developed a theory about inequality and economic growth. Painstakingly collecting a vast amount of data on the national income of the United States, he found that there had been an up-and-down trend in income inequality over the previous century. From the late nineteenth century up to 1929, income inequality had increased. But in the succeeding years, it had fallen sharply, and was continuing to decline more gradually through the 1950s.[1]

Though Kuznets was not a propertarian, and his argument contained many caveats (more on this later), he suggested that the resulting "Kuznets curve" could be partly due to market mechanisms. He argued that capitalist societies would naturally become more unequal as they first developed and low-productivity agricultural workers moved into higher-productivity industrial jobs. But when more than half of the workforce was in industry, inequality would tend to go down.

As usual, the Kuznets curve was stripped of its qualifications and seized on by propertarians as evidence of the justice of capitalism.[2] We had gone through the trials of the choking pollution, the child laborers being dismembered in textile mills, the women being burned to death in sweatshops, and so on, but now that was all over and done with. We were on to the sunlit uplands of equality and prosperity. Economic growth being doled out to all would be the solvent that dissolved class conflict.

Unfortunately, this curve did not last. Starting in the 1970s, income inequality started increasing, and it has continued to do so up to this day. Now, as we saw in chapter 1, the ultra-rich collect about as much of the national income as they did in 1929.

Rising inequality is the inevitable consequence of propertarian policy. Union-busting, deregulation, welfare cuts, and, especially, lowering taxes on the rich divert income to the top. Propertarianism is a tyranny of the rich, and naturally they rig the system to vacuum up as much of the national income as possible. In this chapter, I'll explore how this happened, and how it might be reversed.

One interesting thing about the propertarians' conquest of America is that they insisted that growth would compensate for inequality even as that inequality started to rise. One of their signature slogans was "a rising tide lifts all boats." Or if you prefer culinary metaphors, they said we should "grow the pie" instead of trying to slice it up more evenly. The idea is that growth is more important than transfers or welfare programs, because all classes are *assumed* to share in the fruits of prosperity. But this is not the case. Some simple arithmetic shows that the majority of Americans would have been better off with a much slower rate of growth if it had been better distributed.

Let's examine the bottom half of society. As French economist Thomas Piketty shows in his book *Capital and Ideology*, the bottom 50 percent of Americans went from collecting about 20 percent of national income in the mid-1970s to only 12.5 percent in 2018.[3] (Today the top 10 percent of Americans take about 47 percent of income, and the top 1 percent about 20 percent.)

Suppose we offered the bottom half of American society a choice between their 2018 share of income or their 1970s share of a smaller economy. To return to desserts, this would be like asking Americans whether they would prefer their current slice of the current pie, or a bigger slice of a smaller pie. If we gave the bottom half their 1970s-sized slice, how much could we shrink the economy before it became a bad trade-off for them? If we adjust the data for inflation, in 2018 the national income was 84 percent greater than in 1990— but remember, the bottom half got a far smaller share of that income in 2018.[4] If we do the algebra to determine what the bottom half would receive with a 20 percent share of income going back over the years, we would have to shrink the economy *all the way back to its 1993 size* before this becomes a bad deal.

Of course, this is a rough estimate, and it would not actually be possible to reverse the course of growth in this way. On the contrary, while the bottom 50 percent might get more income in my thought experiment, they would get a great deal *more* than that if we just adjusted the current economy back to its 1970s structure. But the point that growth has *not* benefited all classes equally—that the rising tide in fact floated only the yachts, while the rowboats sank—is unquestionably true. In terms of income, the twenty-six years of growth between 1993 and 2018 have been *worse than useless* for fully half of all Americans.

Why has this happened? Heterodox economists have

argued convincingly that five factors are primarily responsible. First and most important is the decline in taxation on the rich. In their book *The Triumph of Injustice*, economists Emmanuel Saez and Gabriel Zucman muster data showing that the total tax rate (including federal, state, and local taxes) on the richest four hundred Americans has declined from about 70 percent in 1950 to 47 percent in 1980 and just 23 percent in 2018 after the Trump tax cuts—the lowest rate of *anyone* on the income spectrum, including the poorest people in the country.[5] That both mechanically increases the income of the rich, since they have more take-home pay, and leads them to try to increase their income over and above where it previously was—if one is paying 70 percent in tax on every additional dollar of income, then there is little point in trying to grab even more, but if one is paying just 23 percent, it's worth the effort.

Propertarian economists described these high taxes as a bad labor incentive because they pushed people to work less and make less money, thus throttling economic growth. As we saw in chapter 5, they were completely wrong about growth, but in a sense they were right about the incentive. Cutting taxes did indeed incentivize the rich to increase their salaries—but this additional income came *at the expense* of the rest of society, especially at the top end. CEO compensation, for instance, increased by about 1,167 percent between 1978 and 2019, as shown in an analysis from the Economic Policy Institute. Workers, meanwhile, lost out—their incomes grew just 13.7 percent over the same period, and the average ratio between worker and CEO pay grew from 21:1 in 1965 to 31:1 in 1978, 118:1 in 1995, and 320:1 in 2018.[6] And again, as we saw in chapter 4, this development did not cause any growth acceleration—on the contrary, growth sagged because the working classes no longer had the income to buy what they produced.

Even people who are sympathetic to workers can be a bit misleading about what is happening here, sometimes describing it as CEOs simply "bargaining" for better terms. In reality this was an exercise of power. Corporations are hierarchical, authoritarian institutions in which top management has sweeping powers over the workers and how the operation is organized. CEOs (along with other top managers) simply *took* a bigger and bigger chunk of the corporate surplus for themselves.

Realizing this fact clarifies a lot about what happens in American business. For instance, commentators are sometimes confused as to how Wall Street CEOs can possibly command such enormous salaries when they are routinely hauled before investigators or Congress to disclaim any knowledge of their employees' latest instance of money laundering, setting up fake accounts, stealing their customers' homes or cars, and so on.[7] Now, in many cases they are probably lying, and CEOs should at least be responsible for ensuring that criminal behavior is not tolerated even if they are unaware of it. But it is also definitely true that the heads of big banks have little idea of what is happening in most of their operations. JPMorgan Chase, for instance, has almost *$3.4 trillion* in assets.[8] No one person can *possibly* familiarize her- or himself with all the details of such a sprawling operation (he or she would have to examine about $6.4 million worth of accounts every single minute of the year). CEO Jamie Dimon got paid $31.5 million in 2020 not because he was mainly responsible for its gigantic profits that year, but because he is like a king, with everyone else in the bank deferring to his power, and because the bank exercises authoritarian power over much of the economy.[9]

A second related factor is the decline in unionization. Back in the 1970s, about a third of the private sector workforce was unionized.[10] A trade union will naturally mobilize to protect its members' share of the corporate surplus, and so it will oppose bloated executive pay packages or stripping the company's assets to the bone to give them to Wall Street (more on this later). America never had complete unionization, as many European countries continue to have, but that one-third provided a critical counterweight to executive-class power.

That also shows that unions were not just ways to protect workers' raises and benefits; they were a power foundation for egalitarian politics. They added political ballast to the Democratic Party, which up until the 1980s was at least halfheartedly against propertarianism, and extended at least some democratic rights into the workplace. A unionized workplace is one in which workers have some power against authoritarian rule by management.

A third related factor was the destruction of financial regulation. Starting in the 1950s, but accelerating in the 1980s, banks and investment firms gradually clawed their way out from under the New Deal controls that had prevented financial panics since 1933. In the 1980s and 1990s, they got rid of caps on interest rates, bans on interstate banking, bank size requirements, the separation of commercial and investment banking, and countless other rules.[11] As noted before, the result was the return of periodic financial crises (in 1987, 2000, and 2008), but also an increasing share of corporate profits going to Wall Street.

According to propertarian theories, the supposed purpose of finance is to allocate capital—intermediating between savers and borrowers. This should be a relatively low-margin business, especially with the rise of information technology that has made research and communication much, much cheaper. Instead, the cost of intermediation has remained at about 1.5–2 percent for the last century, while financial profits soared.[12]

What actually happened is that Big Finance gradually regeared the corporate sector around short-term profits and speculative gambling. As we saw in previous chapters, during the neoliberal age Wall Street pressure pushed companies away from wages, investment, and research and development and toward disgorging profits to shareholders in the form of dividends and especially share buybacks. Buybacks were not even broadly legal until 1982, when Reagan's Securities and Exchange Commission issued Rule 10B-18.[13] Net share buybacks increased from about nothing in 1980 to reliably 2–4 percent of GDP today—spiking to a high of over 6 percent during the peak of the housing bubble.[14] The 466 companies that were continuously listed on the S&P 500 stock index between 2009 and 2018 spent a sum equal to *92 percent* of their profits on shareholder payouts—52 percent on buybacks and 40 percent on dividends.[15] Many companies have completely ditched any kind of research and development so they can disgorge as much short-term cash as possible. In 2018, 57 percent of companies on the S&P spent nothing at all in this area.[16]

What's more, often companies fund payouts through borrowing. A Roosevelt Institute analysis found that between 2015 and 2017, the restaurant industry spent a sum equal to *136.5 percent* of its profits on share buybacks alone (that is, they spent over a third more than their net income by borrowing and dipping into cash reserves).[17] This kind of thing unsurprisingly weakens companies and sometimes bankrupts them.

Once again, there was a marked political dimension to the rise of Wall Street. Bankers did not just adjust what was happening in terms of dollars and cents; they exercised considerable political domination over these companies and the rest of the economy—in effect arrogating to themselves the regulatory powers that had been abandoned by the state.

In the early 2010s, for instance, the airline JetBlue attempted to make a market play catering to quality: they offered more legroom, no additional fees for checked bags, and better customer service. The investor class threw a tantrum—planting negative stories in the media, producing dour analyses of the move, threatening to sell the company's stock, and so on—demanding the airline stuff more seats into its planes and add more fees. Their demands put pressure on the stock price, and in 2014, after just a couple of years, JetBlue gave in and did exactly that.[18] It's important to note that these moves had not been some kind of attempt at charity from the company's management; they were attempting to improve their reputation and convince customers that it was worth paying a premium for more convenient service, and thereby increase their profits. It takes years for that kind of effort to pay off—indeed, in 2014 the airline was quite profitable, just somewhat less than other airlines. But Wall Street wouldn't even let it try, because the investor class has an unshakable belief that the way to juice profits is by dominating, coercing, and manipulating the customer—a natural expression of propertarian politics. Companies across the country have gotten the message, preemptively puking themselves inside out into the Wall Street maw to stave off an investor attack.

A fourth factor in growing inequality is macroeconomic management. After Federal Reserve chair Paul Volcker broke inflation in the early 1980s by strangling the economy with high interest rates (covered in chapter 4), the Fed gradually shifted away from a policy regime that tried to balance equally between full employment and keeping down inflation, and moved toward one in which stable prices got top priority. The Fed supposedly targets a 2 percent rate of inflation, meaning it should err both above and below that mark as long as it all roughly averages out to around that. But instead it increasingly treated that 2 percent as a ceiling and viewed wage growth as a harbinger of inflation necessitating preemptive interest rate hikes (the one major exception was when chair Alan Greenspan let the late-1990s boom ride).

The mechanical consequence of this is a steady decline in the share of total income going to workers. Labor share generally falls during a recession thanks to unemployment, but it can recover when full employment is reached—but as a matter of arithmetic, this requires a period during which wages grow faster than the economy as a whole (which typically creates inflation), so workers can make up for that lost ground. But if stable prices are the overriding goal of macroeconomic management, and wage increases are viewed as dangerous under any circumstances, then the Fed's behavior will tend to act as a downward ratchet on the labor share. And that is exactly what happened: after the 2000s dot-com crash the labor share of compensation fell sharply to the lowest level recorded since the late 1940s, and fell further still after the 2008 crash.[19]

Labor share of income

Source: Federal Reserve

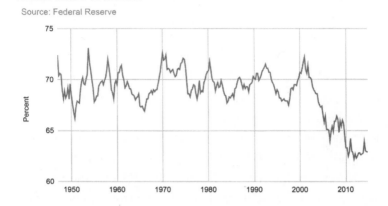

By prioritizing stable prices above full employment, the Fed acted like a sort of constant downward ratchet on the labor market—ignoring falling wages, but panicking at rising ones. Workers thus fell further and further behind.

Finally, there is the brute fact of capital income—that is, money earned from capital gains, dividends, rent payments, and so on. As Thomas Piketty shows in his book *Capital in the Twenty-First Century*, in rich countries the rate of return on wealth has generally been higher than the overall growth rate of the economy (the famous $r > g$ relation), and, as noted before, people tend to save more the more income they make. Second, the wealth-to-income ratio has also risen in rich countries over time. That means absent any countervailing forces, both wealth and income will tend to concentrate over time. Richer people will get more income, which they will use to accumulate more wealth, and so on.[20]

But as Piketty also argues in *Capital and Ideology*, this is not an automatic, mechanical process. The rich have expended enormous political effort to drive down wages and drive up the rate of profit, using techniques like the ones outlined earlier. Indeed, wealth itself is a political construct, and increases in measured wealth often have nothing to do with increases in productive capacity. For instance, countries such as Germany and Sweden have co-determination laws requiring that some of the seats on the boards of publicly traded firms be filled by elected workers of the firm. This makes shares in the company less valuable (and hence decreases national wealth) because they provide less control over the company. But there is no hit to overall productivity in those countries—on the contrary, "greater worker investment in the long-term strategies of German and Swedish firms seems . . . to have increased their productivity," he writes.[21]

Propertarian economists have tried to pin most of the rise in inequality on technological changes—the idea being that newer jobs in services and high-tech industries are more capital-intensive and require higher skills, meaning fewer workers are needed, and people without advanced training will be left behind.[22]

We have already seen the many ways this is a crock. But more important, it leaves out the capacity of the state to compensate for economic developments. Even if it were the case that newer businesses require fewer and more-skilled workers (which is probably overstated, given the extent to which high-tech companies have outsourced labor-intensive work such as website moderation to poorer countries), this could easily be compensated with greater taxation and welfare spending. Let's consider Finland. Inequality is often measured by the "Gini coefficient," a statistical measure in which a coefficient of 0 means every person makes exactly the same income, and a coefficient of 1 means one person collects the entire national income. Finland's Gini coefficient in terms of *market* income—that is, what people receive just from working and owning, outside any government programs—is almost exactly the same as the United States' inequality, at 0.51.[23] But when we include the welfare state, Finland's Gini coefficient falls to 0.26, while America's falls to just 0.39, meaning that the United States has significantly more inequality. Americans could have dialed up the welfare state to achieve a Finnish (or even lower) level of inequality, but propertarians prevented that from happening.

That leads me to a broader point about inequality. The story I've just told is about why, after dropping because of the New Deal, inequality increased once again beginning in the 1970s. But the America of the 1960s, while relatively egalitarian, was still quite unequal in absolute terms. Today the top 1 percent own nearly 40 percent of the national wealth, but back in 1962, they still owned about 33 percent of it.[24] The New Deal was a great egalitarian advance compared with the hideous inequality of 1929, but it was still well short of what could have been achieved.

The deeper truth is that any kind of economic system geared around working and owning, like capitalism, will naturally provide income only to workers and owners. About half of the American population—children, students, the unemployed, people with a work-limiting disability, and retired folks—do not work, and we should not want them to work.[25] (The age of child labor is rightly remembered as a social catastrophe.) Most of them do not own much (or any) wealth either—and as we have seen, under propertarian rule wealth always becomes highly concentrated. Propertarian capitalism causes poverty because whole swaths of the population are cut out of receiving income. A complete economic overhaul is needed to fight inequality.

So what is to be done? We need three broad strategies. First, spread out income from work as broadly as possible. Second, implement a full-dress welfare state to provide income to the population of nonworkers, and to provide basic security for all. Third, democratize wealth—as much as possible of the national wealth should be gradually placed under collective ownership, and its proceeds distributed on a per capita basis.

As usual, Europe provides many examples of how this can be done. Let me start with work. Mass unionization will compress workers' incomes, meaning wages will be boosted up at the bottom and pulled down somewhat at the top. This is a prime goal of all unions, in keeping with the ideal of solidarity and representing all the workers in the firm. We see this in the Nordic countries, where the top tenth of workers make 2.3–2.5 times what the bottom tenth does, compared to the U.S. figure of five times more (see chapter 2).

A full rebuild of the largely collapsed American union movement is outside the scope of this book. However, there are a few straightforward policies that could accomplish a great deal. First, we make it much easier to form a union by repealing the Taft-Hartley Act (which banned sympathy strikes, among other things), banning so-called right-to-work laws (these laws prohibit closed-shop contracts, in which the union and the business agree to make joining the union a condition of employment), and enabling "card check," in which workers are taken to have decided to form a union immediately if a majority of employees sign cards to that effect. Then we strengthen the National Labor Relations Act (NLRA) to add real penalties for violations of labor law—for instance, employers who illegally threaten to fire people for trying to join a union currently face the toothless sanction of having to withdraw their comments and post a notice informing workers of their rights. Scofflaw bosses should face penalties of fines escalating to confiscation of the business for repeat offenses. (This is the basic structure of the Protecting the Right to Organize Act, which at the time of writing had passed the House of Representatives but not the Senate.)

Second, we must change the basic structure of labor law by moving to a sectoral bargaining model. Under the NLRA, workplaces have to be organized individually. That was a fairly viable model in the mid-twentieth century, when huge factories were much more common than they are today. But organizing the widely dispersed retail and service-sector jobs that are more typical today is extremely difficult under this framework, even without the current legal obstacles.

Under sectoral bargaining, union contracts are instead negotiated across an entire sector of the economy. Typically, union representatives bargain with a board of employer representatives, and the government extends the resulting contract across all companies in that sector, regardless of how many union members they have. Thanks to this model, in Austria 98 percent of workers are covered by union contracts, and 99 percent are covered in France (according to the most recent data).[26]

The sectoral bargaining model has shown great success at extending union contract coverage to virtually every employee, but countries with it have also seen large declines in their actual union membership. In Austria union membership is just 26 percent, and in France it is a pitiful 9 percent.[27] Even though almost all workers are covered by union contracts, it is not ideal for a small minority of workers to be conducting negotiations with employers, and very small unions are liable to be crushed by business.

One option to forestall this is for the United States to adopt the aforementioned Ghent system (named after the city in Belgium). Unions started operating unemployment insurance schemes for their members in many countries in the mid-nineteenth century, but in 1901 the Ghent municipal government opted to supplement those union funds with public money. Originally the point was simply to make the unemployment insurance system more secure, but it also provided a large incentive to join a union, because in order to get unemployment benefits workers had to sign up.

Countries including Finland, Sweden, Denmark, and Iceland have versions of this system today, and thus the highest unionization rates in the world (60, 65, 67, and 92 percent, respectively).[28] Typically, to be eligible for unemployment benefits one must join a union, and as a result almost all workers are unionized. (In the Nordics, self-employed people or sole proprietors usually have a different unemployment benefit funded by the state, but many still join unions geared toward that type of work.) It makes a large difference in union density even within Nordic states—Norway, which does not have the Ghent system, has a union density of just 49 percent.

It makes sense for the United States to adopt the Ghent system, but there would be practical challenges given our meager 10 percent union density at present. It would probably take years for unions to even exist to be joined in many workplaces, and that would cut out millions from unemployment in the meantime. However, Iceland has some worthwhile strategies over and above the Ghent system. A recent paper examined its world-record union density (which has actually increased somewhat over the last decade), and argued it was also thanks to closed-shop contracts, a check-off system (where employers automatically deduct union dues from paychecks), outreach to new and especially younger workers, a large unionized state sector, and extra pension and other benefits for members.[29] With some smart tactics, unions themselves can help considerably in keeping their numbers up.

It may be wisest to avoid the Ghent system for a few years, let the union movement return to its former strength, and then roll the system out over time. Or we simply may want to go without it so the unemployment system is as comprehensive as possible. Some trial and error will be necessary to see how high we can get the union membership rate.

At any rate, all this will be challenging at first, as unions will have to be constructed from nothing in many industries. But if the current federal roadblocks are removed, they are sure to spring up quickly, as they did in the 1930s after the passage of the National Labor Relations Act. If it comes time for contract negotiations and a sector simply has no unions whatsoever, then representatives from another sector can be appointed by federal regulators as a temporary stand-in.

Fourth, workers should have representation on corporate boards—also known as worker co-determination. Bernie Sanders has a proposal for 45 percent of board seats to be elected by the workers of the company, but frankly there is no reason they should not get at least half.[30] This would give workers a direct say in corporate governance, and thus a powerful direct lever to raise wages, ratchet down excessive executive pay, and prevent the corporate surplus being kicked out entirely to shareholders.

This will likely improve the productivity of business by

shunting some of the corporate surplus back into research and development, and by improving labor relations within the firm. The relationship between workers and management is always adversarial, but American labor relations have always been exceptionally hostile and routinely violent, with owners viewing any kind of union with furious outrage and workers often logically concluding that their best strategy is to grab the highest wage possible regardless of how the firm is doing. But if workers could in effect become co-managers of the firm, and know for a fact they are getting a reasonable share of the proceeds, they would be much more likely to keep innovation going and quality high so the business could succeed over time. Indeed, workers often know far better than executives (or high-priced management consultants) where the real bottlenecks and inefficiencies in the business processes are.

Fifth, we need a revolution in macroeconomic management. Instead of the Federal Reserve prioritizing stable prices at any cost, and hiking interest rates well before any real sign of inflation is seen, it should have the opposite priority. Instead of the balanced approach of the New Deal age, employment should be the overriding goal, with inflation taking a backseat. Indeed, it is usually fairer to control any inflation spikes with direct credit or price controls (as was done during World War II), rather than by throwing millions out of work and letting market forces do the job. Keeping the economy at full employment as much as possible will protect the labor share of national income and strengthen workers' bargaining position. (To my extreme surprise, Donald Trump's selection to chair the Federal Reserve, Jerome Powell, appears to be largely on board with this agenda.)

Sixth, Wall Street must be brought to heel. Stiff regulations to prevent extractive gambling, bar dangerous overborrowing, foil manipulation of other firms, and keep down bank sizes will do their part, as they did during the New Deal era.

So that's how to take care of workers. Now on to nonworkers. This means a welfare state, the main point of which is to provide income to all categories of nonworkers (which, as noted earlier, is about half the population). Within that, specific welfare programs should be set up for all categories of people who can't or shouldn't work: children, students, the sick or disabled, the unemployed, carers, and retired folks. I covered benefits for unemployment, sickness, disability, and retirement in chapter 6, but the basic point is to provide an income source to all people without labor income. Every benefit should at least provide a poverty-level income so that nobody can possibly fall below that mark.

Matt Bruenig has outlined a strategy for children in his Family Fun Pack proposal. Among other things, this would consist of the following: a "baby box" for new parents containing infant necessities and which can be used as a temporary crib; parental leave, free childcare, and free pre-K, so parents can take time off work when a child is born and then return before school starts (also covered in chapter 6); and, most important, a child allowance of $300 per month for each child. A quasi–child allowance of about this size was actually passed as part of President Biden's pandemic relief package in March 2021, but it has many administrative problems. Instead of simply cutting checks to families, it is structured as an advance payment of the preexisting child tax credit, handled by the IRS. The credit is means-tested based on yearly income (so rich people do not qualify), but it is literally impossible to know what people's income is because people will receive checks before the year is over. Worse, many people whose income is too low for them to be required to file taxes— that is, those who need the money the most—are unknown to the IRS, so the agency will surely miss many of them. Over-payments and underpayments are guaranteed to happen. It would be far better to simply have the Social Security Admin-istration cut checks to all families, and then soak up unneeded payments to the rich by raising their taxes. Remarkably, Sen-ator Mitt Romney (R-Utah) recently wrote a child allowance bill with exactly this structure. The Biden child allowance will expire in 2022, and it will be vital for leftists to get behind a Romney-style design in the effort to make it permanent.[31]

However, income for nonworkers isn't the whole story. We also need universal public benefits that include the whole population—above all, national healthcare through a scheme such as Medicare-for-all, or Britain's National Health Service, as covered in chapter 7. This allows anyone to go to the doctor if they get sick or become injured, without worry-ing about being bankrupted. Free public education, up to at least a traditional university degree, allows all to partake in the fruits of knowledge, and learn the skills they need to get a decent job.

That welfare state should be funded by steeply progressive taxation on both income and wealth, which both provides the resources necessary to operate the welfare programs and does its part to compress incomes. In most of the 1950s and 1960s, for instance, the top marginal tax rate was 91 percent, which kicked in at $200,000 (or about $2 million in today's dollars).[32] The point of such a tax is not to raise revenue but to keep down inequality by basically forbidding people from making more than that amount.

As noted previously, all this implies that the middle and

lower classes will have to pay significant taxes to fund these programs, because the rich will no longer be taking home so much money, and because we want to keep the economy at full employment and production. We will need some combination of income and consumption taxes to get the United States total tax level up in the 40 percent of GDP range or so.

As an aside, people from the modern monetary theory (MMT) school of thought often object to the idea that taxes are needed to "fund" spending. By this view, the government is the ultimate source of funding through its power to print money, and the only reason for taxes is to forestall inflation. This is true on its own terms, but when the economy is operating at full capacity and employment, inflation *will* be a binding constraint. Some MMT followers take the doctrine to say that taxation is not needed at all, but this is categorically false. As previously noted, we want full employment and production as often as possible, and therefore it will be necessary to tax in order to fund new programs—especially gigantic ones like the kind I am talking about. There can be no truly egalitarian economy without broad-based taxation.

Finally, there is wealth. As we've seen, wealth is distributed incredibly unequally—the top 10 percent richest Americans own about three-quarters of the national wealth. There is extreme inequality within that group as well: as noted previously, the top 1 percent own almost 40 percent of all the wealth, and the remainder of the top tenth roughly another 35 percent. The people in the 50–90 percent bracket own about another quarter combined, leaving the bottom half of society with virtually nothing.[33]

Once again Bruenig has a practical solution for this

problem: a social wealth fund.[34] This would levy a variety of taxes on the rich, and sweep in currently owned state assets (like the Tennessee Valley Authority and the vast holdings of federally owned land), to stock up an investment fund collectively owned by the entire nation. After a few years to allow the fund to accumulate a decent total, it would pay out a per-person dividend to each citizen above age seventeen. Varieties of these already exist in practice, and work quite well. Norway has plowed most of its oil revenues into several state funds, which together own assets worth an eye-popping 278 percent of its GDP. Together with its state-owned enterprises (worth another 23 percent of GDP), the Norwegian state owns fully 59 percent of all the wealth in the country. If we exclude owner-occupied housing, the figure rises to 75 percent.[35]

Now, Norway's wealth fund does not pay out universal dividends, likely because the state doesn't want that much purchasing power flooding into the country quickly, which would cause the krone to appreciate and destroy the country's domestic manufacturing base. However, there is a dividend-paying social wealth fund right here in America. The state of Alaska owns about $74 billion in assets, or 148 percent of the state's GDP in 2020, through its Alaska Permanent Fund.[36] It pays out an annual dividend typically between $1,000 and $2,000.[37] It is also, unsurprisingly, extremely popular—79 percent of Alaskans say it is an "important source of income for people in their community," and 64 percent would rather levy an income tax (which Alaska does not have) to plug state budget holes rather than cut the dividend.[38]

Both of these funds were seeded with oil money, but there is no reason that couldn't be done with ordinary tax money.

Indeed, Jay Hammond, who successfully pushed through the Alaskan fund as governor, had previously tried to do the same thing on a smaller scale in local government with taxes.

According to the Bureau of Economic Analysis, in 2019 rental income and payments to asset owners amounted to $3.8 trillion.[39] (This leaves out some business income, but let's be conservative and ignore it.) If we were to scoop up just half the national capital stock into an American social wealth fund, and pay it out on an equal basis to the 255 million people who are eighteen years old or older, that would result in an annual dividend payment on the order of $7,400.[40] That alone would nearly double the current income of someone in the bottom 10 percent of the income distribution.[41]

Some analysts on the left, including my friend Mike Konczal, have argued that a social wealth fund is a bad idea because it would make the United States into a nation of shareholders—a people worried not about improving their workplace but about trying to get more free money from asset returns.[42] This fear is surely overstated. A nation that owned its wealth collectively would be largely neutral between profits and wages, instead of the current system where a tiny powerful minority owning almost all the wealth pushes with all its might to jack up profits. The working class is not going to move heaven and earth to exploit itself—and the gigantic inequality created by concentrated ownership of wealth would be eradicated.

We also might consider building out a larger portfolio of state-owned enterprises. Now, it is hard to imagine the janky American state successfully managing new companies, but on the other hand, it currently owns the United States Postal Service, Amtrak, and the Tennessee Valley Authority and operates them relatively well (or at least it did before President Trump started tearing up the USPS). It's also not as though Comcast and Wells Fargo are doing all that great in terms of providing efficient, low-priced service. Ultimately there is no reason not to have a publicly owned option for, say, telecommunication and banking, just as the Norwegian state owns that country's largest bank and telecom firms, and the only way for the government to get good at managing such services is through practice.

It's impossible to say in advance how equal we might make the United States. The situation of the 1970s, when half the population got 20 percent of income, was superior to the current status quo but still clearly inadequate. While it is probably not possible to have a perfectly even distribution (where every person gets the same income, and thus half the population will get half the income) it would surely be possible to top the 1970s mark. Indeed, European countries have reached 25 percent for the bottom half without creating some kind of crisis.[43] At least 30 percent should be obtainable, if not better.

Americans simply must recognize and internalize that the economy is a collective creation, and there is no reason, moral or technical, that all the citizenry cannot share in the national prosperity. The United States has the worst poverty rate among peer nations not because of any fact of nature but because a tiny minority of propertarians have deliberately arranged our economic institutions to keep a huge chunk of the people in rags. With a few practical, proven reforms, America could become the most equal country in the world.

A NEW COLLECTIVE
AMERICAN FREEDOM

THE IDEA OF "FREEDOM" or "liberty" is the most important concept in the whole history of American politics. Every American child learns in elementary school that colonial
Americans fought a war to break away from British control
because of their tyrannical rule. "The history of the present
King of Great Britain is a history of repeated injuries and
usurpations," reads the Declaration of Independence, "all
having in direct object the establishment of an absolute Tyranny over these States."

It's common in modern times to note the *incredible* gall of the
American revolutionaries. Here was a country where nearly
a fifth of the population was enslaved, and where that slave
labor formed the economic foundation of about half the states,
violently complaining about paying some objectively modest
taxes. The founders were "a small group of unelected, white,
male, land-holding slave owners who also suggested their class
be the only one allowed to vote," George Carlin said in one
of his stand-up comedy routines.[1] "Now that is what's known
as being stunningly—and embarrassingly—full of shit." Europeans were not at all blind to this at the time either. As the

English literary critic Samuel Johnson observed, "How is it that we hear the loudest yelps for liberty among the drivers of Negroes?"[2]

The injustice of slavery was so appalling that even most of the slave-owning Founding Fathers were at least uneasy about the institution. "The whole commerce between master and slave is a perpetual exercise of the most boisterous passions, the most unremitting despotism on the one part, and degrading submissions on the other," wrote Thomas Jefferson in 1781.[3] "Indeed I tremble for my country when I reflect that God is just." George Washington was also more and more troubled by his slave ownership as he got older. His will stipulated that all his slaves should be freed after his death, though legal wrangling meant that many remained in bondage for years. Just one was given his liberty when Washington died—William Lee, who had been Washington's loyal personal servant for decades.[4]

Most of the founders thought that slavery would somehow die out over time, by becoming uneconomical or through increasing moral revulsion. Instead, the opposite happened. With the development of the cotton gin, and as the Industrial Revolution fueled a bottomless British demand for cotton, slavery became enormously profitable, and the doubts many elite slave owners expressed quickly vanished. Instead, as Ulysses S. Grant wrote in his memoirs, "When the institution became profitable, all talk of its abolition ceased where it existed; and naturally, as human nature is constituted, arguments were adduced in its support."[5]

The American South became a slave society—not a society with some slaves, which has been common throughout history, but a society organized *entirely* around slave labor. Slaves did most of the important work, slave-produced commodities were by far the largest national export, and by 1860 slaves were worth more than all the railroads and manufacturing businesses in the country combined.[6]

In 1906, German sociologist Werner Sombart wrote a book titled *Why Is There No Socialism in the United States?* From that day to this many historians and scholars have debated the question—not only why the United States did not permanently develop any kind of revolutionary socialist movement, but also why it did not even develop a labor party, which has been a political keystone in almost every European country for a century. Some have argued that it is the typical American individualist ethos, which made it harder to develop class consciousness because too many laborers expected to become business owners themselves. Others have argued it was the expanding frontier that dissolved class conflict by allowing disgruntled workers to escape to new communities out west.[7]

There is something to each of those explanations. But the main answer, I submit, is the legacy of slavery. On the one hand, this provided an enduring legacy of particularly vicious racism that made it more difficult to unite the American working class; on the other, it created a particularly ferocious brand of conservatism that has been unwilling to accept the kind of class compromises seen in Europe. Today America is falling to pieces because it is in the grip of a propertarian movement that got most of its political backing by exploiting the legacy of slavery. Therefore, to build an America based on collective economics, we must confront that legacy.

There have been three major attempts to create a truly democratic United States based on real freedom and collective economics, and each was eventually brought down by the legacy of slavery. After the Civil War abolished the institution, Radical Republicans such as Thaddeus Stevens argued for an economic and political reordering of the South, to be accomplished by giving freed slaves the vote and distributing former plantation land to them. But moderate Republicans, who were connected to business elites in the North, were leery of redistribution. Property was considered so sacrosanct that not even treason could interfere with it. Most of the slave-owning traitors were allowed to keep their land, and they quickly reconstituted themselves as the South's economic elite.[8]

The Reconstruction regime imposed on the South after the war therefore did not put multiracial democracy on a firm foundation. Under President Ulysses S. Grant, the political rights of the freedmen were indeed defended by federal force—including an aggressive police action by attorney general Amos T. Akerman that successfully destroyed the first Ku Klux Klan—but most southern Black Americans remained impoverished and hence politically vulnerable.[9]

Worse, as Reconstruction progressed, the Republican Party became steadily more attached to propertarianism than they were to defending the victory of the Union in the Civil War. In 1872, a breakaway faction of Liberal Republicans (in the classical sense) ran their own candidate for president on a platform of ending Reconstruction (that is, abandoning Black voters to the Ku Klux Klan) and embracing laissez-faire capitalism. Grant still won reelection, but when a financial crisis and recession struck in 1873, he stuck to economic orthodoxy, vetoing a monetary stimulus bill on propertarian grounds.[10]

If the United States had had even moderately well-functioning democratic institutions, then the logical response to the post-1873 recession would have been for Democrats, who were generally the party of working-class immigrants in the North, to seize the opportunity to swipe Black voters away from the GOP and take power. Leveraging economic crises was often how labor or social democratic parties displaced liberal ones in many European states. And indeed, voters in both the South and the North blamed Republicans for mass unemployment, and Democrats swept the 1874 midterms—the biggest partisan swing in Congress in the entire nineteenth century.[11]

But of course Democrats were much more dedicated to white supremacy than they were to anything else, and so Grant's propertarianism dealt a death blow to Reconstruction. Other Republicans became less and less willing to defend the rights of the freedmen, their most loyal voting bloc. The 1876 election was marred by fraud and violence, as former Confederates did all they could to stop Black people from voting. Republicans and Democrats eventually struck a bargain in which the GOP could keep the presidency but Reconstruction would be ended.

White supremacists thereafter gradually tore down Reconstruction and set up Jim Crow apartheid. Formal segregation was merely the most obvious element of what was a ruthless system of racial domination, enforced by terrorist violence. Hamden Rice, a Black man who grew up in the Jim Crow South, writes that the key feature of Jim Crow "was that *white people, mostly white men, occasionally went berserk, and grabbed random black people, usually men, and lynched them* . . . you may forget or not know that white people also randomly beat black people, and the black people could not fight back, for fear of even worse punishment. This constant low level dread of atavistic violence is what kept the system running. It made life miserable, stressful and terrifying for black people."[12] Many

Black southerners were effectively turned into serfs, trapped by debt, rigged employment contracts, and violent threats into working as sharecroppers on the same cotton plantations for meager wages.

The corrupt bargain of 1876 was eventually extended across the whole white culture. The Civil War was recast not as treason in defense of slavery but somehow as about "states' rights" and defending a noble southern culture against rapacious Yankees. Confederate generals were held up as shining tactical geniuses, while Union ones were smeared as incompetents or drunks who won solely through the weight of numbers. Both sides could agree that instead of an evil slave empire getting the defeat it so richly deserved, the war was more of a tragic national misunderstanding. White historians of the Dunning School libeled the Reconstruction state governments as corrupt failures and argued that the destruction of Black suffrage was good and necessary—a completely preposterous version of history that nevertheless still has powerful influence over high school history curricula to this day.[13]

All this allowed white southerners to convince themselves that they had not started a treasonous war so they could keep human beings as property. It also allowed white northerners to convince themselves they had not shamefully sold out their fellow citizens and thrown away much of the accomplishments of the Civil War bought with oceans of blood.

Propertarianism has never been an ideology that organically takes root among the masses. It took the glue of an ideology of white supremacy to keep a critical mass of the American white population on board with propertarianism as it became hegemonic across the country after 1876. So long as wealthy white racists were allowed to dominate the South, Democrats during the rest of the century did not interfere too much with propertarian domination. Indeed, a faction of "Bourbon Democrats," including President Grover Cleveland, adhered openly to propertarian norms such as the gold standard.

Still, the gruesome dysfunction of the national economy during the Gilded Age (as we saw in chapter 4) created pressures for some kind of economic reform in both parties. There were regular outbreaks of labor militancy during this period (and into the early twentieth century), often put down with psychotic violence by National Guard units or the army. Some labor union and socialist organizers attempted to create a cross-racial coalition of farmers and workers with the Populist movement—an incomplete effort that nevertheless culminated in the nomination of William Jennings Bryan for president in 1896.

Later historians such as Richard Hofstadter would smear the Populists as a group of racist, paranoid cranks. In truth, while they did have problems with prejudice, as Thomas Frank writes in his recent book *The People, No: A Brief History of Anti-Populism*, on balance they were far less racist than the ruling elite at the time, and their economics was also more accurate. In any case, the capitalist class moved heaven and earth to defeat Bryan, spending more as a fraction of the economy than in any election before or since to install William McKinley as president.[14]

Demands for some kind of reform to capitalism would continue to bubble up in both parties through the 1920s, including in the South. That leads us to the second attempt to build a true American democracy, the New Deal. As we saw in chapter 2, this was a complete restructuring of American society and about the closest the country has gotten to a European-style social democracy. Even though Franklin Roosevelt had to include white supremacist Dixiecrats in his political coalition, which meant that segregation was partly built into many of his programs, the New Deal was still a huge leap forward for Black Americans relative to their previous position. About 2 million Black people got jobs in the various New Deal agencies, and Roosevelt cautiously picked at Jim Crow with an order desegregating defense contractors.[15] Most of all, the red-hot war economy sharply narrowed the wage gap between Blacks and whites. Economists J. W. Mason and Andrew Bossie write: "The war period saw by far the greatest convergence of Black and white incomes since Reconstruction. The difference in average wages between Black and white men fell by a staggering 50 points during the 1940s, from white men earning 110 percent more than Black men to a (still substantial) 63 percent more. . . . This is a much faster convergence than in any subsequent decade."[16]

However, race prejudice was a vulnerable crack in the New Deal order, which a coalition of racists and propertarians used to tear it down. Roosevelt had to conduct a delicate balancing act, catering to Blacks in the North and racist whites in the South. So long as he did not openly threaten Jim Crow, the coalition held—indeed, in the 1930s some of the most fervent economic populists were southern Democrats. However, when the rest of the party began unifying against segregation in the 1960s, southern politics turned firmly against any kind of economic egalitarianism and toward the Republican Party.

As we saw in chapter 3, from the moment the New Deal came into being, conservatives began attempting to resurrect Herbert Hoover's propertarian tradition. For a time they were unsuccessful even within the Republican Party. Dwight Eisenhower became president in 1952, and he accepted the New Deal status quo—indeed, he even expanded it in a few places. But the movement against apartheid continued to build strength.

That leads us to the third attempt to build a true American democracy: the civil rights movement. Black Americans and some whites, led by people like Martin Luther King Jr., A. Philip Randolph, John Lewis, Roy Wilkins, Walter Reuther, and Dorothy Height, mounted a political assault on Jim Crow that was eventually successful. Through demonstrations, petitions, sit-ins, and horrifying media spectacles of police beating peaceful marchers, they created pressure that forced President Lyndon Johnson to exercise his legislative legerdemain to force through several sweeping civil rights laws in the mid-1960s.

It's important to emphasize that civil rights activists did not want to stop at mere political rights. They were not at all blind to the economic dimension of Black oppression, and pressed for economic reforms during and after the initial rounds of legislation. The famous 1963 event where King delivered his "I Have a Dream" speech was called the March on Washington for Jobs and Freedom. In 1968, King helped organize the Poor People's Campaign, attempting to unite lower-class people of all races behind a program for low-income housing, full employment, and a guaranteed minimum income. In a 1967 speech, he predicted the struggle would be harder than overthrowing Jim Crow:

> You see, the gains in the first period, or the first era of struggle, were obtained from the power structure at bargain rates; it didn't cost the nation anything to integrate lunch counters. It didn't cost the nation anything to integrate hotels and motels. It didn't cost the nation a penny to guarantee the right to vote. Now we are in

a period where it will cost the nation billions of dollars to get rid of poverty, to get rid of slums, to make quality integrated education a reality. This is where we are now. Now we're going to lose some friends in this period.[17]

King was right. After African Americans had gotten political rights, the movement for economic justice ran into stiff headwinds, and he was assassinated in 1968 while supporting a sanitation workers' strike in Memphis. When he died King was dramatically unpopular—75 percent of Americans disapproved of him, an increase of 25 percentage points from 1963 (also in part because he had spoken out against the Vietnam War).[18]

The rising faction of conservative propertarians seized the opportunity. The explicit strategy from the start was to try to topple the New Deal by welding together a coalition of northern business elites with white racists. This was a tricky task. As journalist Ryan Grim writes:

In order to forge the alliance between the racist Democrats in the South, then, and the business wing of the Republicans in the North, they had to fuse two, unlinked political movements—the drive for segregation and the rollback of the New Deal. That required the South to go along with attacking programs that were extremely popular with the people of the South, and for Northern Republicans to get behind segregation and the preservation of the white Southern way of life.[19]

Highbrow conservative propertarians such as William F. Buckley thus portrayed the fight against civil rights as merely a defense of limited government and states' rights, and heavily implied to the South that anti–New Deal propertarianism was a way to perpetuate white dominance. Business elites could thus convince themselves that they were not simply engaged in an alliance of convenience with gutter racists, and southern voters could be divested of their sympathies for the New Deal programs that, as historian Katherine Rye Jewell writes in *Dollars for Dixie: Business and the Transformation of Conservatism in the Twentieth Century*, had transformed the region from an impoverished backwater to pretty close to a developed-world standard.

Already in 1964 conservatives had gotten one of their own, Barry Goldwater, nominated for president on the Republican ticket. He opposed the Civil Rights Act of that year, supposedly because it would represent an abuse of federal regulatory power. White racists got the real message and swung hard to Goldwater, and as whites were still at that point largely the ones who could vote in the South, he carried southern states from Louisiana to South Carolina—though he was still crushed by Johnson almost everywhere else.

But this "southern strategy" eventually succeeded in building a propertarian majority. During his presidential campaign in 1980, Republican candidate Ronald Reagan spoke a great deal about limited government, but he also kicked off his campaign with a speech about "states' rights" at the fairgrounds near Philadelphia, Mississippi, the town where three civil rights activists had been murdered by white supremacists in 1964. Reagan won handily that year, and won reelection in 1984 by a much larger margin. Republicans eventually gained a hammerlock on all parts of the white South.

Meanwhile, as discussed in chapter 3, a liberal faction of propertarians was infiltrating the Democratic Party and rooting out the old New Deal thinking. Their argument was that in order to compete again, Democrats would have to cater to Reagan-style thinking. As a political matter, this was contestable at best (all the Democratic presidential candidates who lost between 1980 and 1988 were some variety of neoliberal), but the election of Bill Clinton in 1992 cemented their control over the party. Once again big business ruled—gaining power not through an open political argument but by rigging the system so that there were no nonpropertarian options.

But as we have seen, propertarian rule had all the same problems it has always had. America coasted for a while on the previous successes and momentum of the New Deal. It took many years for its key structures to be dismantled or allowed to rot, which allowed many to convince themselves that this time things were different. But by 2008, all the usual morbid symptoms of propertarian tyranny were present—extreme inequality, galloping corruption, sagging growth, and political dysfunction.

To sum up: Over the last 160 years we have seen all attempts to build a truly democratic America brought down because they failed to achieve both political and economic liberty for all citizens. Political liberty alone did not get the job done during Reconstruction or the civil rights movement, but conversely, economic liberty alone in the New Deal did not get the job done either. Only by combining the two can America actually accomplish any of the reforms I have detailed in the preceding chapters.

Such a program will require a new, or rather resurrected, conception of American identity. The United States is a relatively diverse country by European standards—only about 60 percent of us are non-Hispanic whites, and even among white Americans there is a riot of differing immigrant back-grounds.[20] But it is also the case that Americans have a great deal in common. In the main, we broadly share a common culture of movies, TV, music, and food, similar cultural hab-its and traditions, and, outside of the extreme right, a similar faith in democracy. (It's worth noting that a huge chunk of what we consider to be distinctively American culture comes from minority groups—indeed, in the case of music, prac-tically the whole American tradition, from jazz, blues, and rock and roll to funk, disco, and hip-hop, is rooted in Black culture.)

Perhaps most important, we cannot help but share a common history and destiny. In a 1965 debate with William F. Buckley, the writer James Baldwin observed, "We talk about integration in America as though it was some great new conundrum. The problem in America is that we've been integrated for a very long time."[21] If we are to make the United States a functioning country again, much less a decent place to live, there is simply no alternative to developing an idea of American identity that includes everyone in the country. Whites must come to see themselves and their fellow citizens of color as part of a whole.

Some writers (particularly in the Afro-pessimist tradi-tion) are not optimistic about this possibility. In 2014, for instance, Ta-Nehisi Coates wrote that white supremacy is not simply a "means of cleaving poor whites away from blacks. My view on this is that white supremacy is an inter-est in and of itself. It's not clear to me where the politics ends and the bribe begins. I generally think that the left tells itself this story in order to evade the political com-plications of dealing with white supremacy as a sensible, if deeply immoral, choice, as opposed to a con played on gullible white people."[22]

Now, I have an understandable bias against this idea. I am a white American, and frankly I do not want to believe that racism is in any way "sensible" for people like me. However, there is an avalanche of evidence to the contrary as well. There may be a cheap psychological high for whites in believing that Black people are inferior, but the downsides—both moral and physical—are so grotesque that it cannot possibly be worth it. Racism is not exactly a con as such, but an addictive political poison that is literally killing white people by the thousands across the country.

Let me discuss health first. As noted in chapter 7, American life expectancy has declined for five straight years. Research by Anne Case and Angus Deaton published in 2015 found a skyrocketing rate of deaths caused by suicide, alcohol abuse, and drug overdoses, which is now the main reason overall life expectancy is declining (aside from the pandemic, of course).[23] Further work from them found the decline in life expectancy is largely due to these "deaths of despair" happening among people without a college degree, especially middle-aged whites.[24]

There are three obvious proximate factors one can point to here. First is economic inequality. The worst outcomes are seen in deindustrialized communities in the Rust Belt and Appalachia, where factory or coal mining jobs have largely vanished. More broadly, good-paying jobs of any kind have long been scarce across the country for people without a college degree (and increasingly even for people with one). Second is our lousy healthcare system, which charges an arm and a leg for often poor-quality care, and leaves the poorest people out entirely. Third is the opioid

epidemic: Tens of thousands of Americans have died because ruthless drug companies lied about how addictive
their products were, bribed doctors to prescribe as many
pills as possible, and lobbied against states' efforts to protect their citizenry.[25] They found a ready base of customers in impoverished regions that had been abandoned by
the national government. These dope peddlers shipped
9 million pills in just two years to the town of Kermit, West
Virginia—population 382.[26]

Each of these three factors can be directly traced to propertarianism. As we saw in chapter 4, slanted free trade deals
and a dysfunctional trade system obliterated huge chunks of
the American industrial base. Dismantling antitrust policy,
deregulating Wall Street, and slashing taxes on the rich fun-
neled money to the top of the income ladder. Trying to run
as much medical policy through market mechanisms as possible has created a horribly dysfunctional healthcare system,
and propertarian thinking has so infected medical providers
that many have become de facto extortion rackets. That same
profiteering mentality is seen in nakedly predatory drug companies stuffing West Virginia to the gills with addictive pills
with all the speed and efficiency of an advanced assembly line.

It's important to note that deaths of despair are not at
all uncommon among other racial groups, especially Blacks
and Native Americans.[27] Insofar as the gap in life expectancy
between whites and Blacks has apparently closed somewhat
over the last few years, it is mainly because downscale whites
are gradually being shoved into the same pit that the worst-
off minorities have been in for decades.

King witnessed the poisoned chalice of race prejudice personally. In his final sermon before he was murdered, he told
the story of discussing segregation with the white wardens

when he had been jailed in Birmingham. After a time, the conversation turned to the subject of their wages:

> And when those brothers told me what they were earning, I said, "Now, you know what? You ought to be marching with us. You're just as poor as Negroes." And I said, "You are put in the position of supporting your oppressor, because through prejudice and blindness, you fail to see that the same forces that oppress Negroes in American society oppress poor white people. And all you are living on is the satisfaction of your skin being white, and the drum major instinct of thinking that you are somebody big because you are white. And you're so poor you can't send your children to school. You ought to be out here marching with every one of us every time we have a march."[28]

Ulysses S. Grant had a similarly jaundiced view of how slave owners treated the white underclass in the Confederacy. In his memoirs, he wrote:

> The great bulk of the legal voters of the South were men who owned no slaves; their homes were generally in the hills and poor country; their facilities for educating their children, even up to the point of reading and writing, were very limited; their interest in the contest was very meagre—what there was, if they had been capable of seeing it, was with the North; they too needed emancipation. Under the old regime they were looked down upon by those who controlled all the affairs in the interest of slave-owners, as poor white trash

who were allowed the ballot so long as they cast it according to direction.[29]

Incidentally, something like 290,000 southerners died in the Civil War, or about 23 percent of the southern male population aged between twenty and twenty-four in 1860.[30] At any rate, insofar as lower-class whites were actually party to the conspiracy to destroy the New Deal (a contestable argument, since lower-class voter turnout fell sharply during this period), the social carnage thus reaped speaks for itself.[31] However, it is not just material deprivation at work here. The moral legacy of racism also harms white people by implicating them in atrocities, and by cutting off their contact with their fellow citizens.

Indeed, in his debate with Buckley, Baldwin made the provocative argument that what happened to white people under Jim Crow was in some ways even *worse* than what happened to Blacks. White southerners have "been raised to believe," he said, "that no matter how terrible their lives may be . . . and no matter how far they fall, no matter what disaster overtakes them, they have one enormous knowledge in consolation, which is like a heavenly revelation: at least they are not Black." He continued:

Now, I suggest that of all the terrible things that can happen to a human being, that is one of the worst. I suggest that what has happened to white Southerners is in some ways, after all, much worse than what has happened to Negroes there. Because Sheriff Clark in Selma, Alabama, cannot be considered—you know, no one can be dismissed as a total monster. I'm sure he loves his wife, his children. I'm sure, you know, he likes to get drunk. You know, after all, one's got to assume he is visibly a man like me. But he doesn't know what drives him to use the club, to menace with the gun and to use the cattle prod. Something awful must have happened to a human being to be able to put a cattle prod against a woman's breasts, for example. What happens to the woman is ghastly. What happens to the man who does it is in some ways much, much worse.

The "moral lives" of "Alabama sheriffs and poor Alabama ladies—white ladies . . . have been destroyed by the plague called color," he concluded.[32]

One could draw an analogy to a family here. Many readers no doubt know of people who have cut off contact with family members because of prejudice, such as parents who have exiled a child because they turned out to be gay or transgender. The harm in that case goes in both directions—landing hardest on the victim, of course, but also on the bigots who cut themselves off from some of their closest natural human connections for no reason other than prejudice. Many end up racked with guilt for the rest of their lives. Similarly, white Americans who convince themselves that other people are inferior because of the color of their skin (or some such nonsense) cut themselves off from their fellow citizens and curdle their hearts with hate.

Remarkably, it appears that an increasing proportion of the white American citizenry agrees with my argument.

The strength of antiracism has grown steadily among the broader white population since the civil rights movement. In 1969, for instance, just 17 percent of white Americans approved of interracial marriage—but in 2013 it was 84 percent.[33] That tendency has only accelerated in the "Great Awokening" among white liberals since the 2016 election. During the 2020 protests against police brutality after the death of George Floyd, opinion moved even more dramatically. According to a *New York Times* poll, approval of Black Lives Matter increased by 28 points in just two weeks between May and June that year—including a 15-point increase among whites (though it later dipped somewhat).[34] Antiracism has become so strong that even the CEO of Fox News, where the hosts regularly spew barely veiled white supremacy, insists, "We support our Black colleagues and the Black community, as we all unite to seek equality and understanding."[35]

That is a very encouraging development. But so far the economic dimension of democracy has gotten less attention. Propertarian forms of antiracism have gotten wide circulation—during the initial surge of protests after Floyd's death, the book *White Fragility*, by the white diversity consultant Robin DiAngelo, spent weeks atop the *New York Times* bestseller list. This book recommends an individualist, self-help approach to racism, wherein white people are basically supposed to spend all their time doing self-criticism about their own racist thoughts, and constantly ask their friends and colleagues of color whether they are being oppressive.

Again, it's good that white Americans are looking to reduce their culpability in racist oppression, and it's probably healthy for white people to learn to be considerate in their interactions with people of color. But this kind of thinking is not going to create a true American democracy. The practical effect of DiAngelo's advice would be to diversify the upper rungs of the economic elite, while leaving the vast majority of the minority underclass in the same position as before. Fighting racism will require a gigantic overhaul of the economic system in addition to changing individual attitudes.

Take income and wealth. As of 2019, median white household income per household was $72,204, but median Black household income was $45,438; meanwhile, average white wealth per household was $983,400, while average Black wealth was just $142,500.[36] Median white wealth was $162,800, while median Black wealth was a piddling $16,600. Black unemployment is also reliably twice or more that of whites; the rate of uninsurance among the Black nonelderly is nearly 40 percent higher than that of whites; and the Black poverty rate is nearly two and half times greater.[37]

All this economic deprivation intersects heavily with the police brutality and mass incarceration that have gotten so much attention in recent years. Consider incarceration: A study by Bruce Western and Becky Pettit examined a cohort of men born between 1974 and 1979, divided them up by race and educational attainment, and studied how many ended up in jail at some point.[38] Educational attainment is a decent proxy for class, especially in that poverty rates are dramatically higher among high school dropouts. They found that mass incarceration was very heavily concentrated among the poorest African Americans—Black men among this group without a high school degree had an incomprehensible *68 percent* lifetime risk of imprisonment as of 2009.

Cumulative risk of imprisonment by age 30–34 for men born 1975–79, by race and education

Source: Western and Pettit 2010

Lower-class whites were not at all immune from being imprisoned. The incarceration risk for whites without a high school degree in this group was 28 percent—much less than their Black peers, but *twenty-three times* the risk of whites with some college, and more than four times the risk of Blacks with some college.

A similar pattern can be seen in police violence. In a paper for the People's Policy Project, Justin Feldman compiled over 6,400 fatal police shootings and matched them to the poverty rate of the census tract in which they occurred.[39] He found that the rate of shootings was drastically higher in poorer census tracts than in richer ones, for both Blacks and whites (though the discrepancy was mysteriously much less for Latinos).

Moreover, a much greater proportion of Blacks live in the poorest census tracts—36.6 percent as against 9.6 percent of whites. The raw number of shootings also surely understates the class bias in shootings, as presumably there are many more poor people being shot in rich locations than rich people being shot in poor ones.

Once again we see how lower-class whites have lost out horribly under propertarian rule. Using *Washington Post* data, I roughly estimated the rate of police killing by race in 2019.[40] Blacks of course have it worst, at 57 police killings per 10 million people. But the white figure of 20.5 killings is still more than twice as high as the overall figure in Canada, more than ten times that of New Zealand, more than fifteen times that of Germany, and more than *one hundred times* that of Japan.

These data on imprisonment and policing demonstrate the raw side of propertarian tyranny. Some aspects of political domination under a propertarian system are subtle, coming in the form of lower incomes, skinflint social benefits, unemployment, and so on. But as we've seen, propertarian rule also creates vast oceans of social dysfunction and despair. Poverty, in particular, is associated not only with lower life expectancy but also with vastly greater rates of both committing and being victimized by crime. The response to this over recent decades has been to turn police and courts into a force for political repression. American police have become notoriously terrible at solving violent crime—the murder clearance rate (that is, the fraction of murder cases that end in an arrest) has fallen from 91 percent in 1965 to 62 percent in 2018.[41] In cities such as Baltimore it is even worse, at just 32 percent.[42] In the Nordic countries, by contrast, the clearance rate ranges from 83 percent in Sweden to 100 percent in Iceland.[43]

That is because the criminal punishment system today is not designed to solve the problem of crime; rather, it has been designed to warehouse the social dysfunction caused by propertarian rule, and to keep a boot on the neck of the disproportionately Black and brown lower class. It is not that dissimilar from a full-blown dictatorship's secret police.

In previous chapters we have discussed many ways to

redress the inequalities in American society. Building out a proper welfare state, mass unionization, reforming the trade system, clapping Wall Street in regulatory irons, and so on must be part of any effort to extend democracy to the American economy and ease the trauma of propertarian rule. Reforming policing and courts up to, at a minimum, operating as the Nordic ones do would not quite be "defunding the police," as demanded by many activists, but it would amount to replacing them with a categorically different institution. (As an aside, it's important to realize that while police budgets are certainly too high and at least some of that money could be repurposed with no ill effect, police budgets are not remotely large enough to build the kind of institutions mentioned above—that requires a great deal of taxation.)

But the question of wealth deserves special attention. Writers such as Coates have rightly advocated for some form of reparations for slavery, Jim Crow, and the litany of other racist abuses that simultaneously enriched whites and kept Blacks impoverished. Thanks to all that plundering, there is a difference of $15.2 trillion between what Blacks actually possess and what they would have if they had an equal share of the national wealth.[44]

However, this raises some thorny problems. Wealth is not just unequally distributed among races; as we've seen, it is also distributed unequally between classes. The richest 10 percent of both Blacks and whites hold about 75 percent of all the wealth in their respective groups—and the bottom half of both groups have basically none of it. To close the wealth gap, we would have to take $7.6 trillion from the white wealth pile and add it to the Black pile so that both figures meet in the middle. But neither giving out this money on an equal basis nor making the Black wealth distribution the same as the white one is satisfactory. Equal shares of that $7.6 trillion would be $617,000 per Black person, but doing that would open up another racial wealth gap along most of the wealth distribution in favor of Black folks that is *even larger* than the current one favoring whites—and still leave the ultra-rich largely white. And if we distributed it so as to make the Black wealth distribution exactly mirror the white one, we would be giving almost all the money to a small minority of people who are already rich, while half of Black folks would get nothing.

The way through this problem, I suggest, is the social wealth fund approach detailed in chapter 9. By scooping up most of the national wealth into one big pot and distributing the resulting capital income on a per capita basis, there would be almost no wealth inequality either between classes or between races, since it would effectively all be owned collectively. We might consider this a form of reparations for how racial capitalism has harmed the entire working class of all races—poorer whites would benefit too, of course, but to a much lesser extent than poorer Blacks, which is only right and proper. (This would also have the handy property of catering to a much, much larger political coalition.)

That brings me back to freedom. This idea is extraordinarily powerful, and all successful American political movements have oriented themselves around it. This makes sense—after all, it's an attractive notion, and most people would like to be free to do what they like in general. Propertarians have hypnotized Americans with a vision of freedom that amounts to unlimited license for a few—the ability of the ultra-rich to lord over the rest of the population, increasingly including de facto immunity from criminal prosecution.

But any kind of true freedom must be collective. As we saw in chapter 2, it is a priori impossible to have a country free of government coercion, because all economic systems are based on state rules of some kind imposed by force. A society is free, therefore, when the coercive economic rules are arranged through democratic deliberation, in a process that protects civil liberties. True freedom cannot be achieved unless democracy applies throughout society—from the polling station to the workplace.

A particularly stark example of the distinction between propertarian license and collective liberty could be seen during the coronavirus pandemic. Many conservatives angrily insisted that the requirement to wear a mask in public was tyranny, and many groups burned masks in protest. One might as well argue that making murder illegal is an infringement of liberty, because the actual effect of ignoring pandemic control rules was many documented cases of death.[45]

But countries such as Vietnam, New Zealand, Australia, and Taiwan showed a different path.[46] They proved that with some combination of lockdown, travel restrictions, setting up a system to test for the virus, tracing the contacts of positive cases, and isolating them in quarantine, they could completely eradicate the virus. If the whole citizenry stuck together, buckled down, and followed the rules, then after a few weeks something like normal life could and did return. Ironically, communist Vietnam's ultra-aggressive state response meant the government ended up meddling far *less* in citizens' lives than most Western democracies have, at least in terms of pandemic controls. In this as in many other contexts, bold state action is necessary for citizens to be able to live free, normal lives.

At any rate, we have seen that with a total economic reconstruction America could be one of the most pleasant places to live on earth. All workers could have a decent, safe workplace, where they are paid a fair wage and get plenty of time off, and all nonworkers would get income from the state so that they could participate in society. The national wealth would not be controlled by a tiny ultra-rich elite but by everyone through our democratic institutions. All we must do is recognize our helpless interdependence and our commonality with all our fellow citizens.

HOW TO ARGUE WITH
PROPERTARIANS

IN THE SUMMER OF 2011, President Obama was thinking about compromise. The economy had barely started to
grow again in mid-2009, but for the past year the propertarian establishment had been demanding austerity, supposedly
with the goal of cutting the budget deficit. Among them was
Obama himself—in February 2010 he had convened a bipartisan commission to come up with a plan to cut the deficit, chaired by Democratic insider Erskine Bowles and Alan
Simpson, a former Republican senator from Wyoming.[1] (The
commission could not agree on what exactly to do, and failed
to produce a consensus report.)

In August 2010, the *Washington Post* editorial board had
warned that Social Security was no longer taking in enough
revenue to cover its outlays, and in 2037 it would exhaust its
trust fund.[2] They called people downplaying this issue "deniers" and argued for some "combination of revenue increases
and benefit adjustments." In September, William Galston
and Maya MacGuineas published a report for the Brookings Institution arguing for more sweeping austerity.[3] They
predicted that excessive borrowing would "crowd out" private

investment, thereby slowing growth, and interest rates would soon rise, putting a heavy burden on the federal budget. Besides, with healthcare costs growing so quickly, there would be no choice but to cut Medicare at some point.

The federal debt ceiling would be reached at the end of July 2011, and Republicans—who had taken control of the House of Representatives in the 2010 midterm elections—decided to demand austerity in exchange for raising it. This had never happened before in American history, but Obama decided to go along with it. He sought a "Grand Bargain" with Republicans in which he would agree to sweeping cuts to Social Security and Medicare if they would agree to some tax increases.

Supposedly nonpartisan reporters openly slanted their coverage in favor of austerity. In March, Lori Montgomery of *The Washington Post*, citing a Congressional Budget Office estimate showing more borrowing over the next decade, said that the borrowing would have a "negative impact on the nation's budget outlook."[4] In July, she celebrated the news that Obama had decided to agree to slash Social Security and Medicare, writing that this would "defuse the biggest budgetary time bombs that are set to explode as the cost of health care rises and the nation's population ages."[5] That same month, CBS News published an article titled "18 Scary US Debt Facts" (which amounted to the observation that a trillion is a very large number).[6] "The national debt is big and problematic," asserted Rick Newman at *US News & World Report*.[7]

Luckily for the American people, the attempted Grand Bargain quickly unraveled. Obama proposed broad cuts to Medicare, Medicaid, Social Security, government pensions, and various agencies in return for much smaller tax increases.[8] Initially, Speaker of the House John Boehner accepted this rough formula, but he quickly faced an internal rebellion from the extreme right in his own caucus, who rejected any kind of tax increase out of hand, and the deal fell apart.[9] Two years later, Montgomery was still mourning the failure to cut social benefits. The two parties "have done nothing to improve the finances of Social Security and Medicare, programs that already account for more than a third of federal spending and are forecast to push the debt skyward again at the end of the decade as the baby-boom generation retires," she wrote in June 2013.[10]

It's worth taking a step back to emphasize the utter insanity of this fiasco. In the first place, even allowing a negotiation over the debt ceiling was catastrophically irresponsible. Remember, this has nothing to do with spending or borrowing as such; it is simply a legal stipulation that the government can borrow only a specific dollar amount. Indeed, almost no other country even has a debt ceiling, because it is logically assumed that when the legislature passes a budget authorizing some mix of spending and taxation, it has thereby agreed to borrow the balance.

Congress had *already passed* budget measures that required borrowing; Republicans were just taking a legal anachronism dating from World War I and using it to hold the government hostage in order to extract unrelated policy concessions. Obama's countenancing of such behavior set an appalling precedent.

But more important, the policy objective of the Grand Bargain was utter poison. In July 2011 the unemployment rate was 9 percent, and per capita GDP was about 3 percent below its peak in the last quarter of 2007—or perhaps 10 percent below where it would have been if the previous growth trend had continued.[11] What the economy *very obviously* needed was an additional big stimulus to get back to strength. Instead, we had almost the entire political establishment, including the Democratic president and the Republican congressional leadership, agreeing to make things worse in both directions. Obama would have traded huge cuts to some of America's most popular programs, which would slow the economy, in return for tax increases, which would slow it even more. Furthermore, as noted in chapter 2, the world needs a supply of dollar assets to lubricate international trade flows, and if the government refuses to provide them in the form of debt, then they will be obtained by market forces boosting the value of the dollar and boosting up the trade deficit relative to where it otherwise would have been. The United States did indeed gulp down a ton of austerity over the following years, cutting the budget deficit considerably, and, predictably, the trade deficit stayed very high.[12]

All told, this gruesome incident was a world-historical episode of moronic policy incompetence. It's as if your house were on fire, and the mayor and the fire department were arguing furiously about which grade of gasoline should be sprayed on the blaze.

But it was also a striking example of propertarian ideological hegemony, and one we might learn from. At the time, counterarguments from the left were barely heard against the foghorn blast of propaganda that saturated mainstream media and politics. Arguing against such a well-funded school of thought is a very steep uphill battle, but it can and must be done. So in this chapter I'll suggest a number of strategies to counter propertarian claims. Simple argument or rhetoric can't defeat a hegemonic ideology on its own, but it has its place in politics.

One place to start, of course, is with evidence. A central

claim from propertarian deficit scolds is that borrowing must of necessity place a burden on the economy, and that a great deal of borrowing will draw capital away from the rest of the economy, thus crowding out private investment and slowing the rate of growth. This is in keeping with the propertarian vision of the government as basically a parasite feeding on the back of the self-regulating market—indeed, the assumption runs so deep that even when the Obama administration released a paper predicting the results of their Recovery Act stimulus package, their model implied that by 2016 the effects of all the borrowing would be a drag on economic growth relative to where it would be without any stimulus.[13]

But as we saw in chapter 5, the exact opposite of propertarian predictions happened. Interest rates did not rise—on the contrary, the Fed kept its target rate at nearly zero from late 2008 all the way through late 2015.[14] Despite all the massive borrowing, government interest payments as a share of GDP barely budged after the recession, rising from 1.3 percent in 2009 to 1.5 percent in 2011, then falling again to 1.2 percent in 2015 (that share rose somewhat after 2016 thanks to the Trump tax cuts).[15] That 2015 figure was a little more than a third of what the government had been paying in 1991, which itself was not all that high. Indeed, routinely during the Obama presidency demand for government debt was so strong that Treasury bonds sold at interest rates lower than the expected rate of inflation, and occasionally at actual negative rates— literally less than nothing.[16] It's as if you went to the bank and they offered you a $10,000 loan that you could pay back with $9,500 in a few years. You'd be a fool not to take the money, but that's precisely what happened.

The reason, as we've seen, was that thanks largely to the propertarians, the Great Recession was never fully fixed, and the United States remained mired in economic depression. So long as there is excess economic capacity, in the form of idle workers, factories, and so on, the government can borrow without limit. The ultimate result was that following the pro-austerity advice from Galston and MacGuineas created exactly the growth catastrophe they were supposedly trying to avoid.

The hysterical fearmongering from Montgomery about future deficits is similarly blinkered. Now, the projection she worried about so much comes from an assumption of ever-greater increases in healthcare spending, and as I detailed in chapter 7, medical spending is already a severe problem. If it continues on its current track, healthcare cost bloat really will devour the economy. However, it follows that the generosity of Medicare and Medicaid has nothing whatsoever to do with the issue—the problem is *prices*. Cutting benefits for the poor and the elderly will merely shift the costs onto individuals. Montgomery assumes that cutting benefits will help reduce medical spending because propertarian thinking always tries to divorce the state from the economy, but in truth the two are inherently intertwined, and the only way to tackle healthcare prices is through *even more* state action. In any case, any government-side savings from cuts would quickly be eaten up by future price increases anyway.

Incidentally, this is why the propertarian attack on Bernie Sanders's Medicare-for-all plan was so preposterous. American healthcare is already the most expensive in the world by a gigantic margin. Fully $1 trillion per year is flushed down the toilet of administrative inefficiency and profiteering from medical providers and drug companies. As I showed in chapter 7, it would be conceptually trivial to redirect that spending such that all Americans had high-quality health-care, and save a considerable sum to boot.

There is a similar story for Social Security. Here there is also a genuine problem, but it is not nearly so immediate, and again it has nothing to do with the deficit. Propertarians fundamentally misunderstand this issue because they think the problem is about money, when the real problem is demographics.

The *Washington Post* editorial mentioned earlier raised a great deal of fuss about the Social Security trust fund being depleted, but this is totally irrelevant. The reason the program's trust fund is starting to be depleted is that there is an increasing proportion of retirees relative to the population paying payroll taxes compared to previous decades. When someone is retired, they of necessity receive goods and services without working. Therefore, the capacity of a country to support a retired population depends entirely on the size of the working population and how much economic output they are producing. Contrary to the common belief that millennials will not get Social Security because "the money will all be gone," the viability of the program will rest solely on the size and characteristics of the generations coming up behind us.

All retirement scenarios are like this, even private investment accounts. People tend to think that when they have piled up enough financial assets to live on for the rest of their lives, that means they have provided for their own retirement exclusively through their own work, but to be able to retire on your own hoard of money, you still need a population of working people to produce goods and services that you can buy with your assets. Without those workers, your investments are worthless. Indeed, this is also true of how Social Security is currently being funded in part by drawing down its trust fund. This trust fund is stocked with special U.S. Treasury bonds, and in order to fund benefit payments, they are currently being gradually sold off to other investors, the value of whose money must be based on current production.

Social Security itself perpetuates the money myth by structuring its benefits based on past earnings, as if it were a savings account where people get back what they paid in. That is not true either in terms of the benefit formula (many people get back more than what they contributed) or in terms of accounting, as most of the payroll tax revenue taken in by the program is paid right back out again to beneficiaries.[17] At bottom it is a welfare program, not some kind of investment fund.

So in terms of funding Social Security under its current structure, the problem could be fixed easily by bumping the tax rate up a small amount—either by removing the payroll tax cap or by some other method. Indeed, as I outlined in chapter 6, the actual biggest problem with Social Security retirement pensions is they are not generous *enough*. They should be boosted to compensate for the failure of the 401(k) system and the gradual disappearance of private pensions. This would require a slightly higher rate of tax on the working population, but since productivity has been chugging along, there is more than enough production to go around.

A third propertarian error is the treatment of climate change. Senator Marco Rubio, Republican of Florida, whose state is probably the most vulnerable of any in America to unchecked climate change, has grudgingly come around to thinking we may need to do some adaptation—but that's it. "I'm also not going to destroy our economy. There's a reality here. There's a balance on that end of it that we need to be focused on," he said on CNN in 2018.[18]

This attitude is a truly striking false dichotomy. Consider just one aspect of climate change, sea level rise. Miami, the second-largest city in Florida, has an average elevation of just six feet, and much of it is mere inches above sea level.[19] A recent study found that the rate of sea level rise has accelerated over the past twenty-five years, and if it continues at that pace, oceans would be twenty-six inches higher by 2100.[20] The study's lead author, Steve Nerem, further emphasized that this was "almost certainly a conservative estimate," because melting of the Greenland and Antarctic ice sheets is likely to accelerate as time passes. A sea level rise of more than two feet would drown big chunks of Miami, and should some of the worst-case scenarios come to pass, the city would be miles out to sea. What's more, it would be nearly impossible to construct a seawall around the city, because it is built on porous limestone.

Again, we see the classic propertarian brain at work. Government action to fight climate change is seen as something that must slow the economy by definition, rather than what it really is—absolutely necessary to head off economic (and social) calamity. In effect, Rubio would obliterate half his state for a few more years of private fossil fuel profits. However, as covered in chapter 8, it's not just conservatives who fail to grapple with climate change. Liberal propertarians such as William Nordhaus may favor a modest carbon tax to fight climate change, but their orthodox models mean they drastically underrate the possibility of gigantic economic harms from extreme climate events.

So when it comes to climate change, what we can't afford is to keep spewing out greenhouse gas emissions. It is propertarians who should have to come up with the price of deleting half of American agriculture, or building seawalls around our coastal cities, or being forced to engineer new water supplies for cities in the Southwest.

However, evidence can only get us so far. As we saw in chapter 3, propertarians' key rhetorical tactic is not argument but constraining the terms of debate. By the 2010s, practically the whole Washington establishment bought into an ideological framework that automatically produced propertarian conclusions. The result is a general depoliticizing of policy questions—if the budget deficit is bad by definition, then the only argument is about the best way to cut it, not whether it should be cut in the first place. Reporters such as Montgomery had been so thoroughly indoctrinated that they could not even see that they were expressing a contestable opinion, let alone the fact that the opinion was horrendously mistaken.

A related propertarian strategy is trying to naturalize economic outcomes. They tend to portray things such as unemployment or poverty as inevitable developments that can only be addressed (if at all) by massaging the self-regulating market. Again the function is to forestall policy options that might challenge the power of the rich. If Rust Belt towns suffer deindustrialization thanks to a biased global trade system that enables offshoring, it is very convenient for the business owners involved to be able to shrug and say, "It couldn't have been any other way."

So in addition to pointing out the fact that this is not true— the trade system is founded on laws and regulations that could be changed at any time—one should always attack this naturalizing tendency and repoliticize policy questions. There is no such thing as a natural economic system, and if someone is suffering, they can be helped.

The sad truth is that no kind of argumentative strategy can probably get very far with individuals. It is very, very difficult to lever someone out of a frame of mind they have accepted and internalized. This is a disruptive and painful process, and most people will instinctively resist, often angrily. People whose incomes depend on the propertarian status quo, meanwhile—such as the people who work at think tanks funded by fossil fuel barons—will either just lie or talk themselves into believing the arguments are wrong.

However, it is still worth doing. Simply attacking someone's presumptions can put them on the back foot and make them more cautious—especially in the case of "neutral" reporters, who often have no idea why they are writing what they do. What's more, onlookers can be convinced of the truth and justice of collective economics.

So as part of all these arguments, one should attack the propertarian ideological framework at the root, and advance an alternative ideology. In this way we can start building a counterhegemony.

Taxes are a good place to start. Americans have long accepted the idea that, in the words of economist Yanis Varoufakis, "wealth is privately produced and then appropriated by a quasi-illegitimate state, through taxation."[21] By this view, taxes are a simple taking of one's hard-earned wages, for which one receives little benefit; instead the poor (usually coded as Black) are thought to receive the benefits. Republicans are constantly trying to strengthen this anti-tax attitude by making the process of tax filing as onerous as possible.

However, no modern country can possibly exist without *some* kind of welfare state. As the scholar Suzanne Mettler documents in her book *The Submerged State*, the United States has accommodated propertarian ideology by hiding a large proportion of its middle- and upper-class benefits in the tax code. The Treasury Department describes *172* such tax benefits.[22] The Joint Committee on Taxation estimated for the 2021 fiscal year that the top five largest tax credits were the exclusion on employer-sponsored health insurance (at $190 billion), the low rate on capital gains and dividends ($168 billion), tax benefits for defined-benefit retirement pensions ($158 billion), various child tax benefits ($119 billion), and tax benefits for defined-contribution retirement plans such as 401(k) accounts ($109 billion).[23]

Now, these cost figures are likely not quite accurate in terms of what would happen if these benefits were repealed, especially taken together, because people would probably change their behavior to compensate somewhat (though the Center on Budget and Policy Priorities roughly estimated that they reduced federal revenue by $1.5 trillion in 2018—a figure that is more than one and a half times bigger than the cost of Social Security, and more than twice the defense budget).[24]

Nevertheless, a tax benefit is still a government subsidy. Consider an analogy: a condo complex where all the owners have to pay a fee to cover maintenance and so forth. One of the residents loses his main source of income and is scraping by on unemployment. The management wants to help him out, and so they decide to cancel his fee of $500 that year. That has precisely the same effect as handing him a check for $500—he has that much more money in his pocket, and the rest of the residents will have to cover the increment of whatever maintenance expenses come up that year. At bottom, tax subsidies are basically like this—a way to increase someone's disposable income through state action by reducing their tax liability rather than cutting them a check. It's just another way the government can divert income streams around the economy.

One might object that if tax breaks are just another kind of subsidy, what's the big deal? The problem is twofold. First, they are generally unfair. Most of the tax subsidy total consists of deductions (a reduction in your taxable income) or exemptions (when you do not have to pay tax on some income). These are more valuable the more income you have, because you have a greater tax liability to reduce. Certain tax breaks help the rich almost exclusively—more than half of the benefits of the low rate on capital gains and dividends, for instance, flow to the top 0.1 percent.[25]

These kinds of tax benefits are therefore very inefficient, because they pay out inversely to need. If we look at direct state social spending (that is, check-cutting programs like Social Security, not including tax breaks), the United States comes in far below most rich nations, at just 19 percent of GDP in 2018, as compared to France at 31 percent.[26] However, if we include all types of social spending, both public and the private kind enabled by tax benefits, the U.S. figure rises to 30 percent of GDP—the second-highest in the OECD, again just behind France.[27] America actually has a very expensive welfare state; it's just designed horribly.

More important in terms of ideology is that tax subsidies reinforce propertarianism by allowing people to pretend as though they do not benefit from government. In a 2010 paper, Mettler cited polling on the proportion of people on various government programs who report they "have not used a government social program."[28] Tax benefit beneficiaries, unsurprisingly, registered the highest proportion of this false belief, with 64 percent of 529 or Coverdell education tax break recipients and 60 percent of home mortgage interest deduction recipients expressing this belief—as compared to 28 percent of those on Medicaid and 25 percent of those receiving food stamps. Tax subsidies allow people to collect government benefits while still posing as rugged individualists.

Still, those figures for Medicaid and food stamp recipients are bizarrely high, which raises the flip side of this problem—welfare shaming. In an American context, "welfare" refers to means-tested aid for the poor, and it is heavily stigmatized, both in the press and in popular media. For instance, in the 2005 film *Cinderella Man*, the main character views taking government relief aid—during the Great Depression, no less—as so shameful that when he gets some work again, he goes to the relief office and pays back everything he received.

In another book, *The Government-Citizen Disconnect*, Mettler explores this attitude in detail. In an interview with Vox, she explained, "About 44 percent of Americans have unfavorable views of welfare. And the people who have very unfavorable views about welfare have strong attitudes about government that are shaped by this view. They believe that welfare is unfair, or that undeserving people are receiving it, and that deserving people like themselves are not getting anything."[29] This kind of stigmatizing is no doubt a big reason why even some people on food stamps—which is about the most blatant and intrusive kind of social program it is possible to imagine—think of themselves as not receiving any government aid. It's also the main reason why something like a quarter of people who are eligible for food stamps do not actually enroll. "Stigma seems to be a big barrier to participation," a welfare researcher told NBC News in 2013.[30]

In reality, of course, 100 percent of the American citizenry is a beneficiary of some kind of government program, and none more so than the rich. Propertarianism is the ideological underpinning that allows people living high on the government hog to look down on the poor, who feel guilty about being on benefits that are meager indeed compared to those lavished on the top 1 percent. And overall, the welfare state thus constructed is both threadbare and incredibly pricey.

Americans must come to understand that for the vast majority of us, taxes are not only about redistribution but also a way to fund things we *all* have to pay for. Currently we pay quite a substantial sum in tax, and then on top of that we are forced to pay still more for private health insurance, retirement, childcare, and so on. As we saw in chapter 9, the main purpose of the welfare state is to provide income to all nonworkers. But only a small proportion of that nonworking population is that way for their whole lives. Most nonworkers are at a particular point in their life cycle, such as children, students, parents, and the elderly, or have suffered a turn of bad luck, such as the unemployed.

Collective economics is based on social solidarity. This is not just about caring for the worst-off in society but also about caring for everyone, including yourself. Under a classic social democratic welfare state, my family receives child benefits when I am young, I receive a student allowance when I am in college, and I receive family benefits when I have children, all funded mainly by the middle-aged people in their prime working years. Then, when I have reached my top working years in turn, I pay taxes to care for the kids coming up behind me, as well as the now-elderly people who looked after me when I was in need. With such a lens, one should look at the payroll tax report card the Social Security Administration sends you from time to time with pride—proof that you are doing your part to prevent the elderly and disabled from starving.

The coronavirus pandemic actually provided some encouraging evidence that Americans will respond to a collective economics message under the right circumstances. The March 2020 CARES Act contained $1,200 checks for most individuals, which the IRS sent out without people having to apply (for the most part). Despite being only a modest portion of the bill, the checks quickly seized public attention and became one of the most popular programs in American history. Polls consistently found support at around 78 percent, including *two-thirds of Republicans.*[31] Journalists such as myself discovered that including the phrase "$1,200 checks" in a headline was practically guaranteed to produce a gusher of web traffic, and random people took to pestering Capitol Hill reporters online with questions about when the next round would be coming. It demonstrates that at least one fundamental part of collective economics—handing out free money through the welfare state—is popular so long as it isn't poisoned with propertarian ideology. It turns out that even Americans like getting free money, so long as they aren't brutally shamed for it and don't have to jump through a million flaming hoops first.

Another reasonable rhetorical strategy is uncovering the hidden motivations for propertarian arguments, as a way of mounting a frontal attack on their legitimacy. When someone advances an argument for cutting Medicare or Social Security that obviously makes no sense on its own terms, or when they predict something, the exact opposite happens, but they continue to advocate the same idea, it is natural to speculate about their real motivations.

As we saw in previous chapters, propertarian ethics is designed at all points to reinforce the political domination of the capitalist class. Therefore, for example, propertarians will tend to oppose any kind of welfare state program that makes unemployment less unpleasant, because by their lights the point of government is to force people into working for business making profits. The *Washington Post* argument about the Social Security trust fund is particularly striking in this respect, because it amounts to saying "unless we cut benefits, we will have to cut benefits." Cutting benefits, it seems, was the overriding goal. Another tell could be seen when Alan Simpson (co-chair of the deficit-cutting commission mentioned earlier) compared Social Security to "a milk cow with 310 million tits," and another when the commission's partial report (not endorsed by all its members) endorsed large tax cuts for the rich and corporations along with hikes for the middle class.[32] It couldn't be more obvious that the deficit was merely a fig leaf—the whole miserable thing was propertarianism through and through.

Socialized healthcare programs such as Medicare come under attack for the same reason: because where government is providing some service, private business could be making a profit doing a worse job. Indeed, Medicare has been partially privatized for exactly this reason, with the introduction of Medicare Advantage—a program that allows private insurers to provide worse Medicare service at a dramatically higher cost.

This also ties into a related warped view in the Washington establishment of what constitutes "responsible" government. American political elites tend to regard wise policymaking as forcing through unpopular decisions to inflict pain on the citizenry. There are times when that is necessary, such as with wartime rationing. But most of the time today this amounts to a sort of political sadism—as in Obama's Grand Bargain mentioned earlier, a stupid and pointless idea that would have deeply harmed tens of millions of people. Propertarians tried to make it a bipartisan compromise to launder the responsibility between both parties.

It is worth excavating the motivations here, but this realization can equally well be used to create blunt, cutting slogans such as "They're trying to steal your retirement." Lefties achieved some success when they dubbed the Bowles-Simpson group the "cat food commission," implying it would force poor retirees to survive on cat food.

The value of sheer repetition should also not be underestimated when it comes to political rhetoric. Most people are not at all familiar with the details of policy or political negotiation, and any one person is vanishingly unlikely to read any particular article or hear a single speech. But advocates can compensate for that by repeating the same point as often as possible, or by making it again every time a new applicable situation comes up. With each additional repetition there is a chance that a new person will hear the idea. As the Republican political consultant Frank Luntz advises his candidates about communicating a message: "You say it again, and you say it again, and you say it again, and you say it again, and you say it again, and then again and again and again and again, and about the time that you're absolutely sick of saying it is about the time that your target audience has heard it for the first time."[33]

That leads to the final aspect of contesting propertarian arguments: simply running them over. We should muster evidence, argument, rhetoric, and repetition to build our own conventional wisdom that can replace the existing one.

Once again, Social Security provides an illustrative example. In late 2012, a great many leftists had become roundly sick of simply defending Social Security from cuts, and started considering the opposite idea: that benefits should instead be expanded. One of the first was the old-school blogger Duncan Black, better known by his pseudonym, Atrios. On his widely read blog, and in a column in *USA Today*, he used all the tactics I have articulated to argue for "MOAR SOCIAL SECURITY," as he put it in several posts.[34] He argued convincingly that America was facing a looming retirement crisis because traditional pensions had vanished, private retirement accounts were not working out, and Social Security was not nearly generous enough to fill in the gap, especially for lower-income folks. He lambasted people who had blinded themselves to the crisis so that they could keep down taxes on the rich. On his blog, he posted over and over about the idea, keeping the issue bubbling. Progressive politicians including Bernie Sanders and Elizabeth Warren took up the call, joined by activists, progressive groups, and other writers (I participated in a small way at the time).

After the Grand Bargain failed, this group effort began to chip away at the propertarian consensus. Democratic politicians started to feel the pressure (especially in that many constituents contacted them) and began to distance themselves from efforts to cut Social Security. When Elizabeth Warren gave a speech endorsing a benefit increase, and that resulted in a deranged attack in *The Wall Street Journal* from the propertarian think tank Third Way, even many moderate Democrats who supported the group stood behind Warren, and one disavowed the think tank.

The effort got further momentum with Bernie Sanders's 2016 presidential campaign. This brought huge attention to his aggressive agenda, which included a big boost to benefits, especially when it turned out he was giving Hillary Clinton a run for her money. By January 2016, the notoriously staid and cautious *New York Times* editorial board was endorsing an increase in benefits, and by June President Obama had signed on as well.[35] All told, it was a remarkably quick about-face—but it would not have happened without those years of ideological trench war and popular mobilization.

Another example can be seen in the early New Deal. When Franklin Roosevelt took office, he wanted to be "a balance wheel between management and labor," as historian William Leuchtenburg writes in his book *Franklin D. Roosevelt and the New Deal: 1932–1940*.[36] He had long emphasized economic interdependence, and he wanted the capitalist class to participate in his programs. But business would of course have none of it—they wanted to dominate everyone else as they had before 1933. They cooperated with extreme reluctance if at all, and in 1935 the Chamber of Commerce openly denounced the New Deal, which both soured Roosevelt on the capitalists and opened an opportunity for his more left-wing advisers and allies in Congress. (One of Roosevelt's greatest strengths as a politician, given the bizarre American constitutional system, was his ability to turn hard to the left when it was to his political advantage to do so.) Harvard's Felix Frankfurter, an antitrust advocate, argued that the time had come to attack business. Leuchtenburg writes:

> The Harvard professor insisted that the attempt at business-government co-operation had failed, and urged Roosevelt to declare war on business. Once the president had understood that business was the enemy, he would be free to undertake the Brandeisian program to cut the giants down to size: by launching

antitrust suits, and by taxing large corporations more stiffly than small business.[37]

This led to the Second New Deal of 1935, the most radical period in Roosevelt's presidency. He and his allies in Congress set up Social Security, helped unions, jacked up taxes on the rich, and passed several other measures:

> By Black Monday [May 27, 1935], the president had already begun to move decisively in a new direction. . . . Roosevelt insisted on the passage of four major pieces of legislation: the social security bill, the Wagner labor proposal, a banking bill, and a public-utility holding company measure. A few days later, he added a fifth item of "must" legislation: a "soak the rich" tax scheme. In addition, he demanded a series of minor measures, some of them highly controversial, which in any other session would have been regarded a major legislation. . . . Thus began the "Second Hundred Days." Over a long period Congress debated the most far-reaching reform measures it had ever considered. In the end, Roosevelt got every item of significant legislation he desired.[38]

By the time of his reelection campaign in 1936, Roosevelt was campaigning openly against the business class. In a campaign speech at Madison Square Garden that year, he said, "They had begun to consider the Government of the United States as a mere appendage to their own affairs. We know now that Government by organized money is just as dangerous as Government by organized mob. Never before in all our history have these forces been so united against one candidate as they stand today. They are unanimous in their hate for me—and I welcome their hatred."[39] He won in a landslide even bigger than in 1932.

Finally, I want to emphasize that political argument is not some kind of magic solvent here. We can't defeat propertarianism with just one weird trick. But argument has its place. In the first instance, it is important to actually be correct on the facts and understand how policy works. An ideology of collective economics must not be divorced from reality—the Soviet Union shows that one can get immense power out of a utopian ideology that purports to be the master key for all history and politics, but if reality diverges too much from the ideology, it eventually cracks apart. Conversely, Soviet Communism, nineteenth-century classical liberalism, and late twentieth-century neoliberalism demonstrate that a hegemonic ideology can continue inflicting terrible damage for a long time even when most of its predictions do not bear fruit. We don't want that either.

But argument can still move belief and change people's views, even when things seem to be going well. And in times of crisis, when advocates of the status quo are discredited or even questioning their own beliefs and the mass of the population is confused and looking for answers, critics can advance by leaps and bounds. Intellectuals are far from the most important part of any collective economics movement (that would be labor unions), but they still provide the important functions of contesting policy arguments and translating the movement's demands into workable policy.

Today is certainly a time of crisis. The 2008 crisis broke the legitimacy of the propertarian consensus, and the coronavirus pandemic has ground up most of the remaining shards. The millennials just reaching middle age today are probably the most left-wing generation in American history, rivaled only by Generation Z, coming up behind us.[40] Donald Trump, with his record of tax cuts for the rich and catastrophic bungling of the pandemic, has discredited the right-wing propertarianism of the Republican Party.

At the time of writing, Joe Biden—previously known as the handmaiden of the credit card industry in the Senate and a guy who was buddy-buddy with Dixiecrat segregationists— was shaping up to be the most left-wing president since Lyndon Johnson at least. In March 2021, Democrats, who had just fifty votes in the Senate, passed a $1.9 trillion pandemic relief package—more than twice the size of Obama's Recovery Act—with $1,400 checks and a huge expansion of the child tax credit that basically turned it into a social democratic child allowance. The overall effect, if implemented perfectly, would be to cut child poverty in half.[41] This change was made for only one year (thanks to goofball Senate rules), but Democrats and left-wing groups immediately began gearing up to make it permanent.

That said, the Biden administration and the rest of the Democratic Party are still full of people who were deeply implicated in all the neoliberal atrocities of the last forty years. If and when the pandemic is gone, calls for austerity will likely return. It has seldom been more important to press the case for collective economics on all fronts. The Democrats will probably have to be dragged kicking and screaming to the promised land, but with a strong enough tug, they might just get there.

ACKNOWLEDGMENTS

I would like to thank my agent, Erik Hane at Headwater Literary Management, who helped me develop the idea for this book, and my editor, Kevin Reilly, along with the rest of the great staff at St. Martin's Press. Thanks are also due to Steve Randy Waldman for comments and suggestions on an early draft. Most of all, I must thank Chelsea Chamberlain for putting up with me, and providing innumerable helpful suggestions, while I was writing.

ACKNOWLEDGMENTS

NOTES

Introduction

1. Suze Orman, "Start Here," https://www.suzeorman.com/start-here.
2. Dave Ramsey, Financial Peace, https://www.financialpeace.com/.
3. Gregory Wallace, "Airlines and TSA Report 96% Drop in Air Travel as Pandemic Continues," CNN, April 9, 2020, https://www.cnn.com/2020/04/09/politics/airline-passengers-decline/index.html.
4. Federal Reserve Bank of St. Louis data tool FRED, series on savings rate, https://fred.stlouisfed.org/series/PSAVERT.
5. Ibid., series on unemployment claims, https://fred.stlouisfed.org/series/ICSA; ibid., series on unemployment rate, https://fred.stlouisfed.org/series/UNRATE/.
6. Ibid., series on GDP, https://fred.stlouisfed.org/series/GDPC1/.
7. Ibid., series on consumer spending as a share of GDP, https://fred.stlouisfed.org/series/DPCERE1Q156NBEA.
8. Nick Paumgarten, "The Scold," *New Yorker*, February 21, 2016, https://www.newyorker.com/magazine/2016/02/29/mr-money-mustache-the-frugal-guru.
9. Luke Darby, "Why Does the Trump Administration Keep Seizing Hospitals' Coronavirus Supplies?," *GQ*, April 8, 2020, https://www.gq.com/story/trump-admin-confiscating-coronavirus-supplies.
10. Kelsey Snell, "What's Inside the Senate's $2 Trillion Coronavirus Aid Package," NPR, March 26, 2020, https://www.npr.org/2020/03/26/821457551/whats-inside-the-senate-s-2-trillion-coronavirus-aid-package.

11. "Benefits in Unemployment, Share of Previous Income," OECD, https://data.oecd.org/benwage/benefits-in-unemployment-share-of-previous-income.htm.

12. Amelia Thomson-DeVeaux, "Many Americans Are Getting More Money from Unemployment Than They Were from Their Jobs," *FiveThirtyEight*, May 15, 2020, https://fivethirtyeight.com/features/many-americans-are-getting-more-money-from-unemployment-than-they-were-from-their-jobs/.

13. Francis Fukuyama, "The End of History?," *National Interest*, no. 16 (Summer 1989): 3–18, https://www.jstor.org/stable/24027184?seq=1.

14. Jason Silverstein, "Mitch McConnell Would Rather Let States Declare Bankruptcy Than Receive More Federal Aid," CBS News, April 23, 2020, https://www.cbsnews.com/news/mitch-mcconnell-states-bankruptcy-federal-aid/.

15. Jason Easley, "Lindsey Graham Vows to Cut Off Unemployment Benefits to the Jobless," *PoliticsUSA*, April 29, 2020, https://www.politicususa.com/2020/04/29/lindsey-graham-vows-to-cut-off-unemployment-benefits-to-the-jobless.html.

16. Senator Portman press release, May 13, 2020, https://www.portman.senate.gov/newsroom/portman-difference/cnbc-portman-discusses-importance-testing-safely-reopen-ohio-holding.

17. Greg Iacurci, "Dems, GOP Continue to Spar over Extension of Extra $600 in Unemployment Benefits," CNBC, June 11, 2020, https://www.cnbc.com/2020/06/11/dems-gop-spar-over-extension-of-extra-600-in-unemployment-benefits.html.

Chapter 1: A History of a Self-Immolating Idea

1. Transcript of Brookings Institution event, April 2018, https://www.brookings.edu/wp-content/uploads/2018/04/biden-transcript.pdf.

2. Kevin D. Williamson, "The Father-Führer," *National Review*, March 28, 2016, https://www.nationalreview.com/magazine/2016/03/28/father-f-hrer/.

3. Adam Smith, *The Wealth of Nations*, 1776, p. 27.

4. Ibid., p. 419.

5. Ibid., p. 716.

6. Karl Marx and Friedrich Engels, *Manifesto of the Communist Party*, 1848.

7. Smith, *The Wealth of Nations*, pp. 724–760.

8. Karl Polanyi, *The Great Transformation*, 1945, p. 3.

9. Eric Hobsbawm, *The Age of Revolution*, 1996, p. 34.

10. Barry Eichengreen and Marc Flandreau (eds.), *The Gold Standard in Theory and History*, 1997.

11. Ibid.

12. Polanyi, *The Great Transformation*, p. 223.

13. Matthew C. Klein and Michael Pettis, *Trade Wars Are Class Wars*, 2020, pp. 3–10.

14. Goedele de Keersmaeker, *Polarity, Balance of Power and International Relations Theory*, 2016, p. 90.

15. Stephen Broadberry, Johann Custodis, and Bishnupriya Gupta, "India and the Great Divergence: An Anglo-Indian Comparison of GDP per Capita, 1600–1871," *Explorations in Economic History* 55 (January 2015): 58–75, http://eprints.lse.ac.uk/56838/.

16. Amartya Sen, *Poverty and Famines*, 1981.

17. Henry Clay, "The American System," February 1832, https://www.senate.gov/artandhistory/history/resources/pdf/AmericanSystem.pdf.

18. Reuven Glick and Ramon Moreno, "Government Intervention and the East Asian Miracle," *FRBSF Economic Letter*, July 11, 1997, https://www.frbsf.org/economic-research/publications/economic-letter/1997/july/government-intervention-and-the-east-asian-miracle/.

19. Antonio Gramsci, *Selections from the Prison Notebooks*, 1999, p. 506.

20. Normal Angell, *The Great Illusion*, 1910.

21. Ibid., p. 302.

22. William Philpott, *Bloody Victory*, 2009.

23. Eugene Rogan, *The Fall of the Ottomans*, 2016.

24. John Maynard Keynes, *The Economic Consequences of Mr. Churchill*, 1925.

25. Klein and Pettis, *Trade Wars Are Class Wars*, p. 194.

26. Federal Reserve Bank of St. Louis data tool FRED, series on industrial production, https://fred.stlouisfed.org/series/INDPRO/; ibid., series on unemployment rate, https://fred.stlouisfed.org/series/M0892AUSM156SNBR.

27. Roger Middleton, "British Monetary and Fiscal Policy in the 1930s,"

Oxford Review of Economic Policy 26, no. 3 (2010): 414–441, https://academic.oup.com/oxrep/article-pdf/26/3/414/1054720/grq024.pdf; Nicholas H. Dimsdale, Nicholas Horsewood, and Arthur van Riel, "Unemployment in Interwar Germany: An Analysis of the Labor Market, 1927–1936," *Journal of Economic History* 66, no. 3 (September 2006): 778–808, https://www.jstor.org/stable/3874859.

28. Kevin O'Rourke, "Government Policies and the Collapse in Trade During the Great Depression," VoxEU, November 27, 2009, https://voxeu.org/article/government-policies-and-collapse-trade-during-great-depression.

29. John Kenneth Galbraith, *The Great Crash 1929*, 2009, p. 183.

30. Ibid., p. 186.

31. Middleton, "British Monetary and Fiscal Policy in the 1930s."

32. William L. Patch Jr., *Heinrich Brüning and the Dissolution of the Weimar Republic*, 1998.

33. Eric Rauchway, *Winter War*, 2018, pp. 10–12.

34. Eric Rauchway, *The Great Depression and the New Deal*, 2008.

35. Herbert Hoover, *Freedom Betrayed*, 2012.

36. Michał Kalecki, "Political Aspects of Full Employment," *Political Quarterly*, 1943.

37. President Clinton news conference, July 31, 1996, https://www.youtube.com/watch?v=2Ypufy3nA44&ab_channel=clintonlibrary42.

38. John Q. Barrett, "'That One' and 'That Man,'" *History News Network*, November 2008, https://historynewsnetwork.org/article/55697.

39. Sally Denton, *The Plots Against the President*, 2012.

40. R. J. Overy, *The Nazi Economic Recovery 1932–1938*, 1996.

Chapter 2: Collective Economics

1. Eugene Kiely, "'You Didn't Build That,' Uncut and Unedited," Factcheck.org, July 23, 2012, https://www.factcheck.org/2012/07/you-didnt-build-that-uncut-and-unedited/.

2. Maddison Project Database, version 2018: Jutta Bolt, Robert Inklaar, Herman de Jong, and Jan Luiten van Zanden, "Rebasing 'Maddison': New Income Comparisons and the Shape of Long-Run Economic Development," Maddison Project working paper 10, 2018, https://www.rug.nl/ggdc/historicaldevelopment/maddison/releases/maddison-project-database-2018.

3. Robert K. Merton, "Singletons and Multiples in Scientific Discovery: A Chapter in the Sociology of Science," *Proceedings of the American Philosophical Society* 105, no. 5 (1961): 470–486, https://www.jstor.org/stable/985546?seq=1.

4. William F. Ogburn and Dorothy Thomas, "Are Inventions Inevitable? A Note on Social Evolution," *Political Science Quarterly* 37, no. 1 (March 1922): 83–98, https://www.jstor.org/stable/2142320.

5. Stephen H. Cutcliffe, "Holley, Alexander Lyman," *American National Biography*, https://doi.org/10.1093/anb/9780198606697.article.1300778.

6. Tim Hartford, "Killed for Spying: The Story of the First Factory," BBC, July 10, 2019, https://www.bbc.com/news/business-48533696.

7. Mark Stephens, "How Steve Jobs Got the Ideas of GUI from XEROX," clip from *Triumph of the Nerds*, 1996, https://www.youtube.com/watch?v=J33pVRdxWbw.

8. National Center for Education Statistics, *Digest of Education Statistics*, Table 205.10, 2019, https://nces.ed.gov/programs/digest/d19/tables/dt19_205.10.asp?current=yes; Anu Partanen, "What Americans Keep Ignoring About Finland's School Success," *The Atlantic*, December 29, 2011, https://www.theatlantic.com/national/archive/2011/12/what-americans-keep-ignoring-about-finlands-school-success/250564/.

9. "Characteristics of Postsecondary Students," National Center for Education Statistics, April 2020, https://nces.ed.gov/programs/coe/indicator_csb.asp.

10. Matthew Karnitschnig, Deborah Solomon, Liam Pleven, and Jon E. Hilsenrath, "U.S. to Take Over AIG in $85 Billion Bailout; Central Banks Inject Cash as Credit Dries Up," *Wall Street Journal*, September 16, 2008, https://www.wsj.com/articles/SB122156561931242905.

11. Dominic Holland et al., "Structural Growth Trajectories and Rates of Change in the First 3 Months of Infant Brain Development," *JAMA Neurology* 71, no. 10 (2014): 1266–1274, doi:10.1001/jamaneurol.2014.1638.

12. George P. Murdock and Caterina Provost, "Factors in the Division of Labor by Sex: A Cross-Cultural Analysis," *Ethnology* 12, no. 2 (April 1973): 203–225, https://www.jstor.org/stable/3773347.

13. Daron Acemoglu, "Economic Growth: Lectures 2 and 3: The Solow Growth Model," November 2011, https://economics.mit.edu/files/7181.

14. John Bates Clark, *The Distribution of Wealth: A Theory of Wages, Interest and Profits*, 1899, p. 1.

15. Anthony Fleming, "Ice Ages in the Geological Record," *Indiana Geological and Water Survey of Indiana University*, https://igws.indiana.edu /Surficial/IceAge.

16. Robert M. Solow, "Technical Change and the Aggregate Production Function," *Review of Economics and Statistics* 39, no. 3 (August 1957): 312–320, https://www.jstor.org/stable/1926047.

17. Bryan Caplan, "Defending Desert," *EconLog*, April 2006, https://www .econlib.org/archives/2006/04/defending_deser.html; N. Gregory Mankiw, "Defending the One Percent," *Journal of Economic Perspectives* 27, no. 3 (Summer 2013): 21–34, https://scholar.harvard.edu/files /mankiw/files/defending_the_one_percent_1.pdf; Tyler Cowen, "Are CEOs Paid Their Value Added?," *Marginal Revolution*, November 29, 2011, https://marginalrevolution.com/marginalrevolution /2011/11/are-ceos-paid-their-value-added.html.

18. Amartya Sen, "Just Deserts," *New York Review of Books*, March 4, 1982, http://www.nybooks.com/articles/archives/1982/mar/04/just -deserts/.

19. Ha-Joon Chang, *Globalisation, Economic Development & the Role of the State*, 2002.

20. Robert Solow, "Chapter 9 Neoclassical Growth Theory," *Handbook of Macroeconomics*, 1999, pp. 637–667, https://www.sciencedirect.com /science/article/pii/S1574004899010125.

21. Joan Robinson, *Introduction to the Theory of Employment*, 1969, p. 10.

22. Thomas Piketty, "Of Productivity in France and in Germany," *Le Monde*, January 9, 2017, https://www.lemonde.fr/blog/piketty/2017 /01/09/of-productivity-in-france-and-in-germany/.

23. "Integrated Macroeconomic Accounts," Bureau of Economic Analysis, https://apps.bea.gov/iTable/iTable.cfm?reqid=14&step=1#reqid =14&step=3&isuri=1&1403=6201.

24. "Ag and Food Sectors and the Economy," United States Department of Agriculture, https://www.ers.usda.gov/data-products/ag -and-food-statistics-charting-the-essentials/ag-and-food-sectors -and-the-economy.aspx.

25. Timothy Cogley, "Monetary Policy and the Great Crash of 1929: A Bursting Bubble or Collapsing Fundamentals?," *FRBSF Economic Letter*, March 26, 1999, https://www.frbsf.org/economic-research

/publications/economic-letter/1999/march/monetary-policy
-and-the-great-crash-of-1929-a-bursting-bubble-or-collapsing
-fundamentals/.

26. Federal Reserve Bank of St. Louis Bank data tool FRED, series on PCE deflator, https://fred.stlouisfed.org/series/DPCERE1Q156NBEA.

27. Ingrid Robeyns, "The Capability Approach," *Stanford Encyclopedia of Philosophy* (Winter 2016), https://plato.stanford.edu/archives /win2016/entries/capability-approach/.

28. John Rawls, "Justice as Fairness: Political Not Metaphysical," *Philosophy and Public Affairs* 14, no. 3 (Summer 1985): 223–251, https://www .jstor.org/stable/2265349.

29. *New Republic*, August 12, 1996.

30. OECD data series on social spending, https://data.oecd.org/socialexp /social-spending.htm.

31. "Labor Market Subsidy," Kela, https://www.kela.fi/web/en/labour -market-subsidy.

32. OECD data series on labor force participation rate, https://data.oecd .org/emp/labour-force-participation-rate.htm.

33. OECD data series on collective bargaining coverage, https://stats .oecd.org/Index.aspx?DataSetCode=CBC.

34. Tim Van Rie, Ive Marx, and Jeroen Horemans, "Ghent Revisited: Unemployment Insurance and Union Membership in Belgium and the Nordic Countries," *European Journal of Industrial Relations* 17, no. 2 (2011): 125–139, https://journals.sagepub.com/doi/abs/10.1177 /0959680111400895/.

35. "Industrial Relations in Austria: Background Summary," European Trade Union Institute, October 13, 2016, https://www.etui.org/covid -social-impact/austria/industrial-relations-in-austria-background -summary.

36. Matt Bruenig, "Market Incomes Will Always Produce Hideous Inequality," *People's Policy Project*, March 28, 2019, https://www .peoplespolicyproject.org/2019/03/28/market-incomes-will-always -produce-hideous-inequality/.

37. "Business Lobby Proposes Minimum Wage in Finland," *Uutiset*, September 22, 2019, https://yle.fi/uutiset/osasto/news/business_lobby _proposes_minimum_wage_in_finland/10983185.

38. Thomas Piketty, "Wealth Inequality: Europe & the U.S. 1900–2015," http://piketty.pse.ens.fr/files/ideology/pdf/F10.4.pdf; ibid., "Wealth

Inequality: The Top Percentile, 1900–2015," http://piketty.pse.ens.fr /files/ideology/pdf/F10.5.pdf.

39. Matt Bruenig, "Social Wealth Fund for America," *People's Policy Project*, 2018, https://www.peoplespolicyproject.org/projects/social-wealth -fund/.

40. Jay Greene, "How Amazon's Quest for More, Cheaper Products Has Resulted in a Flea Market of Fakes," *Washington Post*, November 14, 2019, https://www.washingtonpost.com/technology/2019/11 /14/how-amazons-quest-more-cheaper-products-has-resulted-flea -market-fakes/.

Chapter 3: How Neo-Propertarianism Conquered the World

1. Roger E. A. Farmer, "How New Keynesian Economics Betrays Keynes," *Evonomics*, https://evonomics.com/new-keynesian-economics -betrays-keynes/.

2. John Maynard Keynes, "The Keynes Plan," International Monetary Fund, February 1996, https://www.elibrary.imf.org/view/IMF071 /15395-9781451972511/15395-9781451972511/ch01.xml?language =en&redirect=true.

3. Michael Ellman and S. Maksudov, "Soviet Deaths in the Great Patriotic War: A Note," *Europe-Asia Studies* 46, no. 4 (1994): 671–680, https:// www.tandfonline.com/doi/abs/10.1080/09668139408412190.

4. Department of Veterans Affairs, "America's Wars," November 2020, https://www.va.gov/opa/publications/factsheets/fs_americas_wars .pdf.

5. Maddison Project Database, version 2018.

6. Michael J. Hogan, *The Marshall Plan*, 1987.

7. Vincent Bevins, *The Jakarta Method*, 2020.

8. Burton A. Abrams, "How Richard Nixon Pressured Arthur Burns: Evidence from the Nixon Tapes," *Journal of Economic Perspectives* 20, no. 4 (Fall 2006): 177–188, https://pubs.aeaweb.org/doi/pdf/10.1257 /jep.20.4.177.

9. Catherine R. Schenk, "The Origins of the Eurodollar Market in London: 1955–1963," *Explorations in Economic History* 35 (1998): 221– 238, https://www.sfu.ca/~poitras/EEH_Eurodollar_98.pdf.

10. Scott Newton, "Sterling, Bretton Woods, and Social Democracy, 1968–1970," *Diplomacy and Statecraft* 24, no. 3 (September 2013):

427–455, https://www.researchgate.net/publication/263412198
_Sterling_Bretton_Woods_and_Social_Democracy_1968–1970.

11. Sebastian Mallaby, *More Money Than God*, 2010.

12. Michael Carson and John Clark, "Asian Financial Crisis," Federal Reserve Bank of New York, https://www.federalreservehistory.org/essays/asian-financial-crisis.

13. World Bank data series on Indonesia GDP, https://data.worldbank.org/indicator/NY.GDP.MKTP.CD?locations=ID.

14. Michael D. Bordo, Dominique Simard, and Eugene N. White, "France and the Bretton Woods International Monetary System 1960 to 1968," in James Reis (ed.), *International Monetary Systems in Historical Perspective*, 1995, pp. 155–180, https://link.springer.com/chapter/10.1007%2F978-1-349-24220-7_8.

15. Adam Tooze, "Framing Crashed (10): 'A New Bretton Woods' and the Problem of 'Economic Order'—Also a Reply to Adler and Varoufakis," February 9, 2019, https://adamtooze.com/2019/02/09/framing-crashed-10-a-new-bretton-woods-and-the-problem-of-economic-order-also-a-reply-to-adler-and-varoufakis/.

16. Robert E. Lucas Jr., "Econometric Policy Evaluation: A Critique," *Carnegie-Rochester Conference Series on Public Policy* 1 (1976): 19–46, https://doi.org/10.1016/S0167-2231(76)80003-6.

17. Thomas J. Sargent and Neil Wallace, "Rational Expectations and the Theory of Economic Policy," *Journal of Monetary Economics* 2, no. 2 (April 1976): 169–183, https://doi.org/10.1016/0304-3932(76)90032-5.

18. Dan Froomkin, "Cass Sunstein: The Obama Administration's Ambivalent Regulator," *HuffPost*, June 13, 2011, https://www.huffpost.com/entry/cass-sunstein-obama-ambivalent-regulator-czar_n_874530.

19. George Stadler, "Real Business Cycles," *Journal of Economics Literature* 32 (December 1994): 1750–1783, http://faculty.econ.ucdavis.edu/faculty/kdsalyer/LECTURES/Ecn200e/Stadler.pdf.

20. R. M. Sapolsky and R. J. Share, "Emergence of a Peaceful Culture in Wild Baboons," *PLOS Biology* 2, no. 4 (2004): e124, https://journals.plos.org/plosbiology/article?id=10.1371/journal.pbio.0020124.

21. Polanyi, *The Great Transformation*, p. 49.

22. Ibid., p. 51.

23. William A. Jackson, *Markets*, 2019.

24. Christopher Boehm, *Hierarchy in the Forest*, 2001.

25. Quinn Slobodian, *Globalists*, 2018, p. 44.

26. Ibid., 271.

27. "What Is the Fiscal Compact Treaty?," *Irish Times*, February 28, 2012, https://www.irishtimes.com/news/what-is-the-fiscal-compact-treaty-1.701082.

28. Federal Reserve Bank of St. Louis data tool FRED, data series on Greek unemployment, https://fred.stlouisfed.org/series/LRUNTTTTGRQ156S.

29. Yanis Varoufakis, *Adults in the Room*, 2017.

30. Yanis Varoufakis, "Why We Must Save the EU," *The Guardian*, April 5, 2016, https://www.theguardian.com/world/2016/apr/05/yanis-varoufakis-why-we-must-save-the-eu.

31. Corey Robin, "Nietzsche, Hayek, and the Meaning of Conservatism," *Jacobin*, June 26, 2013, https://www.jacobinmag.com/2013/06/nietzsche-hayek-and-the-meaning-of-conservatism/.

32. *Report of the Chilean National Commission on Truth and Reconciliation*, United States Institute of Peace, February 2000, https://www.usip.org/sites/default/files/resources/collections/truth_commissions/Chile90-Report/Chile90-Report.pdf; Larry Rohter, "Colonel's Death Gives Clues to Pinochet Arms Deals," *New York Times*, June 19, 2006, https://www.nytimes.com/2006/06/19/world/americas/19chile.html?ex=1308369600en=964a159db7c0d614ei=5088partner=rssnytemc=rss.

33. John Maynard Keynes, *The General Theory of Employment, Interest, and Money*, 2018, p. 286.

34. Ibid.

35. Steve Randy Waldman, "Not a Monetary Phenomenon," *Interfluidity*, September 5, 2013, https://www.interfluidity.com/v2/4561.html.

36. Paul Stephen Dempsey, "The Rise and Fall of the Civil Aeronautics Board—Opening Wide the Floodgates of Entry," *Transportation Law Journal* 11, no. 1 (1979): 91–185, https://papers.ssrn.com/sol3/papers.cfm?abstract_id=2233081; Dempsey, "The Rise and Fall of the Interstate Commerce Commission: The Tortuous Path from Regulation to Deregulation of America's Infrastructure," *Marquette Law Review* 96, no. 4 (Summer 2012): 1151–1189, https://scholarship.law

.marquette.edu/cgi/viewcontent.cgi?referer=https://www.google
.com/&httpsredir=1&article=5129&context=mulr;The.

37. Scott McCartney, "Kennedy Pushed Airline Deregulation, Changed U.S. Air Travel," *Wall Street Journal*, August 26, 2009, https://www.wsj.com/articles/BL-MSB-4933.

38. Dan Rather Reports, "Haul or High Water," June 8, 2010, https://www.youtube.com/watch?v=A1iN-a0cvsQ&ab_channel =DanRatherReports.

39. Michael Collins, "Did Deregulation Work?," *IndustryWeek*, October 26, 2016, https://www.industryweek.com/the-economy/regulations /article/22007281/did-deregulation-work; Michael H. Belzer, *Sweatshops on Wheels*, 2000, https://global.oup.com/academic/product /sweatshops-on-wheels-9780195128864?cc=us&lang=en&; Paul Stephen Dempsey, *Flying Blind: The Failure of Airline Deregulation*, 1990, https://files.epi.org/2014/flying-blind.pdf.

40. Joseph A. McCartin, *Collision Course*, 2013.

Chapter 4: Casting the False Prophets of Growth out of the Economic Temple

1. William McBride, "What Is the Evidence on Taxes and Growth?," Tax Foundation, December 18, 2012, https://taxfoundation.org /what-evidence-taxes-and-growth.

2. Ron Haskins, "Balancing Work and Solidarity in the Western Democracies," Brookings Institution, October 28, 2010, https://www .brookings.edu/research/balancing-work-and-solidarity-in-the -western-democracies/.

3. Charlie Peters, "A Neo-Liberal's Manifesto," *Washington Monthly*, September 1982, https://www.washingtonpost.com/archive /opinions/1982/09/05/a-neo-liberals-manifesto/21cf41ca-e60e -404e-9a66-124592c9f70d/.

4. Thomas Friedman, *The Lexus and the Olive Tree*, 1999, p. 130.

5. Ibid.

6. Ibid.

7. Milton Friedman, "Nobel Lecture: Inflation and Unemployment," *Journal of Political Economy* 85, no. 3 (June 1977): 451–472, https:// www.journals.uchicago.edu/doi/abs/10.1086/260579.

8. Federal Reserve Bank of St. Louis Bank data tool FRED, series

on effective federal funds rate, https://fred.stlouisfed.org/series /fedfunds.

9. Steven Rattner, "Volcker Asserts U.S. Must Trim Living Standard," *New York Times*, October 18, 1979, https://www.nytimes.com /1979/10/18/archives/volcker-asserts-us-must-trim-living-standard -warns-of-inflation.html.

10. "Paul Volcker, Fed Chair Who Fought Runaway Inflation, Has Died at Age 92," CBS/AP, December 9, 2019, https://www.cbsnews.com /news/paul-volcker-died-federal-reserve-chairman-fought-runaway -inflation-dead-age-92-cause-of-death-not-released-2019-12-09/.

11. "Should the Government Adopt Long-Term Wage and Price Controls for Selected Unions and Industries?," *The Advocates*, 1971, view on "John Kenneth Galbraith on Regulations (1971)," https://www .youtube.com/watch?v=Ev8zRbEHUAk.

12. Federal Reserve Bank of St. Louis data tool FRED, series on unemployment rate, https://fred.stlouisfed.org/series/UNRATE/.

13. "The Productivity–Pay Gap," Economic Policy Institute, July 2019, https://www.epi.org/productivity-pay-gap/.

14. Emmanuel Saez, "Income and Wealth Inequality: Evidence and Policy Implications," Neubauer Collegium Lecture, October 2014, https://eml.berkeley.edu/~saez/lecture_saez_chicago14.pdf.

15. William Easterly, "What Did Structural Adjustment Adjust? The Association of Policies and Growth with Repeated IMF and World Bank Adjustment Loans," *Journal of Development Economics* 76, no. 1 (February 2005): 1–22, https://doi.org/10.1016/j.jdeveco.2003.11 .005.

16. Robert J. Barro and Jong-Wha Lee, "IMF Programs: Who Is Chosen and What Are the Effects?," *Journal of Monetary Economics* (October 2005), https://scholar.harvard.edu/barro/publications/imf -programs-who-chosen-and-what-are-effects.

17. Robert Naiman and Neil Watkins, "A Survey of the Impacts of IMF Structural Adjustment in Africa: Growth, Social Spending, and Debt Relief," Center for Economic and Policy Research, April 1999, https://cepr.net/documents/publications/debt_1999_04.htm.

18. Michael Tomasky, *Bill Clinton*, 2017, p. 78.

19. Teresa Ghilarducci and Aida Farmand, "What's Not to Like About the EITC? Plenty, It Turns Out," *American Prospect*, June 28, 2019, https://prospect.org/economy/like-eitc-plenty-turns-out/.

20. Joseph Stiglitz, "The Roaring Nineties," *The Atlantic*, October 2002, https://www.theatlantic.com/magazine/archive/2002/10/the -roaring-nineties/302604/.

21. Richard W. Stevenson, "To Greenspan, 90's Bubble Was Beyond Reach of Fed," *New York Times*, August 31, 2002, https://www .nytimes.com/2002/08/31/business/to-greenspan-90-s-bubble-was -beyond-reach-of-fed.html.

22. Federal Reserve Bank of St. Louis data tool FRED, series on unem- ployment rate, https://fred.stlouisfed.org/series/UNRATE/; ibid., series on personal consumption expenditures deflator, https://fred .stlouisfed.org/series/DPCERD3Q086SBEA.

23. Ibid., series on manufacturing employment, https://fred.stlouisfed .org/series/MANEMP.

24. Wayne M. Morrison and Marc Labonte, "China's Currency Pol- icy: An Analysis of the Economic Issues," Congressional Research Service, December 19, 2011, https://www.everycrsreport.com/files /20111219_RS21625_dbbcbc4260c002d7e8e6e608b5abdd644d4f6c 12.pdf.

25. Elaine X. Grant, "TWA—Death of a Legend," *St. Louis Maga- zine*, July 28, 2006, https://www.stlmag.com/TWA-Death-Of-A -Legend/.

26. Robert Skidelsky, *Keynes*, 2010, p. 117.

27. Federal Reserve Bank of St. Louis data tool FRED, series on real GDP, https://fred.stlouisfed.org/series/GDPC1/.

28. Chester Bowles, *Tomorrow Without Fear*, 1946, p. 21.

29. Ibid., p. 23.

30. Marriner Eccles, *Beckoning Frontiers*, 1951, p. 76.

31. John Kenneth Galbraith, *The Great Crash 1929*, pp. 177–178.

32. Steve Randy Waldman, "Inequality and Demand," *Interfluidity*, Janu- ary 24, 2013, https://www.interfluidity.com/v2/3830.html.

33. Milton Friedman, *A Theory of the Consumption Function*, 1957.

34. Noah Smith, "Offensiveness Does Not Make You a Better Econo- mist," *Noahpinion*, March 12, 2012, https://noahpinionblog.blogspot .com/2012/03/offensiveness-does-not-make-you-better.html.

35. Paul Krugman, "Inequality and Recovery," *The Conscience of a Liberal*, January 20, 2013, https://krugman.blogs.nytimes.com/2013/01/20 /inequality-and-recovery/.

36. Christopher D. Carroll, "Why Do the Rich Save So Much?," NBER, May 1998, https://www.nber.org/papers/w6549.

37. "#12 Hearst family," *Forbes*, December 16, 2020, https://www.forbes.com/profile/hearst/?list=families&sh=6e23532b533d.

38. J. W. Mason, "Disgorge the Cash: The Disconnect Between Corporate Borrowing and Investment," Roosevelt Institute, 2015, http://jwmason.org/wp-content/uploads/2015/05/Disgorge-the-Cash.pdf.

39. Maureen Tkacik, "Crash Course," *New Republic*, September 18, 2019, https://newrepublic.com/article/154944/boeing-737-max-investigation-indonesia-lion-air-ethiopian-airlines-managerial-revolution.

40. Julie Johnsson and Ryan Beene, "Internal Boeing Messages Say 737 Max 'Designed by Clowns,'" *Bloomberg*, January 10, 2020, https://www.bloomberg.com/news/articles/2020-01-10/-incredibly-damning-boeing-messages-show-employee-unease-on-max.

41. Peter Bernstein and Annalyn Swan (eds.), *All the Money in the World*, 2007.

42. "America's Concentration Crisis," Open Markets Institute, 2019, https://concentrationcrisis.openmarketsinstitute.org/.

43. Claire Kelloway, "How to Close the Democrats' Rural Gap," *Washington Monthly*, January/February/March 2019, https://washingtonmonthly.com/magazine/january-february-march-2019/how-to-close-the-democrats-rural-gap/.

44. Ryan Grim and Paul Blumenthal, "Peter Peterson Spent Nearly Half a Billion in Washington Targeting Social Security, Medicare," *HuffPost*, May 15, 2012, https://www.huffpost.com/entry/peter-peterson-foundation-half-billion-social-security-cuts_n_1517805.

45. Keach Hagey and Suzanne Vranica, "How Covid-19 Supercharged the Advertising 'Triopoly' of Google, Facebook and Amazon," *Wall Street Journal*, March 19, 2021, https://www.wsj.com/articles/how-covid-19-supercharged-the-advertising-triopoly-of-google-facebook-and-amazon-11616163738.

46. Savannah Jacobson, "The Most Feared Owner in American Journalism Looks Set to Take Some of Its Greatest Assets," *Columbia Journalism Review*, June 29, 2020, https://www.cjr.org/special_report/alden-global-capital-medianews-tribune-company.php.

47.   Josh Marshall, "A Serf on Google's Farm," *Talking Points Memo*, September 1, 2017, https://talkingpointsmemo.com/edblog/a-serf-on
-googles-farm.

Chapter 5: Social Growth

1.   Peter D. Meltzer, "Sotheby's Scores Big with Bill Koch's $21.9 Million Wine Auction," *Wine Spectator*, May 24, 2016, https://www
.winespectator.com/articles/sothebys-koch-53198.

2.   Frederik Balfour, "Mystery Owner's Wine Collection Draws $29.8 Million at Auction," *Bloomberg*, March 29, 2019, https://www
.bloomberg.com/news/articles/2019-03-29/mystery-owner-to-sell
-26-million-of-wine-at-hong-kong-auction.

3.   *Report on the Economic Well-Being of U.S. Households in 2018*, Federal Reserve, May 2019, https://www.federalreserve.gov/publications/files
/2018-report-economic-well-being-us-households-201905.pdf.

4.   Robert Frank, "Bottle of Wine Sells for a Record $558,000," CNBC, November 15, 2018, https://www.cnbc.com/2018/10/15/bottle-of
-wine-sells-for-record-breaking-558000.html.

5.   Arion McNicoll, "Move Over Abramovich: Meet 'Azzam,' the World's Largest, Fastest Superyacht," CNN, July 18, 2013, https://www.cnn
.com/travel/article/move-over-abramovich-azzam/index.html.

6.   Julie Reynolds, "How Many Palm Beach Mansions Does a Wall Street Tycoon Need?," *The Nation*, September 27, 2017, https://www
.thenation.com/article/how-many-palm-beach-mansions-does-a
-wall-street-tycoon-need/.

7.   Julie Reynolds, "The Man Behind the Curtain, Part 1," *News Matters*, https://dfmworkers.org/the-man-behind-the-curtain/.

8.   "2019 AHAR: Part 1—PIT Estimates of Homelessness in the U.S.," Department of Housing and Urban Development, January 2020, https://www.hudexchange.info/resource/5948/2019-ahar-part-1
-pit-estimates-of-homelessness-in-the-us/.

9.   Richard White, *Railroaded*, 2012, p. 517.

10.   Richard White, *The Republic for Which It Stands*, 2019, p. 478.

11.   Ibid., p. 529.

12.   Scott Martelle, *Blood Passion*, 2008.

13.   White, *The Republic for Which It Stands*, p. 531.

14. Charles P. Kindleberger and Robert Aliber, *Manias, Panics, and Crashes*, 2005.

15. Robert A. Rosenblatt, "GAO Estimates Final Cost of S&L; Bailout at $480.9 Billion," *Los Angeles Times*, July 13, 1996, https://www.latimes.com/archives/la-xpm-1996-07-13-fi-23615-story.html; Bureau of Labor Statistics inflation calculator, https://www.bls.gov/data/inflation_calculator.htm.

16. Chris Alden, "Looking Back on the Crash," *The Guardian*, March 10, 2005, https://www.theguardian.com/technology/2005/mar/10/newmedia.media.

17. Jared Bernstein, "The Jobless Recovery," Economic Policy Institute, March 25, 2003, https://www.epi.org/publication/issuebriefs_ib186/.

18. Matthieu Royer, "Collateralized Debt Obligations—an Overview," Professional Risk Managers International Association, http://www.staff.city.ac.uk/~pilbeam/CDOsexplained1.pdf.

19. Michael Lewis, *The Big Short*, 2010.

20. Michael Powell, "Bank Accused of Pushing Mortgage Deals on Blacks," *New York Times*, June 6, 2009, https://www.nytimes.com/2009/06/07/us/07baltimore.html.

21. Federal Reserve Bank of St. Louis data tool FRED, series on residential investment, https://fred.stlouisfed.org/series/A011RE1Q156NBEA.

22. Ben S. Bernanke, "The Crisis as a Classic Financial Panic," Speech at Fourteenth Jacques Polak Annual Research Conference, November 2013, https://www.federalreserve.gov/newsevents/speech/bernanke20131108a.htm.

23. Adam Tooze, *Crashed*, 2017.

24. Bureau of Labor Statistics, data series on civilian unemployment rate, https://www.bls.gov/charts/employment-situation/civilian-unemployment-rate.htm.

25. Ryan Cooper and Matt Bruenig, "Foreclosed: Destruction of Black Wealth During the Obama Presidency," *People's Policy Project*, 2017, https://www.peoplespolicyproject.org/wp-content/uploads/2017/12/Foreclosed.pdf.

26. Reed Hundt, *A Crisis Wasted*, 2019, pp. 206–207.

27. Tommy Andres, "Divided Decade: How the Financial Crisis

Changed Housing," *Marketplace*, December 17, 2018, https://www
.marketplace.org/2018/12/17/what-we-learned-housing/.

28. David Dayen, *Chain of Title*, 2016.

29. Department of Justice, Municipal Bonds Investigation 2014, https://
www.justice.gov/atr/division-update/2014/municipal-bonds
-investigation; Department of Justice press release, "Deutsche Bank
Agrees to Pay $7.2 Billion for Misleading Investors in Its Sale of Res-
idential Mortgage-Backed Securities," January 17, 2017, https://www
.justice.gov/opa/pr/deutsche-bank-agrees-pay-72-billion-misleading
-investors-its-sale-residential-mortgage-backed; Securities and Exchange Commission press release, "Goldman Sachs to Pay Record $550
Million to Settle SEC Charges Related to Subprime Mortgage CDO,"
July 15, 2010, https://www.sec.gov/news/press/2010/2010-123.htm.

30. Department of Justice press release, "HSBC Holdings Plc. and HSBC
Bank USA N.A. Admit to Anti-Money Laundering and Sanctions
Violations, Forfeit $1.256 Billion in Deferred Prosecution Agree-
ment," December 11, 2012, https://www.justice.gov/opa/pr/hsbc
-holdings-plc-and-hsbc-bank-usa-na-admit-anti-money-laundering
-and-sanctions-violations.

31. Michael R. Crittenden, "Lawmakers Demand Docs over 'Too Big
to Jail' Banks," *Wall Street Journal*, March 10, 2013, https://www.wsj
.com/articles/BL-WB-37966.

32. Securities and Exchange Commission press release, "Wells Fargo
to Pay $500 Million for Misleading Investors About the Success of
Its Largest Business Unit," February 21, 2020, https://www.sec.gov
/news/press-release/2020-38.

33. Federal Reserve Bank of St. Louis data tool FRED, series on private
investment, https://fred.stlouisfed.org/series/A011RE1Q156NBEA.

34. Zachary D. Carter, "Obama's $400,000 Wall Street Speech
Is Completely in Character," *HuffPost*, April 26, 2017, https://
www.huffpost.com/entry/obama-wall-street-speech-400k_n
_5900bf16e4b0af6d718ab7b9; Ryan Dezember, "Former Trea-
sury Secretary Timothy Geithner Is Now a Private-Equity Firm
Executive," *Wall Street Journal*, April 6, 2018, https://www.wsj.com
/articles/former-treasury-secretary-timothy-geithner-is-now-a
-buyout-firm-executive-1523021400.

35. Bowles, *Tomorrow Without Fear*, p. 21.

36. David Cannadine, *Mellon: An American Life*, 2006.

37. Bill Dupor, "The Recovery Act of 2009 vs. FDR's New Deal: Which Was Bigger?," Federal Reserve Bank of St. Louis, February 10, 2017, https://www.stlouisfed.org/publications/regional-economist/first _quarter_2017/the-recovery-act-of-2009-vs-fdrs-new-deal-which -was-bigger.

38. Jason Scott Smith, *A Concise History of the New Deal*, 2014.

39. Claude Fischer, "Labor's Laboring Effort," *Berkeley Blog*, September 9, 2010, https://blogs.berkeley.edu/2010/09/09/labor%E2%80%99s -laboring-effort/.

40. *America Builds: The Record of PWA*, 1939, p. 27, https://archive.org /details/americabuilds00unitrich/page/n5/mode/2up.

41. Ibid., p. 8; Erick Trickey, "The Grand Coulee Powers On, 75 Years After Its First Surge of Electricity," *Smithsonian Magazine*, March 22, 2016, https://www.smithsonianmag.com/history/grand-coulee -powers-75-years-after-its-first-surge-electricity-180958524/?no-ist.

42. "WPA Pays Up and Quits," *New York Times*, July 1, 1943.

43. *Census of Agriculture*, 1940, p. 22, https://web.archive.org/web /20200816172323/http://usda.mannlib.cornell.edu/usda /AgCensusImages/1940/03/01/1270/Table-01.pdf.

44. Theodore Saloutos, "New Deal Agricultural Policy: An Evaluation," *Journal of American History* 61, no. 2 (September 1974): 394–416, https://www.jstor.org/stable/1903955?seq=1.

45. White, *The Republic for Which It Stands*, p. 478.

46. Doris Goodwin, "The Way We Won: America's Economic Breakthrough During World War II," *American Prospect*, December 19, 2001, https:// prospect.org/health/way-won-america-s-economic-breakthrough -world-war-ii/.

47. Rauchway, *Winter War*, p. 5.

48. Sean Fleming, "US Life Expectancy Is Falling—Here's Why," World Economic Forum, January 2, 2020, https://www.weforum.org/agenda /2020/01/us-life-expectancy-decline/.

49. William Cronon, *Nature's Metropolis*, 1992, pp. 109–118.

Chapter 6: The Broken American Labor System

1. Federal Reserve Bank of St. Louis data tool FRED, series on hours worked, https://fred.stlouisfed.org/series/B4701C0A222NBEA; OECD

data series on hours worked, https://data.oecd.org/emp/hours-worked .htm.

2. "Maternity and Paternity at Work," International Labour Organization, 2014, https://www.ilo.org/wcmsp5/groups/public/—dgreports/—dcomm/—publ/documents/publication/wcms_242615.pdf.

3. Lyman Stone, "How Many Kids Do Women Want?," Institute for Family Studies, June 1, 2018, https://ifstudies.org/blog/how-many -kids-do-women-want.

4. Timothy W. Martin, "The Champions of the 401(k) Lament the Revolution They Started," *Wall Street Journal*, January 2, 2017, https://www.wsj.com/articles/the-champions-of-the-401-k-lament -the-revolution-they-started-1483382348.

5. Dan Caplinger, "Does Social Security Still Have a Minimum Benefit?," *Motley Fool*, March 3, 2019, https://www.fool.com/retirement /2019/03/03/does-social-security-still-have-a-minimum-benefit .aspx.

6. Robert Argento, Victoria L. Bryant, and John Sabelhaus, "Early Withdrawals from Retirement Accounts During the Great Recession," Federal Reserve, https://www.federalreserve.gov/pubs/feds /2013/201322/201322pap.pdf.

7. OECD data series on labor force participation rate, https://data.oecd .org/emp/labour-force-participation-rate.htm.

8. Deborah Thorne et al., "Graying of U.S. Bankruptcy: Fallout from Life in a Risk Society," Indiana Legal Studies Research Paper No. 406, August 2018, https://papers.ssrn.com/sol3/papers.cfm ?abstract_id=3226574.

9. "For How Long Are Workers Guaranteed Paid Sick Leave?," WORLD Policy Analysis Center, 2019, https://worldpolicycenter .org/policies/for-how-long-are-workers-guaranteed-paid-sick -leave.

10. "California Paid Sick Leave: Frequently Asked Questions," California Department of Industrial Relations, March 2017, https://www .dir.ca.gov/dlse/Paid_Sick_Leave.htm; David J. Santeusanio and Stephanie M. Merabet, "Paid Family and Medical Leave Benefits Available to Massachusetts Employees on Jan. 1, 2021," *Holland & Knight Alert*, December 21, 2020, https://www.hklaw.com/en /insights/publications/2020/12/paid-family-and-medical-leave -benefits-available-to-massachusetts; "Sickness Benefit (Sykepenger)

for Employees," *Nav*, August 12, 2020, https://www.nav.no/en/home /benefits-and-services/Sickness-benefit-for-employees.

11. Melissa Linebaugh, "How Much in Social Security Disability Benefits Can You Get?," *NOLO*, https://www.nolo.com/legal-encyclopedia /how-much-social-security-disability-ssdi-benefits-can-you-get .html.

12. Beatrice Adler-Bolton, "Fighting for Disability Benefits," *Sick Note*, March 9, 2021, https://www.sicknote.co/p/guest-post-fighting-for -disability.

13. Matt Bruenig, "The Best Way to Eradicate Poverty: Welfare Not Jobs," *People's Policy Project*, September 18, 2018, https://www .peoplespolicyproject.org/2018/09/18/the-best-way-to-eradicate -poverty-welfare-not-jobs/.

14. "Employee Benefits in the United States Summary," Bureau of Labor Statistics, September 24, 2020, https://www.bls.gov/news.release /ebs2.nr0.htm.

15. "There's a New Holiday Act on Its Way," *Azets*, https://www.azets .dk/eng/news/new_holiday_act/; "Denmark—Sickness Benefit," European Commission, https://ec.europa.eu/social/main.jsp?catId =1107&langId=en&intPageId=4489.

16. Matt Bruenig, "Family Fun Pack," *People's Policy Project*, 2019, https:// www.peoplespolicyproject.org/projects/family-fun-pack/.

17. Emily Brandon, "How Much You Will Get from Social Security," *US News* & *World Report*, January 11, 2021, https://money.usnews.com /money/retirement/social-security/articles/how-much-you-will-get -from-social-security.

18. "Benefit Calculation Examples for Workers Retiring in 2021," Social Security Administration, https://www.ssa.gov/OACT/ProgData /retirebenefit2.html.

19. Nicholas Kristof, "Profiting from a Child's Illiteracy," *New York Times*, December 7, 2012, https://www.nytimes.com/2012/12 /09/opinion/sunday/kristof-profiting-from-a-childs-illiteracy .html.

20. "Selected Data from Social Security's Disability Program," Social Security Administration, https://www.ssa.gov/OACT/STATS /dibStat.html.

21. David Card, Jochen Kluve, and Andrea Weber, "What Works? A

Meta Analysis of Recent Active Labor Market Program Evaluations," *Journal of the European Economic Association* 16, no. 3 (June 2018): 894–931, https://academic.oup.com/jeea/article-abstract/16/3/894/4430618?redirectedFrom=fulltext.

22. "The Recession of 2007–2009," Bureau of Labor Statistics, February 2012, https://www.bls.gov/spotlight/2012/recession/pdf/recession_bls_spotlight.pdf.

23. Bureau of Labor Statistics, data series on construction employment, https://data.bls.gov/timeseries/CES2000000001?amp%253bdata_tool=XGtable&output_view=data&include_graphs=true.

24. "Focus on Productivity: Construction Industries," Bureau of Labor Statistics, https://www.bls.gov/lpc/construction.htm.

25. OECD data series on tax revenue, https://data.oecd.org/tax/tax-revenue.htm.

26. "Child Care Costs in the United States," Economic Policy Institute, https://www.epi.org/child-care-costs-in-the-united-states/; Liz Hamel et al., "The Burden of Medical Debt: Results from the Kaiser Family Foundation/New York Times Medical Bills Survey," Kaiser Family Foundation, January 5, 2016, https://www.kff.org/health-costs/report/the-burden-of-medical-debt-results-from-the-kaiser-family-foundationnew-york-times-medical-bills-survey/; Zack Friedman, "Student Loan Debt Statistics in 2021: A Record $1.7 Trillion," *Forbes*, February 20, 2021, https://www.forbes.com/sites/zackfriedman/2021/02/20/student-loan-debt-statistics-in-2021-a-record-17-trillion/.

27. Steven Pinker, *The Better Angels of Our Nature*, 2011.

28. John Maynard Keynes, "The Economic Possibilities of Our Grandchildren," in *Essays in Persuasion*, 2009, pp. 199, 201.

Chapter 7: The Hell of American Healthcare

1. Sarah Kliff and Jessica Silver-Greenberg, "How Rich Hospitals Profit from Patients in Car Crashes," *New York Times*, February 1, 2021, https://www.nytimes.com/2021/02/01/upshot/rich-hospitals-profit-poor.html.

2. Anna Almendrala, "The Air Ambulance Billed More Than His Surgeon Did for a Lung Transplant," *Kaiser Health News*, November 6, 2019, https://khn.org/news/the-air-ambulance-billed-more-than-his-surgeon-did-for-a-lung-transplant/.

3. Elizabeth Lawrence, "Veteran's Appendectomy Launches Excruciating Months-Long Battle over Bill," *Kaiser Health News*, August 25, 2020, https://khn.org/news/bill-of-the-month-veteran-appendectomy-complication-long-battle-over-bill/.

4. David U. Himmelstein et al., "Medical Bankruptcy: Still Common Despite the Affordable Care Act," *American Journal of Public Health* 109, no. 3 (February 6, 2019): 431–433, https://ajph.aphapublications.org/doi/10.2105/AJPH.2018.304901?eType=EmailBlastContent&eId=a5697b7e-8ffc-4373-b9d2-3eb745d9debb&amp.

5. OECD data series on health spending, https://data.oecd.org/healthres/health-spending.htm; Federal Reserve Bank of St. Louis data tool FRED, series on real GDP, https://fred.stlouisfed.org/series/GDPC1/.

6. "National Health Expenditures 2019 Highlights," Centers for Medicare and Medicaid Services, https://www.cms.gov/files/document/highlights.pdf.

7. Irene Papanicolas, Liana R. Woskie, and Ashish K. Jha, "Health Care Spending in the United States and Other High-Income Countries," *Journal of the American Medical Association* 319, no. 10 (March 13, 2018): 1024–1039, https://jamanetwork.com/journals/jama/article-abstract/2674671.

8. Ibid.

9. OECD data series on life expectancy at birth, https://data.oecd.org/healthstat/life-expectancy-at-birth.htm.

10. Fleming, "US Life Expectancy Is Falling—Here's Why."

11. OECD data series on infant mortality rates, https://data.oecd.org/healthstat/infant-mortality-rates.htm; Papanicolas et al., "Health Care Spending in the United States and Other High-Income Countries."

12. Sarah Kliff and Margot Sanger-Katz, "Bottleneck for U.S. Coronavirus Response: The Fax Machine," *New York Times*, July 13, 2020, https://www.nytimes.com/2020/07/13/upshot/coronavirus-response-fax-machines.html.

13. Dean Baker, "The Problem of Doctors' Salaries," *Politico*, October 25, 2017, https://www.politico.com/agenda/story/2017/10/25/doctors-salaries-pay-disparities-000557/.

14. Rabah Kamal and Cynthia Cox, "How Do Healthcare Prices and Use in the U.S. Compare to Other Countries?," *Health System Tracker*,

May 8, 2018, https://www.healthsystemtracker.org/chart-collection/how-do-healthcare-prices-and-use-in-the-u-s-compare-to-other-countries/.

15. Melanie Evans, "What Does Knee Surgery Cost? Few Know, and That's a Problem," *Wall Street Journal*, August 21, 2018, https://www.wsj.com/articles/what-does-knee-surgery-cost-few-know-and-thats-a-problem-1534865358.

16. Ge Bai and Gerard F. Anderson, "Extreme Markup: The Fifty US Hospitals with the Highest Charge-to-Cost Ratios," *Health Affairs*, June 2015, https://www.healthaffairs.org/doi/full/10.1377/hlthaff.2014.1414.

17. "Note Exempt Items, Taxpayers Are Told; Some Gifts, Life Insurance and Veterans' Pensions on List," *New York Times*, January 16, 1943, https://www.nytimes.com/1943/01/16/archives/note-exempt-items-taxpayers-are-told-some-gifts-life-insurance-and.html.

18. "Federal Subsidies for Health Insurance Coverage for People Under Age 65: 2018 to 2028," Congressional Budget Office, May 2018, https://www.cbo.gov/system/files/2018-06/53826-healthinsurancecoverage.pdf.

19. "Origins and Evolution of Employment-Based Health Benefits," in M. J. Field and H. J. Shapiro (eds.), *Employment and Health Benefits: A Connection at Risk*, 1993, https://www.ncbi.nlm.nih.gov/books/NBK235989/.

20. Ibid.

21. Ezekiel J. Emanuel, *Reinventing American Health Care*, 2014.

22. Louise Norris, "Understanding the ACA's Subsidy Cliff," *Verywell Health*, January 24, 2021, https://www.verywellhealth.com/aca-subsidy-cliff-4770899.

23. Lauren Clason, Emily Kopp, and Mary Ellen McIntire, "Ten Years into Obamacare, Cost and Access Issues Abound," *Roll Call*, March 10, 2020, https://www.rollcall.com/2020/03/10/ten-years-into-obamacare-cost-and-access-issues-abound/.

24. Jon Walker, "Fixing the ACA Exchanges Only Makes Them Worse," *People's Policy Project*, April 4, 2018, https://www.peoplespolicyproject.org/2018/04/04/fixing-the-aca-exchanges-only-makes-them-worse/.

25. Brooks Jackson, "CBO's Obamacare Predictions: How Accurate?,"

FactCheck.org, March 13, 2017, https://www.factcheck.org/2017/03 /cbos-obamacare-predictions-how-accurate/.

26. Rachel Garfield, Kendal Orgera, and Anthony Damico, "The Coverage Gap: Uninsured Poor Adults in States That Do Not Expand Medicaid," Kaiser Family Foundation, January 21, 2021, https:// www.kff.org/medicaid/issue-brief/the-coverage-gap-uninsured -poor-adults-in-states-that-do-not-expand-medicaid/.

27. Joan Biskupic, "The Inside Story of How John Roberts Negotiated to Save Obamacare," CNN, March 25, 2019, https://www.cnn.com /2019/03/21/politics/john-roberts-obamacare-the-chief/index .html.

28. Jon Walker, "The Almost Big F*cking Deal in the COVID Relief Bill," *American Prospect*, March 9, 2021, https://prospect.org/health /covid-relief-bill-health-insurance-subsidy-cliff/.

29. "2020 Employer Health Benefits Survey," Kaiser Family Foundation, October 8, 2020, https://www.kff.org/report-section/ehbs-2020 -summary-of-findings/.

30. Ibid.

31. Donna Rosato, "How Paying Your Doctor in Cash Could Save You Money," *Consumer Reports*, May 4, 2018, https://www.consumerreports .org/healthcare-costs/how-paying-your-doctor-in-cash-could-save -you-money/.

32. Paul Kane and Rachel Bade, "'I'm Agnostic': Pelosi Questions Whether Medicare-for-All Can Deliver Benefits of Obamacare," *Washington Post*, April 4, 2019, https://www.washingtonpost.com /politics/im-agnostic-pelosi-questions-whether-medicare-for -all-can-deliver-benefits-of-obamacare/2019/04/04 /fe2942c0-56ed-11e9-aa83-504f086bf5d6_story.html?utm_term =.91064f4bbfe0.

33. Paul Krugman, "What's Next for Progressives?," *New York Times*, August 7, 2017, https://www.nytimes.com/2017/08/07/opinion /healthcare-single-payer-children.html.

34. Jonathan Chait, "Bernie Sanders's Bill Gets America Zero Percent Closer to Single Payer," *Intelligencer*, September 13, 2017, https:// nymag.com/intelligencer/2017/09/sanderss-bill-gets-u-s-zero -percent-closer-to-single-payer.html.

35. Elizabeth Austic et al., "Insurance Churning," University of Michigan Center for Healthcare Research and Transformation, Novem-

ber 2016, https://poverty.umich.edu/research-publications/policy
-briefs/insurance-churning/.

36. "November 2020 Medicaid & CHIP Enrollment Data Highlights," Medicaid.gov, https://www.medicaid.gov/medicaid/program
-information/medicaid-and-chip-enrollment-data/report-highlights
/index.html.

37. Daniel McDermott, Cynthia Cox, Robin Rudowitz, and Rachel
Garfield, "How Has the Pandemic Affected Health Coverage in
the U.S.?," Kaiser Family Foundation, December 9, 2020, https://
www.kff.org/policy-watch/how-has-the-pandemic-affected-health
-coverage-in-the-u-s/.

38. Matt Bruenig, "New Poll Finds Voters Strongly Oppose Employer Insurance," *People's Policy Project*, October 24, 2019, https://
www.peoplespolicyproject.org/2019/10/24/new-poll-finds-voters
-strongly-oppose-employer-insurance/.

39. Leila Fadel et al., "As Hospitals Lose Revenue, More Than a Million Health Care Workers Lose Jobs," NPR, May 8, 2020, https://
www.npr.org/2020/05/08/852435761/as-hospitals-lose-revenue
-thousands-of-health-care-workers-face-furloughs-layoff.

40. Matt Bruenig, "Medicare for America Will Force People Off Their
Insurance," *People's Policy Project*, March 21, 2019, https://www
.peoplespolicyproject.org/2019/03/21/medicare-for-america-will
-force-people-off-their-insurance/.

41. Scott Simon and Heidi Glenn, "'Just the Right Policy': Pete Buttigieg
on His 'Medicare for All Who Want It' Plan," NPR, November 8,
2019, https://www.npr.org/2019/11/08/774716877/just-the-right
-policy-pete-buttigieg-on-his-medicare-for-all-who-want-it-plan.

42. Jon Walker, "Biden Wants to Expand the ACA. Blue States Can't Figure Out How to Run It in the First Place," *The Intercept*, March 6, 2020,
https://theintercept.com/2020/03/06/biden-campaign-health-care
-platform-affordable-care-act/.

43. Fred Schulte, David Donald, and Erin Durkin, "Why Medicare Advantage Costs Taxpayers Billions More Than It Should," Center for Public Integrity, January 14, 2015, https://publicintegrity.org/health/why
-medicare-advantage-costs-taxpayers-billions-more-than-it-should/.

44. "A Life-Saving Hepatitis C Cure with an $84,000 Price Tag,"
BBC News, July 22, 2014, https://www.bbc.com/news/blogs
-echochambers-28429585.

45. "Imagining the Post-Antibiotics Future," *FERNnews*, November 20, 2013, https://medium.com/@fernnews/imagining-the-post-antibiotics-future-892b57499e77.

46. Godfrey S. Bbosa et al., "Antibiotics/Antibacterial Drug Use, Their Marketing and Promotion During the Post-Antibiotic Golden Age and Their Role in Emergence of Bacterial Resistance," *Health* 6, no. 5 (February 2014), http://dx.doi.org/10.4236/health.2014.65059.

47. Lawrence Wright, "The Plague Year," *New Yorker*, December 28, 2020, https://www.newyorker.com/magazine/2021/01/04/the-plague-year.

48. Uwe Reinhardt, "The Pricing of U.S. Hospital Services: Chaos Behind a Veil of Secrecy," *Health Affairs* 25, no. 1 (January/February 2006), https://www.healthaffairs.org/doi/10.1377/hlthaff.25.1.57.

49. Matt Bruenig, "US Workers Are Highly Taxed When You Count Health Premiums," *People's Policy Project*, April 8, 2019, https://www.peoplespolicyproject.org/2019/04/08/us-workers-are-highly-taxed-when-you-count-health-premiums/.

50. *Our Care 2019*, Veterans of Foreign Wars, September 2019, https://vfworg-cdn.azureedge.net/-/media/VFWSite/Files/Advocacy/VFW-Our-Care-2019.pdf.

Chapter 8: The Social Climate

1. Neela Banerjee, John H. Cushman Jr., David Hasemyer, and Lisa Song, *Exxon: The Road Not Taken*, 2015, https://insideclimatenews.org/content/Exxon-The-Road-Not-Taken.

2. "CO_2 Emissions from the USSR," U.S. Department of Energy Carbon Dioxide Information Analysis Center, https://cdiac.ess-dive.lbl.gov/trends/emis/usr.html.

3. Philip Micklin, "The Aral Sea Disaster," *Annual Review of Earth and Planetary Sciences*, May 30, 2007, https://www.annualreviews.org/doi/abs/10.1146/annurev.earth.35.031306.140120.

4. Adam Voiland, "Methane Matters," *Earth Observatory*, March 8, 2016, https://earthobservatory.nasa.gov/features/MethaneMatters.

5. Piers Forster et al., "Changes in Atmospheric Constituents and in Radiative Forcing," Intergovernmental Panel on Climate Change,

2018, https://www.ipcc.ch/site/assets/uploads/2018/02/ar4-wg1 -chapter2-1.pdf.

6. Qiancheng Ma, "Greenhouse Gases: Refining the Role of Carbon Dioxide," Goddard Institute for Space Studies, March 1998, https:// web.archive.org/web/20210306193037/https://www.giss.nasa.gov /research/briefs/ma_01/.

7. Michael Mann et al., "Influence of Anthropogenic Climate Change on Planetary Wave Resonance and Extreme Weather Events," *Scientific Reports*, March 27, 2017, https://www.nature.com/articles /srep45242.

8. Ian Joughin, Benjamin E. Smith, and Brooke Medley, "Marine Ice Sheet Collapse Potentially Under Way for the Thwaites Glacier Basin, West Antarctica," *Science*, May 16, 2014, https://science.sciencemag .org/content/344/6185/735; Pierre Deschamps et al., "Ice-Sheet Collapse and Sea-Level Rise at the Bølling Warming 14,600 Years Ago," *Nature*, 483 (March 2012): 559–564, https://www.nature.com /articles/nature10902.

9. Steven C. Sherwood and Matthew Huber, "An Adaptability Limit to Climate Change Due to Heat Stress," *Proceedings of the National Academy of Sciences*, May 25, 2010, https://www.pnas.org/content/107/21/9552.

10. Gerard D. McCarthy et al., "Atlantic Meridional Overturning Circulation," *MCCIP Science Review*, 2017, http://mural.maynoothuniversity .ie/12060/.

11. William D. Nordhaus and Andrew Moffat, "A Survey of Global Impacts of Climate Change: Replication, Survey Methods, and a Statistical Analysis," Cowles Foundation for Research in Economics, July 2017, https://cowles.yale.edu/sites/default/files/files/pub/d20/d2096.pdf.

12. William Nordhaus, "Revisiting the Social Cost of Carbon," *Proceedings of the National Academy of Sciences*, January 31, 2017, https://www .pnas.org/content/early/2017/01/30/1609244114.

13. Rebecca Lindsey, "Climate Change: Atmospheric Carbon Dioxide," National Oceanic and Atmospheric Administration, August 14, 2020, https://www.climate.gov/news-features /understanding-climate/climate-change-atmospheric-carbon -dioxide; NOAA Mauna Loa data series, "Trends in Atmospheric Carbon Dioxide," https://www.esrl.noaa.gov/gmd/ccgg/trends/; William Nordhaus, "Projections and Uncertainties About Climate Change in an Era of Minimal Climate Policies," *American Economic*

Journal 10, no. 3 (2018): 333–360, https://pubs.aeaweb.org/doi /pdfplus/10.1257/pol.20170046.

14.   Christopher B. Field et al., "Climate Change 2014: Impacts, Adaptation, and Vulnerability," Intergovernmental Panel on Climate Change, 2014, p. 14, https://www.ipcc.ch/site/assets/uploads/2018 /02/ar5_wgII_spm_en.pdf.

15.   Nordhaus and Moffat, "A Survey of Global Impacts of Climate Change."

16.   "GDP, Current Prices," 2020 data, International Monetary Fund, https://www.imf.org/external/datamapper/NGDPD@WEO /OEMDC/ADVEC/WEOWORLD/AFQ.

17.   Stephen Schneider, "What Is the Probability of 'Dangerous' Climate Change," *Understanding and Solving the Climate Change Problem*, https://stephenschneider.stanford.edu/Climate/Climate_Impacts /WhatIsTheProbability.html.

18.   Trevor Houser and Hannah Pitt, "Preliminary US Emissions Estimates for 2019," Rhodium Group, January 7, 2020, https://rhg.com /research/preliminary-us-emissions-2019/.

19.   "France Carbon (CO2) Emissions 1960–2021," *MacroTrends*, https:// www.macrotrends.net/countries/FRA/france/carbon-co2-emissions; Federal Reserve Bank of St. Louis data tool FRED, series on French GDP per capita, https://fred.stlouisfed.org/series/NYGDPPCAPKDFRA.

20.   "Denmark—CO2 Emissions per Capita," Knoema, https://knoema .com/atlas/Denmark/CO2-emissions-per-capita; Federal Reserve Bank of St. Louis data tool FRED, series on Danish GDP per capita, https://fred.stlouisfed.org/series/NYGDPPCAPKDDNK.

21.   "Special Report: Global Warming of 1.5 °C," Intergovernmental Panel on Climate Change, 2018, https://www.ipcc.ch/sr15/.

22.   "Energy and the Environment Explained: Where Greenhouse Gases Come From," U.S. Energy Information Administration, 2020, https://www.eia.gov/energyexplained/energy-and-the-environment /where-greenhouse-gases-come-from.php; "Draft Inventory of U.S. Greenhouse Gas Emissions and Sinks: 1990–2019," U.S. Environmental Protection Agency, https://www.epa.gov/ghgemissions/draft -inventory-us-greenhouse-gas-emissions-and-sinks-1990-2019.

23.   Hannah Ritchie, "Sector by Sector: Where Do Global Greenhouse Gas Emissions Come From?," *Our World in Data*, September 18, 2020, https://ourworldindata.org/ghg-emissions-by-sector.

24. U.S. Environmental Protection Agency, "Global Greenhouse Gas Emissions Data," https://www.epa.gov/ghgemissions/global-green house-gas-emissions-data.

25. "Electricity Explained: Electricity Generation, Capacity, and Sales in the United States," U.S. Energy Information Administration, https://www.eia.gov/energyexplained/electricity/electricity-in-the -us-generation-capacity-and-sales.php.

26. Marcy de Luna and Amanda Drane, "What Went Wrong with the Texas Power Grid?," *Houston Chronicle*, February 16, 2021, https:// www.houstonchronicle.com/business/energy/article/Wholesale -power-prices-spiking-across-Texas-15951684.php.

27. David Chandler, "Explaining the Plummeting Cost of Solar Power," *MIT News*, November 20, 2018, http://news.mit.edu/2018 /explaining-dropping-solar-cost-1120.

28. Anil Markandya and Paul Wilkinson, "Electricity Generation and Health," *The Lancet*, September 15, 2007, https://www.thelancet.com /journals/lancet/article/PIIS0140-6736(07)61253-7/fulltext.

29. Diane Cardwell and Jonathan Soblem, "Westinghouse Files for Bankruptcy, in Blow to Nuclear Power," *New York Times*, March 29, 2017, https://www.nytimes.com/2017/03/29/business/westinghouse -toshiba-nuclear-bankruptcy.html.

30. Robert Hargraves and Ralph Moir, "Liquid Fluoride Thorium Reactors: An Old Idea in Nuclear Power Gets Reexamined," *American Scientist* 98, no. 4 (July–August 2010): 304–313, https://www.jstor .org/stable/27859537.

31. Ibid.

32. Robin Cowan, "Nuclear Power Reactors: A Study in Technological Lock-in," *Journal of Economic History* 50, no. 3 (September 1990): 541–567, https://www.jstor.org/stable/2122817.

33. Kevin Bullis, "Can ARPA-E Solve Energy Problems?," *Technology Review*, March 5, 2012, https://www.technologyreview.com/2012/03 /05/187280/can-arpa-e-solve-energy-problems/.

34. Mahesh Venkataraman et al., "Zero-Carbon Steel Making: The Opportunities and Role of Australia in Nurturing a 'Green Steel' Industry," Energy Change Institute, December 19, 2019, https://energy.anu.edu .au/files/green_steel_working_paper_Complete%20Dec%202019.pdf.

35. *Technology Roadmap—Low-Carbon Transition in the Cement Industry*, International Energy Agency, April 2018, https://www.iea.org

/reports/technology-roadmap-low-carbon-transition-in-the-cement
-industry.

36. Takayuki Higuchi et al., "Development of a New Ecological Concrete with CO_2 Emissions Below Zero," *Construction and Building Materials* 67 (September 30, 2014): 338–343, https://www.sciencedirect.com/science/article/abs/pii/S0950061814000531.

37. Tabbi Wilberforce et al., "Outlook of Carbon Capture Technology and Challenges," *Science of the Total Environment*, 657 (March 20, 2019): 56–72, https://www.sciencedirect.com/science/article/abs/pii/S004896971834779X.

38. "Transit Street Design Guide," National Association of City Transportation Officials, https://nacto.org/publication/transit-street-design-guide/introduction/why/designing-move-people/; Christopher MacKechnie, "What Is the Passenger Capacity of Different Modes of Transit?," *liveaboutdotcom*, January 25, 2019, https://www.liveabout.com/passenger-capacity-of-transit-2798765; Dan Zhou et al, "Estimating Capacity of Bicycle Path on Urban Roads in Hangzhou, China," 94th Annual Meeting of the Transportation Research Board, 2015, https://nacto.org/wp-content/uploads/2016/04/5_Zhou-Xu-Wang-and-Sheng-Estimating-Capacity-of-Bicycle-Path-on-Urban-Roads-in-Hangzhou-China_2014.pdf.

39. "NHTSA Releases 2019 Crash Fatality Data," National Highway Traffic Safety Administration, December 18, 2020, https://www.nhtsa.gov/press-releases/roadway-fatalities-2019-fars.

40. Aaron Gordon, "Zombie Miles and Napa Weekends: How a Week with Chauffeurs Showed the Major Flaw in Our Self-Driving Car Future," *Jalopnik*, November 15, 2017, https://jalopnik.com/zombie-miles-and-napa-weekends-how-a-week-with-chauffe-1839648416.

41. Norman Garrick, "Burying a 1950s Planning Disaster," *Bloomberg CityLab*, September 1, 2016, https://www.bloomberg.com/news/articles/2016-09-01/burying-rochester-s-inner-loop-a-1950s-era-planning-disaster.

42. Eleonore Voisard, "Will This Be the First European City to Ban Cars?," *BBC Reel*, March 11, 2021, https://www.bbc.com/reel/video/p08n2hwl/will-this-be-the-first-european-city-to-ban-cars-.

43. Brady Seals and Andee Krasner, *Gas Stoves: Health and Air Quality Impacts and Solutions*, Rocky Mountain Institute, 2020, https://rmi.org/insight/gas-stoves-pollution-health.

44. OECD data series on municipal waste, generation, and treatment, 2018 figures, https://stats.oecd.org/Index.aspx?DataSetCode=MUNW.

45. Tim Dickinson, "Planet Plastic," *Rolling Stone*, March 3, 2020, https://www.rollingstone.com/culture/culture-features/plastic-problem-recycling-myth-big-oil-950957/.

46. Amory Lovins, "Reinventing Fire," Rocky Mountain Institute, 2014, https://rmi.org/insight/reinventing-fire/.

47. Cynthia C. Kelly, *The Manhattan Project*, 2020.

48. *World Resources Report: Creating a Sustainable Food Future*, World Resources Institute, July 2019, https://research.wri.org/wrr-food.

49. Vaclav Smil, *Feeding the World*, 2000.

50. Patrick Lloyd-Smith, "A Note on the Robustness of Aggregate Ecosystem Service Values," *Ecological Economics* 146 (April 2018): 778–780, https://www.sciencedirect.com/science/article/abs/pii/S0921800917310480.

51. Thomas P. Holmes et al., "A Synthesis of the Economic Values of Wilderness," *Journal of Forestry* 114, no. 3 (June 2015): 320–328, https://academic.oup.com/jof/article/114/3/320/4599815.

52. Hannah Ritchie and Max Roser, "Greenhouse Gas Emissions," *Our World in Data*, https://ourworldindata.org/greenhouse-gas-emissions.

53. Jacob Fawcett, "A Global Green New Deal for the Developing World," *People's Policy Project*, June 17, 2019, https://www.peoplespolicyproject.org/2019/06/17/global-green-new-deal-for-the-developing-world/.

54. "Fourth National Climate Assessment," U.S. Global Change Research Program, 2018, https://nca2018.globalchange.gov/.

Chapter 9: Inequality, Explained

1. Simon Kuznets, "Economic Growth and Income Inequality," *American Economic Review* 45, no. 1 (March 1955): 1–28, https://www.jstor.org/stable/1811581.

2. Binyamin Appelbaum, *The Economists' Hour*, 2019.

3. Thomas Piketty, *Capital and Ideology*, 2018, http://piketty.pse.ens.fr/files/ideology/pdf/F11.1.pdf.

4. Federal Reserve Bank of St. Louis data tool ALFRED, series on inflation-adjusted gross national income, https://alfred.stlouisfed.org/graph/?g=q9aK.

5. Emanuel Saez and Gabriel Zucman, *The Triumph of Injustice*, 2020.

6. Lawrence Mishel and Jori Kandra, "CEO Compensation Surged 14% in 2019 to $21.3 Million," Economic Policy Institute, August 18, 2020, https://www.epi.org/publication/ceo-compensation-surged -14-in-2019-to-21-3-million-ceos-now-earn-320-times-as-much-as-a -typical-worker/.

7. Emily Glazer and Christina Rexrode, "Wells Fargo CEO Testifies Before Senate Banking Committee," *Wall Street Journal*, September 20, 2016, https://www.wsj.com/articles/wells-fargo-ceo-testifies -before-senate-banking-committee-1474390303.

8. "JPMorgan Chase & Co.," *Wall Street Journal*, 2020, https://www.wsj .com/market-data/quotes/JPM/financials/annual/balance-sheet.

9. Sergei Klebnikov, "Jamie Dimon's Salary Rises to $31.5 Million in 2019, amid Record Bank Profits," *Forbes*, January 24, 2020, https:// www.forbes.com/sites/sergeiklebnikov/2020/01/24/jamie-dimons -salary-rises-to-315-million-in-2019-amid-record-bank-profits/.

10. Michelle F. Davis, "JPMorgan Keeps Dimon's Pay Steady at $31.5 Million for 2020," *Bloomberg*, January 21, 2021, https://www .bloomberg.com/news/articles/2021-01-21/jpmorgan-keeps-ceo -dimon-s-pay-steady-at-31-5-million-for-2020.

11. Matthew Sherman, "A Short History of Financial Deregulation in the United States," Center for Economic and Policy Research, July 2009, https://www.cepr.net/documents/publications/dereg -timeline-2009-07.pdf.

12. Thomas Philippon, "Has the US Finance Industry Become Less Efficient? On the Theory and Measurement of Financial Intermediation," *American Economic Review* 105, no. 4 (April 2015): 1408–1438, https:// www.aeaweb.org/articles?id=10.1257/aer.20120578.

13. "Division of Trading and Markets: Answers to Frequently Asked Questions Concerning Rule 10b-18 ('Safe Harbor' for Issuer Repurchases)," Securities and Exchange Commission, https://www.sec.gov /divisions/marketreg/r10b18faq0504.htm.

14. Joseph W. Gruber and Steven B. Kamin, "Corporate Buybacks and Capital Investment: An International Perspective," IFDP Notes, Federal Reserve, April 11, 2017, https://www.federalreserve.gov/econres /notes/ifdp-notes/corporate-buybacks-and-capital-investment-an -international-perspective-20170411.htm.

15. William Lazonick et al., "Financialization of the U.S. Pharmaceutical Industry," Institute for New Economic Thinking, December 2, 2019,

https://www.ineteconomics.org/perspectives/blog/financialization-us-pharma-industry.

16. William Lazonick, Mustafa Erdem Sakinç, and Matt Hopkins, "Why Stock Buybacks Are Dangerous for the Economy," *Harvard Business Review*, January 7, 2020, https://hbr.org/2020/01/why-stock-buybacks-are-dangerous-for-the-economy.

17. Irene Tung and Katy Milani, "Curbing Stock Buybacks: A Crucial Step to Raising Worker Pay and Reducing Inequality," Roosevelt Institute, July 31, 2018, https://rooseveltinstitute.org/curbing-stock-buybacks-crucial-step/.

18. Hugo Martin and Christine Mai-Duc, "JetBlue Cutting Legroom, Adding Checked-Bags Fee for Some Fliers," *Los Angeles Times*, November 19, 2014, https://www.latimes.com/business/la-fi-jetblue-bag-fees-legroom-20141120-story.html.

19. "The Labor Share of Income and Equilibrium Unemployment, Accessible Data," Federal Reserve, https://www.federalreserve.gov/econresdata/notes/feds-notes/2015/labor-share-of-income-and-equilibrium-unemployment-accessible-20150608.html#fig3.

20. Thomas Piketty, *Capital in the Twenty-First Century*, 2014, ch. 5.

21. Thomas Piketty, *Capital and Ideology*, p. 435.

22. Philippe Aghion, Peter Howitt, and Giovanni L. Violante, "General Purpose Technology and Wage Inequality," *Journal of Economic Growth* 7 (December 2002): 315–345, https://link.springer.com/article/10.1023/A:1020875717066.

23. Matt Bruenig, "Market Incomes Will Always Produce Hideous Inequality," *People's Policy Project*, March 28, 2019, https://www.peoplespolicyproject.org/2019/03/28/market-incomes-will-always-produce-hideous-inequality/.

24. Edward N. Wolff, "Household Wealth Trends in the United States, 1962 to 2016: Has Middle Class Wealth Recovered?," National Bureau of Economic Research, November 2017, https://www.nber.org/papers/w24085.

25. Matt Bruenig, "The Best Way to Eradicate Poverty: Welfare Not Jobs," *People's Policy Project*, September 18, 2019, https://www.peoplespolicyproject.org/2018/09/18/the-best-way-to-eradicate-poverty-welfare-not-jobs/.

26. OECD data series on collective bargaining, https://stats.oecd.org/Index.aspx?DataSetCode=CBC.

27. OECD data series on union membership, https://stats.oecd.org /Index.aspx?DataSetCode=TUD.

28. Ibid.

29. Gylfi Dalmann Aðalsteinsson and Þórhallur Örn Guðlaugsson, "Trade Union Density in Iceland," *Icelandic Review of Politics and Administration* 15, no. 1 (2019), http://www.irpa.is/article/view/a.2019.15.1.4.

30. Bernie Sanders, "Corporate Accountability and Democracy," https:// berniesanders.com/issues/corporate-accountability-and-democracy/.

31. Matt Bruenig, "Romney's Child Allowance Improves on Biden Proposal," *People's Policy Project*, February 4, 2021, https://www .peoplespolicyproject.org/2021/02/04/romneys-child-allowance -improves-on-biden-proposal/.

32. "Federal Individual Income Tax Rates History: Nominal Dollars," Tax Policy Center, https://files.taxfoundation.org/legacy/docs/fed _individual_rate_history_nominal.pdf; BLS Inflation Calculator, 1954 figures, https://www.bls.gov/data/inflation_calculator.htm.

33. Thomas Piketty, data series on wealth concentration, http://piketty .pse.ens.fr/files/ideology/pdf/F13.10.pdf.

34. Matt Bruenig, "Social Wealth Fund for America," *People's Policy Project*, 2018, https://www.peoplespolicyproject.org/projects/social -wealth-fund/.

35. Ibid.

36. Alaska Permanent Fund Corporation, https://apfc.org/.

37. "Summary of Dividend Application and Payments," Alaska Department of Revenue, https://pfd.alaska.gov/Division-Info/Summary-of -Applications-and-Payments.

38. "New Poll Results Confirm Widespread Support for Alaska's Permanent Fund Dividend," Omidyar Network, 2017, https://omidyar.com /news/new-poll-results-confirm-widespread-support-for-alaskas -permanent-fund-dividend/.

39. "National Income and Product Accounts," Bureau of Economic Analysis, https://apps.bea.gov/iTable/iTable.cfm?reqid=19&step =3&isuri=1&nipa_table_list=58&categories=survey.

40. "United States Quick Facts," U.S. Census Bureau, https://www .census.gov/quickfacts/fact/table/US/PST045219.

41. PK, "Income Percentile Calculator for the United States," *DQYDJ*, https://dqydj.com/income-percentile-calculator/.

42. Mike Konczal, "I Do Not Understand Why the Left Should Want a Sovereign Wealth Fund," *Medium*, August 28, 2018, https://medium .com/@rortybomb/i-do-not-understand-why-the-left-should-want-a -sovereign-wealth-fund-a2e64e82126e.

43. Thomas Piketty, data series on income trends over time, http:// piketty.pse.ens.fr/files/ideology/pdf/F11.1.pdf.

Chapter 10: A New Collective American Freedom

1. George Carlin, *You Are All Diseased*, 1999.

2. Samuel Johnson, "Taxation No Tyranny," 1775.

3. Thomas Jefferson, *Notes on the State of Virginia*, 1801.

4. "10 Facts About Washington & Slavery," Mount Vernon Estate, https:// www.mountvernon.org/george-washington/slavery/ten-facts-about -washington-slavery/.

5. Ulysses S. Grant, *Memoirs of Ulysses S. Grant*, 1885, reprint 2020, p. 97.

6. Thomas Piketty and Gabriel Zucman, "Capital Is Back: Wealth-Income Ratios in Rich Countries 1700–2010," Paris School of Economics, July 26, 2013, http://www.parisschoolofeconomics.com /zucman-gabriel/capitalisback/PikettyZucman2013WP.pdf.

7. Eric Foner, "Why Is There No Socialism in the United States?," *History Workshop*, no. 17 (Spring 1984): 57–80, https://www.jstor.org /stable/4288545.

8. Eric Foner, *Reconstruction*, 2002.

9. Ibid., pp. 454–458.

10. Ibid., pp. 521–522.

11. Ibid., p. 523.

12. Hamden Rice, "Most of You Have No Idea What Martin Luther King Actually Did," *Daily Kos*, August 29, 2011, https://www.dailykos .com/stories/2011/8/29/1011562/-.

13. John David Smith and J. Vincent Lowery (eds.), *The Dunning School*, 2013.

14. Thomas Frank, *The People, No*, 2020; Seth Masket, "More Spending on Presidential Elections and the Peculiar Case of 1896," *Enik Rising*, March 2, 2012, http://enikrising.blogspot.com/2012/03/more -spending-on-presidential-elections.html.

15. "African Americans," *Living New Deal*, https://livingnewdeal.org /what-was-the-new-deal/new-deal-inclusion/african-americans-2/;

Franklin D. Roosevelt, "Executive Order 8802—Prohibition of Discrimination in the Defense Industry," June 25, 1941, http://docs .fdrlibrary.marist.edu/od8802t.html.

16. J. W. Mason and Andrew Bossie, "Public Spending as an Engine of Growth and Equality: Lessons from World War II," Roosevelt Institute, September 23, 2020, https://rooseveltinstitute.org/publications /public-spending-as-an-engine-of-growth-and-equality-lessons-from -world-war-ii/.

17. Martin Luther King Jr., Hungry Club Address, May 10, 1967, https://www.theatlantic.com/magazine/archive/2018/02/martin -luther-king-hungry-club-forum/552533/.

18. James C. Cobb, "Even Though He Is Revered Today, MLK Was Widely Disliked by the American Public When He Was Killed," *Smithsonian Magazine*, April 4, 2018, https://www.smithsonianmag .com/history/why-martin-luther-king-had-75-percent-disapproval -rating-year-he-died-180968664/.

19. Ryan Grim, "National Review Is Trying to Rewrite Its Own Racist History," *The Intercept*, July 5, 2020, https://theintercept.com/2020 /07/05/national-review-william-buckley-racism/.

20. "United States Quick Facts," U.S. Census Bureau, https://www .census.gov/quickfacts/fact/table/US/PST045219.

21. Cambridge University debate, James Baldwin vs. William F. Buckley, 1965, https://www.youtube.com/watch?v=oFeoS41xe7w.

22. Ta-Nehisi Coates, "Books for the Horde: *The New Jim Crow*, Chapter One," *The Atlantic*, September 17, 2014, https://www.theatlantic.com /politics/archive/2014/09/books-for-the-horde-the-new-jim-crow -chapter-one/380350/.

23. Anne Case and Angus Deaton, "Rising Morbidity and Mortality in Midlife Among White Non-Hispanic Americans in the 21st Century," *Proceedings of the National Academy of Sciences*, November 2, 2015, https:// www.pnas.org/content/112/49/15078.

24. Anne Case and Angus Deaton, *Deaths of Despair and the Future of Capitalism*, 2020.

25. David Armstrong, "Sackler Embraced Plan to Conceal OxyContin's Strength from Doctors, Sealed Testimony Shows," *ProPublica*, February 21, 2017, https://www.propublica.org/article/richard -sackler-oxycontin-oxycodone-strength-conceal-from-doctors-sealed -testimony; Debbie Cenziper et al., "They Looked at Us Like an

Easy Target," *Washington Post*, October 18, 2019, https://www
.washingtonpost.com/graphics/2019/investigations/west-virginia
-opioid-legal-battle-foster-care/; Chris McGreal, "Doctor Who Was
Paid by Purdue to Push Opioids to Testify Against Drugmaker,"
The Guardian, April 10, 2019, https://www.theguardian.com/us
-news/2019/apr/10/purdue-opioids-crisis-doctor-testify-against
-drugmaker.

26. Lewis Beale, "Welcome to Kermit, WV, Pop. 382 and 9 Million
Pain Meds," *Daily Beast*, April 11, 2020, https://www.thedailybeast
.com/welcome-to-mud-lick-wv-pop-382-and-9-million-pain
-meds.

27. Peter A. Muennig et al., "America's Declining Well-Being, Health,
and Life Expectancy: Not Just a White Problem," *American Journal of
Public Health* 108, no. 12 (December 2018): 1626–1631, https://www
.ncbi.nlm.nih.gov/pmc/articles/PMC6221922/.

28. Martin Luther King Jr., "Drum Major Instinct," February 4,
1968, https://kinginstitute.stanford.edu/encyclopedia/drum-major
-instinct.

29. Grant, *Memoirs of Ulysses S. Grant*, p. 96.

30. J. David Hacker, "A Census-Based Count of the Civil War Dead,"
Civil War History 57, no. 4 (December 2011): 307–348, https://muse
.jhu.edu/article/465917.

31. Richard Valelly, "Vanishing Voters," *American Prospect*, December 5,
2000, https://prospect.org/power/vanishing-voters/.

32. Baldwin–Buckley debate, 1965, https://www.youtube.com/watch?v
=oFeoS41xe7w.

33. Frank Newport, "In U.S., 87% Approve of Black-White Marriage,
vs. 4% in 1958," Gallup, July 25, 2013, https://news.gallup.com/poll
/163697/approve-marriage-blacks-whites.aspx.

34. Nate Cohn and Kevin Quealy, "How Public Opinion Has Moved
on Black Lives Matter," *New York Times*, June 10, 2020, https://www
.nytimes.com/interactive/2020/06/10/upshot/black-lives-matter
-attitudes.html.

35. Lachlan Cartwright, "Fox News Staff Erupts over Network Racism: Bosses 'Created a White Supremacist Cell,'" *Daily Beast*,
July 18, 2020, https://www.thedailybeast.com/fox-news-staffers
-erupt-over-tucker-carlsons-racism-say-bosses-created-a-white
-supremacist-cell.

36. Jessica Semega et al., "Income and Poverty in the United States: 2019," Census Bureau, September 15, 2020, https://www.census.gov/library /publications/2020/demo/p60-270.html; Neil Bhutta et al., "Disparities in Wealth by Race and Ethnicity in the 2019 Survey of Consumer Finances," FEDS Notes, September 28, 2020, https://www.federalre serve.gov/econres/notes/feds-notes/disparities-in-wealth-by-race-and -ethnicity-in-the-2019-survey-of-consumer-finances-20200928.htm.

37. "Poverty Rate by Race/Ethnicity," Kaiser Family Foundation, https:// www.kff.org/other/state-indicator/poverty-rate-by-raceethnicity/ ?currentTimeframe=0&sortModel=%7B%22colId%22:%22Locat ion%22,%22sort%22:%22asc%22%7D; "Uninsured Rates for the Nonelderly by Race/Ethnicity," Kaiser Family Foundation, https:// www.kff.org/uninsured/state-indicator/rate-by-raceethnicity/ ?currentTimeframe=0&sortModel=%7B%22colId%22:%22Location %22,%22sort%22:%22asc%22%7D.

38. Bruce Western and Becky Pettit, "Incarceration & Social Inequality," *Daedalus* (Summer 2010), https://www.amacad.org/publication /incarceration-social-inequality.

39. Justin Feldman, "Class and Racial Inequalities in Police Killings," *People's Policy Project*, June 23, 2020, https://www.peoplespolicyproject .org/2020/06/23/class-and-racial-inequalities-in-police-killings/.

40. Ryan Cooper, "What About Police Violence Against White People?," *The Week*, June 9, 2020, https://theweek.com/articles/918849/what -about-police-violence-against-white-people.

41. "America's Declining Homicide Clearance Rates 1965–2019," Murder Accountability Project, http://www.murderdata.org/p/reported -homicide-clearance-rate-1980.html.

42. Jessica Anderson, "Baltimore Ending the Year with 32% Homicide Clearance Rate, One of the Lowest in Three Decades," *Baltimore Sun*, December 30, 2019, https://www.baltimoresun.com /maryland/baltimore-city/bs-md-ci-crime-policy-20191230 -zk2v2auuhbgq3f7zsh3t7rt6cm-story.html.

43. Martti Lehti et al., "Nordic Homicide Report," University of Helsinki, 2019, https://helda.helsinki.fi/bitstream/handle/10138/306217 /Katsauksia_37_Lehti_etal_2019.pdf?sequence=5 &isAllowed=y.

44. Matt Bruenig, "The Racial Wealth Gap Is About the Upper Classes," *People's Policy Project*, June 29, 2020, https://www.peoplespolicyproject .org/2020/06/29/the-racial-wealth-gap-is-about-the-upper-classes/.

45. Virginia Langmaid, "Maine Wedding Outbreak Offers a Cautionary Covid-19 Tale for the Holidays," CNN, November 12, 2020, https://www.cnn.com/2020/11/12/health/maine-wedding-holidays-covid/index.html.

46. David Wallace-Wells, "How the West Lost COVID: How Did So Many Rich Countries Get It So Wrong? How Did Others Get It So Right?," *Intelligencer*, March 15, 2021, https://nymag.com/intelligencer/2021/03/how-the-west-lost-covid-19.html.

Chapter 11: How to Argue with Propertarians

1. "President Obama Establishes Bipartisan National Commission on Fiscal Responsibility and Reform," White House Press Secretary, February 18, 2010, https://obamawhitehouse.archives.gov/the-press-office/president-obama-establishes-bipartisan-national-commission-fiscal-responsibility-an.

2. "Whatever the Deniers Say, Social Security Needs Reform Soon," *Washington Post*, August 11, 2010, https://www.washingtonpost.com/wp-dyn/content/article/2010/08/10/AR2010081005524.html.

3. William A. Galston and Maya MacGuineas, "The Future Is Now: A Balanced Plan to Stabilize Public Debt and Promote Economic Growth," Brookings Institution, September 30, 2010, https://www.brookings.edu/wp-content/uploads/2016/06/0930_public_debt_galston.pdf.

4. Lori Montgomery, "More Than 60 Senators Call on Obama to Join Deficit-Reduction Talks," *Washington Post*, March 18, 2011, https://www.washingtonpost.com/business/economy/cbo-obama-policies-would-require-deficits-of-95-trillion-through-2021/2011/03/18/ABnyUfq_story.html.

5. Lori Montgomery, "In Debt Talks, Obama Offers Social Security Cuts," *Washington Post*, July 6, 2011, https://www.washingtonpost.com/business/economy/in-debt-talks-obama-offers-social-security-cuts/2011/07/06/gIQA2sFO1H_story.html.

6. Carla Fried, "4 Critical Reasons Why You Should Care About the Budget Deficit," CBS News, November 19, 2010, https://www.cbsnews.com/news/4-critical-reasons-why-you-should-care-about-the-budget-deficit/.

7. Rick Newman, "Who to Blame for the Debt Fiasco," *US News*,

July 15, 2011, https://www.usnews.com/news/blogs/rick-newman /2011/07/15/who-to-blame-for-the-debt-fiasco.

8. Matt Bai, "Obama vs. Boehner: Who Killed the Debt Deal?," *New York Times*, March 28, 2012, https://www.nytimes.com/2012/04/01 /magazine/obama-vs-boehner-who-killed-the-debt-deal.html.

9. Sahil Kapur, "How Tea Party Absolutism Cost the GOP a Huge Win in Entitlements," *Talking Points Memo*, February 21, 2014, https://talkingpointsmemo.com/dc/how-tea-party-absolutism-cost -republicans-a-huge-win-on-entitlements.

10. Lori Montgomery, "Urgency on Debt Issue Fades, but Underlying Danger Remains," *Washington Post*, June 7, 2013, https://www .washingtonpost.com/business/economy/urgency-on-debt-issue -fades-but-underlying-danger-remains/2013/06/07/4b83350e -cf85–11e2–8845-d970ccb04497_story.html.

11. Federal Reserve Bank of St. Louis data tool FRED, series on unemployment rate, https://fred.stlouisfed.org/series/UNRATE/; ibid., series on real per capita GDP, https://fred.stlouisfed.org/series /A939RX0Q048SBEA.

12. Ibid., series on trade balance, https://fred.stlouisfed.org/series /BOPGSTB.

13. Christina Romer and Jared Bernstein, "The Job Impact of the American Recovery and Reinvestment Plan," Council of Economic Advisers, January 9, 2009, https://www.politico.com/pdf/PPM116 _obamadoc.pdf.

14. Federal Reserve Bank of St. Louis data tool FRED, series on effective federal funds rate, https://fred.stlouisfed.org/series/fedfunds.

15. Ibid., series on federal interest payments as a share of GDP, https:// fred.stlouisfed.org/series/FYOIGDA188S.

16. Richard G. Anderson and Yang Liu, "How Low Can You Go? Negative Interest Rates and Investors' Flight to Safety," Federal Reserve Bank of St. Louis, January 1, 2013, https://www.stlouisfed.org /publications/regional-economist/january-2013/how-low-can-you -go-negative-interest-rates-and-investors-flight-to-safety.

17. Louis Jacobson, "Medicare and Social Security: What You Paid Compared with What You Get," *PolitiFact*, February 1, 2013, https:// www.politifact.com/article/2013/feb/01/medicare-and-social -security-what-you-paid-what-yo/.

18. Carla Baranauckas, "Marco Rubio Says He Won't 'Destroy Our Economy' for Climate Change," *HuffPost*, October 14, 2018, https://www.huffpost.com/entry/marco-rubio-says-he-wont-destroy-our-economy-for-climate-change_n_5bc3af1de4b040bb4e837770.

19. Jeff Goodell, "Miami: How Rising Sea Levels Endanger South Florida," *Rolling Stone*, August 30, 2013, https://www.rollingstone.com/feature/miami-how-rising-sea-levels-endanger-south-florida-200956/.

20. Katie Weeman and Patrick Lynch, "New Study Finds Sea Level Rise Accelerating," *Global Climate Change*, February 13, 2018, https://climate.nasa.gov/news/2680/new-study-finds-sea-level-rise-accelerating/.

21. Yanis Varoufakis, "How I Became an Erratic Marxist," *The Guardian*, February 18, 2015, https://www.theguardian.com/news/2015/feb/18/yanis-varoufakis-how-i-became-an-erratic-marxist.

22. "Tax Expenditures," U.S. Treasury Department Office of Tax Analysis, October 19, 2018, https://home.treasury.gov/system/files/131/Tax-Expenditures-FY2020.pdf.

23. "The Tax Policy Center's Briefing Book," Tax Policy Center, https://www.taxpolicycenter.org/briefing-book/what-are-largest-tax-expenditures.

24. "Policy Basics: Federal Tax Expenditures," Center on Budget and Policy Priorities, updated December 8, 2020, https://www.cbpp.org/research/federal-tax/policy-basics-federal-tax-expenditures.

25. Chuck Marr, Samantha Jacoby, and Kathleen Bryant, "Substantial Income of Wealthy Households Escapes Annual Taxation or Enjoys Special Tax Breaks," Center on Budget and Policy Priorities, November 13, 2019, https://www.cbpp.org/research/federal-tax/substantial-income-of-wealthy-households-escapes-annual-taxation-or-enjoys.

26. OECD data series on direct social spending, https://data.oecd.org/socialexp/social-spending.htm.

27. OCED data series on social expenditure, https://stats.oecd.org/Index.aspx?DataSetCode=SOCX_AGG.

28. Suzanne Mettler, "Reconstituting the Submerged State: The Challenges of Social Policy Reform in the Obama Era," *Perspectives on Politics*, August 23, 2010, https://www.cambridge.org/core/journals

/perspectives-on-politics/article/reconstituting-the-submerged-state
-the-challenges-of-social-policy-reform-in-the-obama-era/12485025
2051794EB3E1AE87E1D082C8.

29. Sean Illing, "Why So Many People Who Need the Government Hate It," *Vox*, December 21, 2019, https://www.vox.com/2018/8/17 /17675100/suzanne-mettler-government-citizen-disconnect-welfare.

30. Jonel Aleccia, "Broke and Ashamed: Many Won't Take Handouts Despite Need," NBC News, March 23, 2013, https://www.nbcnews .com/feature/in-plain-sight/broke-ashamed-many-wont-take -handouts-despite-need-v17327439.

31. Maggie Astor, "A Poll Shows Most Americans, Including Many Republicans, Support $1,400 Stimulus Checks," *New York Times*, February 3, 2021, https://www.nytimes.com/2021/02/03/us/stimulus -check-polls.html.

32. Ryan Grim, "Alan Simpson: Social Security Is 'a Milk Cow with 310 Million Tits,'" *HuffPost*, August 24, 2010, https://www.huffpost.com /entry/alan_simpson_social_security_n_693277; Paul Krugman, "The Hijacked Commission," *New York Times*, November 11, 2010, https://www.nytimes.com/2010/11/12/opinion/12krugman.html.

33. "The Persuaders," *Frontline*, November 2004, https://www.pbs.org /wgbh/pages/frontline/shows/persuaders/interviews/luntz.html.

34. Duncan Black, "MOAAAAAAAAAAAAR SOCIAL SECURITY," *Eschaton*, February 4, 2013, https://www.eschatonblog.com /2013/02/moaaaaaaaaaaaar-social-security.html.

35. Daniel Marans, Arthur Delaney, and Ryan Grim, "Barack Obama Once Proposed Cutting Social Security. Here's What Changed His Mind," *HuffPost*, June 8, 2016, https://www.huffpost.com /entry/barack-obama-grand-bargain-social-security-expansion_n _5751f92de4b0eb20fa0e0142.

36. William Leuchtenburg, *Franklin D. Roosevelt and the New Deal*, 2009, p. 109.

37. Ibid., 150.

38. Ibid.

39. Franklin D. Roosevelt, "Speech at Madison Square Garden," October 31, 1936, https://millercenter.org/the-presidency/presidential -speeches/october-31-1936-speech-madison-square-garden.

40. Michael Kazin, "Alexandria Ocasio-Cortez and America's Most Liberal Generation," *New York Times*, March 31, 2021, https://www

.nytimes.com/2021/03/29/books/review/the-aoc-generation-david
-freedlander.html.

41. Zachary Parolin et al., "The Potential Poverty Reduction Effect of the
American Rescue Plan," March 11, 2021, Center on Poverty and Social Policy at Columbia University, https://static1.squarespace.com
/static/5743308460b5e922a25a6dc7/t/604aa2465cfc4a35b8a1c236
/1615503943944/Poverty-Reduction-Analysis-American-Rescue
-Plan-CPSP-2021.pdf.

INDEX